Teaching
Children
Music

in the ELEMENTARY SCHOOL

Teaching
Children
Music

in the ELEMENTARY SCHOOL

Third Edition

Louise Kifer Myers
CONSULTANT IN MUSIC EDUCATION

PRENTICE-HALL, INC. *Englewood Cliffs, N. J.*

1961

Current printing (last digit):

14 13 12 11 10 9 8 7 6 5

© *1950, 1956, 1961, by*
PRENTICE-HALL, INC.
Englewood Cliffs, N. J.

Library of Congress
Catalog Card No.: 61-14700

PRINTED IN THE UNITED STATES OF AMERICA
89172-C

Preface

This book is a guide for teaching *all* the children through music and for teaching that part of the music program usually directed by the elementary classroom teacher. Its plan, briefly, is to capitalize on children's *natural* interest in music and using their *natural* equipment for making music by providing experiences in sequence that will result in their musical development.

For *all* the children, we hope they will become acquainted with the entire world of music—singing and singers, composing and composers, rhythms and dancers, conducting and conductors, instruments and instrumentalists. Children make this acquaintance by becoming singers, composers, dancers, conductors, and instrumentalists themselves.

Since the classroom teacher is the key person in a program designed to bring out the natural musicality of *all* the children, the development of the teacher's innate musicality should be basic in that person's training, and the skills should be acquired through experiences comparable to those suggested for children.

The music specialist's role in a program for *all* the children demands an expertness in the areas of teaching, curriculum, and child growth and development equal to that in music. For that reason, suggestions for training the music specialists must include experience that will interpret the realities of a school music program for *all* the children.

Grade-level standards of accomplishment are not set up because musical growth is the result of experience—and musical experience, unfortunately, does not accrue automatically with being in a grade in school. Instead, successive experiences in each of the areas of the music program (with standards by which growth in each area may be evaluated) are given so teachers will be able (1) to analyze competency in each phase and (2) to provide a "next" experience for growth and development.

Ability to read music is one of the goals of the elementary school music program. It results from or is the composite of several skills. Each of these several skills is developed independently in order to reduce the complexity of learning to read. For example, learning to interpret the duration aspect of notes is related to movement, and learning to interpret the level aspect of notes is related to identical groups of tones in songs children know. There is an emphasis on *likeness* and *sameness* rather than on difference. Paced through weeks of experience, mastery of these subsidiary skills makes the desired goal easier to attain.

The annotated bibliography is divided into sections, primarily to show the various areas that must conjoin to make possible child growth and development through music.

The following are suggestions for using this book in methods classes:

1. Consider Chapters 1 and 2 as a presentation of the philosophy of guiding experiences in music. Refer to them often in

connection with other chapters. Consider Chapter 10 as the summary.

2. Use the activities included in the sections "For Discussion," "Things to Do," and "Suggestions for Teachers" as the basis for gaining personal skills. "Things to Do" is concerned with starting activity in singing and movement for children as well as college students.

3. The need for a common background of song material becomes apparent when facts of music need to be illustrated. The illustrative material herein is from *Music Fundamentals Through Song*, which could well become the song repertoire for both students and children. Students should relate the facts learned from these songs to material in a child's book.

4. To study music fundamentals and to strengthen music-reading skill, proceed with *students* as is suggested for children in Chapters 4 and 7. This material is excellent, too, for orienting music majors to the way of music in the elementary school. Use the songs suggested in Chapter 3. Use the same creative approach, rather than a technical approach.

5. Precede and follow the study of major areas by student observation of prearranged demonstrations of children, engaged in activity in the same area. Use telecast teaching as a basis for discussion when possible.

6. Periodic testing of personal skills and mastery of content is advisable.

7. Space the opportunity for hearing non-European-style music. For example, play American Indian music for ten minutes during several class sessions, while students check the list of characteristics given; *then* suggest that they use the objective terms in discussing what they hear. Ideally, getting acquainted with this type of music should result from an interest in the culture of the people to whom it belongs.

It is indeed a pleasure to acknowledge again my indebtedness to those teachers all over the country who were willing to discuss with me what material should be included in this book. To those who suggested more "technical facts," the rules and suggestions for deriving the facts are here. I wrote *Music Fundamentals Through Song*, a song-, text-, work-book so students could learn the facts and acquire the skills by the same methods outlined in this book. To those who suggested including lists of certain songs or where specific dances, for example, can be found, what better way is there of getting acquainted with available material than by searching for a specific? I am grateful to those who gave me permission to use their material, especially to Miss E. Marion Dorward. Without the encouragement of my husband, Alonzo F. Myers, this edition of *Teaching Children Music in the Elementary School* would neither have been attempted, nor completed.

LOUISE KIFER MYERS

Table of

Contents

I *A Program for Elementary
School Music*

II *Implementing the Program*

Teaching
Children
Music

in the ELEMENTARY SCHOOL

—————— I

A Program

for Elementary

School Music

Music in

Today's Schools

Since the day early man directed conscious attention to the sounds he could make, he was attracted by them. Later, these sounds were organized into patterns called "music." Musicologists tell us that every group known to anthropologists and historians has had music.

Some of the noblest, some of the most compelling thoughts of the ages have been expressed through the medium of tone. Although music has a universal quality, it is one of the individual's most cherished personal possessions. The expressions of great musicians, just as the works of art in the museum, seem to belong to him—his to enjoy and delight in. Some people express their own ideas through music, whereas others are satisfied to listen to the expressions of another.

Because of its place in the lives of all people and the joy

individuals have experienced in their association with it, music is given a prominent place in the school program. It becomes a part of the day's activities in school because it is a part of life. It has its natural contribution to make in helping one to gain an understanding of peoples and things; it has its natural contribution to make in bringing joy to those who hear it.

In helping one become informed about other groups, music can contribute to the idea that people the world over are alike despite differences in skin color, language, and habits of eating and dressing; music can contribute to the concept of "likeness" by showing that the feelings of those of other peoples, as expressed in music, are much the same as ours. Music, by capturing and preserving the mood of the dance, can contribute to an understanding of a society in which the minuet was popular; it can broaden our understanding of the life of serfs and slaves through *The Volga Boatmen* or a Negro work song. Because of its power to help one in understanding people, music is an important phase of the program in today's schools.

Because of the joy—emotional and intellectual—that music has brought to man through the ages, those who make the broad plans for music hope that children's contact with music will be satisfying and increasing, never annoying, never decreasing. What are the joys—emotional and intellectual—that music has brought to man through the ages? Music has contributed to the joy of self-expression through singing and playing musical instruments, through writing songs, and through bodily movements to music—dancing. Through music's emotional appeal, through understanding the music itself, and through an awareness of all that makes skill in performance possible has come the joy of listening to the expressions of others. Music in today's schools hopes to introduce, amplify, and enhance these joys.

MUSIC IN TODAY'S SCHOOLS

In today's schools children become aware of music, experiment with it, and get acquainted with it through a variety of experiences. The relationship between the two—children and music—is fostered by those who believe that children should be aware of the number of ways in which music can add to their enjoyment of life. For some, this enjoyment will come by expressing the elements of music—rhythm, melody, harmony, mood, form—through bodily movement. Some will prefer singing alone or in groups; others will choose to play instruments. Children with creative powers will use them to write songs.

The prime purpose of the music program is to present such a variety of experiences that each child may discover some phase of musical activity he will really enjoy and which will make him a happier, more complete person. A visit to several schoolrooms will demonstrate the variety of musical activities from which choices can be made.

In a sixth-grade room a small group of children is busily engaged in studying pictures in the books they have collected to get ideas for costuming figures for their marionette show of *Die Meistersinger;* another group is planning and working on a huge mural depicting life in the Middle Ages. Several children are writing the script for the play, and others are deciding which phonograph records and how much music from each to use at certain points in the production. You enjoy hearing the sixth-grade pianist teach the *Prize Song* to the sixth-grade "Walter." The girl-teacher softly plays a simplified version of the song while "Walter" sings his melody. Very seriously they assert that when it comes time for the contest in the play, the phonograph record will be used to win the contest.

In another room a group of children is creating a tune for a classmate's poem. The result of the original creative effort is discussed: "The words ask a question; the music should do the same"; "Those words need very gay music that skips"; or, "The words just tumble down, and so must the music." This is a group effort, so the group contributes ideas.

In the music room children are seated on the floor watching the telecast of a singer of folk songs. He accompanies his singing on a guitar—and, obviously, had invited children to "play" along with him, because each child is strumming on an imaginary instrument. Now he says, "The next song is *Great Big House in New Orleans.* I shall sing an introduction to show how fast it goes. If you know it, sing along with me softly." If we could stay a while longer, we would hear several children play on the piano the tones of an oft repeated phrase of the song.

Downstairs, the children in the second grade are learning to play Autoharps. As one child plays, the teacher stands nearby, singing with the class. While the group sings, each child plays his own make-believe harp with a graceful stroke on the measure accent, practicing for his turn to play the real instrument. You can almost see an idea in the head of one child: he is looking at the melody bells, seeming to plan which keys to play on *that* instrument instead of strumming on his harp.

In any of these or other rooms children might be found carefully analyzing the piano keyboard or its mechanism, studying the relation between keys and tones so that they will understand the "why" of a key signature or how to make simple musical instruments; they might be reading new songs to be sung at a "concert" for a neighboring class; or they might be listening to the story of Dukas' *The Sorcerer's Apprentice* and then to the music itself, later discussing its possibilities for dramatization.

Children in today's schools learn by doing. They learn music by making music. They make music while learning. They make it by singing and playing—by playing flutes, Autoharps, drums, bells, xylophones, rattles, and tone blocks. They learn in choirs, glee clubs, bands, orchestras, harmonica clubs, and in class and private lessons. Making music is the *bait* or *lure* to learning. Bait for what? Interest, enthusiasm, enjoyment, and desire to know more.

Yes, children *make* music while learning. They *learn* music while making. These lures to learning become the best of all motivation in getting the learners to want to do the things music in today's school hopes to teach them. Learning is paced throughout the program, and follows an orderly sequence. Basic skills are developed so that they function in later learning and so they can support further learning.

True, some critics would say this picture of the music program has in it some activities that are definitely nonmusical. Costuming a marionette, music? Certainly not, but the costumes of opera singers contribute to the beauty and meaning of an opera and to the enjoyment of the audience. It does not seem likely that the child who has had a satisfying experience in making a marionette and designing its costume for a class production of *Die Meistersinger* will definitely and permanently turn against music. Making a drum, music? Certainly not, but writing a score for a drum and playing it is. Planning a dramatization for *The Sorcerer's Apprentice*, music? Certainly not, but a dramatization involves an awareness of and a knowledge of the music. As a matter of fact, such a dramatization to the music and interpretation of the music is the result of listening many times to the composition and of actually knowing it and of being able to anticipate some passages. Going through a pipe organ, music? Examining the inside of a piano, music? Certainly not, but how much more meaningful organ and piano music becomes as the result of knowing how tones are produced. It does not seem likely that gaining such information will cause a child to decide that never again of his own volition will he listen to the playing of a piano or an organ.

What a contrast to the program of another day. Too often, the philosophy in presenting drills and exercises seemed to be "Here it is. It's good for you—so, take it or leave it." A good many left it. They liked music—but *that* wasn't their idea of music. They just were not interested.

Think for a few minutes about the things adults and children do when they are interested. They pursue their interests, they investigate, they experiment, and they learn. Because of their interest in airplanes, makers of model airplanes *learn* as they work; because of their interest in social dancing, people *learn* to dance; because of their interest in football, men *learn* to play. Most of the things we do that are not required of us we do because we are interested in them. There is no fear that a rich musical program—one that is varied, one that gives opportunity for experimentation and investigation—will result in little or no learning. As a matter of fact, such a program is quite likely to result in lasting knowledge and far-reaching interests.

THE "WHY" OF THE PROGRAM

The planned activities of the music program are related as nearly as possible to children's natural interest in music and music-making. There is considerable evidence that children are naturally musical.

Consider a baby. He comes into the world specially equipped, it seems, for music. He is attracted by sound (that is what music is—sound) and he is soothed by it. He has ears to hear it and the capacity for remembering it. He is pleased at being moved to its regular rhythm. Moreover, he comes equipped with a built-in musical instrument—some say, the most beautiful of all instruments—a voice.

Consider a two- or three- or four-year-old. He is a maker of music—he makes up and sings his own songs and sings the songs of others, and is captivated by real and toy instruments. He listens and responds. Sometimes he listens with rapt attention. Sometimes what he hears makes him dance.

Max Schoen in his *Psychology of Music* [1] says that musical aptitudes are of two kinds: those for reception of music (musicality) and those for making music (talent). Children are born with the capacity for *receiving* music and *making* it. Observation of little children confirms that they are naturally receptive to music and have aptitude for making it. Those who are responsible for music today have planned it so as to extend and expand this natural musicality and to develop this natural talent. The program is based on another fact, too.

It is a fact: Each child, each of *us*, is a social being as well as an emotional being, a physical being, a creative being, a

[1] Max Schoen, *Psychology of Music*, New York: The Ronald Press, 1940.

spiritual being, an intellectual being. There is some area of music that fits and appeals to each of these beings. Combinations of these areas can appeal to several of these beings. Making music with others, for example, *can* appeal to and *can* satisfy several of the beings that is a child. Listening to music or moving to music *can* please several of the beings that is a child.

The idea that *today* is important to children is paramount. Although it is true that development, growth and aim are inherent in the very word "program," children learn for *now*. They learn for doing today—they do not learn against the time thirteen years from today when they just might need to know. They make music today and they know they will make it on the close tomorrow—the future they comprehend and that has real meaning for them.

Thus, music starts with children—their natural musicality and their innate talent. Just as with other items of natural equipment, though, children come into the world with their musical equipment at various levels of development—some have better memories for tone, some have prettier voices, some have more muscular control, some have a finer sense of rhythm than others. So consider the level of development and provide activity to improve and refine it. Development is planned along lines that appeal to the intellectual being and all the other beings that is a child, as well.

"Children are naturally musical"—some of you may have almost violent reactions and say: "She never saw that fifth-grade class of mine!" or "If they are naturally musical, why do I have to work so hard?" or "If she had been there yesterday!" True, she does not actually know that fifth-grade class; she believes you work hard and conscientiously; and she can understand that yesterday was a trial. However, of this she is confident: If those who are responsible for the contact between children and music (1) concentrate on developing children's natural aptitudes for music through activities appealing to *all* the beings that is a child, and (2) utilize to the fullest the implications of the fact that *pre*-school children and music seem to complement each other and seem to be made for each other, then, *school* children and their music will dovetail, too.

CHILD GROWTH THROUGH MUSIC

Through its variety of activities, today's school hopes to contribute to the physical, intellectual, social, spiritual, creative, and emotional growth of all elementary school children, and to extend and develop their natural equipment for making and enjoying music.

Primary Grades

Singing together is valuable experience for individual children in their early school experiences. These little egoists need the discipline imposed by singing with the group and by unquestioningly following the simple directions of the leader. This activity is spoiled by unthinking effort on the part of any of those who participate. Individual creative effort has its important place—but this is *not* the place. When the concept of group singing is established, each child will understand that the tonal line to which he must adhere is an exact line and one that he must follow to the best of his ability. The rules of *this* game demand that each person abandon his own ideas for the moment and conform exactly to a pattern that has been set.

Of course, children do not know that group singing is an excellent means by which they may pool their individual efforts to arrive at a designated goal. For them, singing with other children should be only a pleasurable activity to which they contribute as best they can. It is probably one of the few opportunities they have to join simultaneously with the whole group in carrying on a common project. Even working or playing with a small group is often a new experience for first-graders. In what other circumstances can they get the experience and discipline of working with a group of thirty or forty?

Singing alone or with a small group contributes to child

growth, too. Some children who have certain speech difficulties or who are painfully shy seem to lose themselves in their song. While singing alone, they make their most creditable individual effort. Since singing alone differs very little from singing with a group, it is still a welcome variation and takes care of the short attention span of little children. This activity disciplines the most uninhibited child; to sing a given song, he is forced to keep within the tonal pattern of that song.

The muscular control of little children is poor. They need to be guided into activities that will develop their big muscles. Swinging along in the manner of a lumbering elephant will help them gain control over their big muscles. Bouncing and catching a large ball to music requires no small amount of timing and muscular coordination, and attaining such timing and co-ordination is fun. Bodily movements plus dramatization plus music are known as rhythms, and rhythms, selected because of the contribution they make to large-muscle growth and control, aid in the physical development of children.

Rhythms, moreover, *can* be the motivation for careful observation of motion. How does an airplane fly? How does a steam shovel work? How does a turkey walk? How does a shoemaker fix shoes? How does a farmer plant his seeds? How can one know these things unless he observes? The results of such observations—knowing *how*—add to the ever-increasing volume of facts the child is gathering. There is a place for fantasy, but the child needs to become aware of reality, of the way things are. When he knows, he will not hesitate to dramatize his ideas because knowledge gives him a sense of security.

Intermediate Grades

The disciplines demanded by group singing prevailing in the intermediate grades have become even more exacting. Routine in learning songs and in singing has become established. The musical experiences of the primary grades provide a foundation upon which refinement of interpretation can be built. Because children in these grades have a deep feeling of attachment for children of their own age and sex, choruses and/or glee clubs of boys or girls are important to them. Because this is the age of gangs, chums, and best friends, smaller singing groups can be started.

This period of rapid physical growth is accompanied by better muscular control. Since children now have command of their large muscles, rhythms will help to develop control of smaller muscles. Not only can rhythmic activities aid in this development, but music is an element that helps dissolve self-consciousness. Ability to manipulate the body without thought of body is desirable, and musical accompaniment is an aid. In trying to fit a folk-dance step to its corresponding measure of music or in carrying out a bit of rhythmic play in a given musical space, the child cannot concentrate on anything except getting the thing done. There is no time to think of self.

Music makes possible an extensive area for intellectual growth for intermediate grade children. They have a keen curiosity and a desire to collect things and facts. The more mature children have acquired enough confidence to investigate alone. Since the mere act of "going to school" has lost its glamour, those in charge of the school program need to provide motivation for learning by including the wide field of the arts in their program.

Music offers another medium for creative effort. Composing tunes, playing musical instruments, dancing—all these play an important part in the development of the whole child.

MUSICAL GROWTH FOR *ALL* THE CHILDREN

The music program explores the broad field of musical activities. It is the hope that children will find at least one phase that will add to their pleasure as children and later as adults—not only find it but also pursue it with the idea of learning more. There are certain experiences *all* children must have in order to make choices. But when unusual ability and interest are discovered, these must be developed, too—in bands, orchestras, and choruses and by class and private lessons. Sometimes classroom teachers can assume some of the responsibility for guiding them—if not, special music teachers are needed. Other classroom teachers direct only those activities related to the musical growth of *all* the children in the daily music program.

What actual experience in music do we wish for *all* the children in a classroom? What should the music program include so as to give them a complete awareness of the realm of this art? What skills do they need in order to grow musically?

Music—a Universal Language

"Universal" implies *all* and *everywhere*. Musicologists tell us that each group of people known to anthropologists and historians has had music. Whether or not we like the music of China or the music of India is unimportant—this music has pleased the inhabitants of these countries for hundreds of years. As a matter of fact, it pleased them long before *our* pattern of music started to take shape before the Middle Ages. True, the music of some other groups scarcely conforms to our idea of music, but our opinion here, too, is of little consequence. All people everywhere have and have had their music. Music is and always has been a language.

We wish for children an awareness of music as a language, as a means by which feelings, ideas and emotions are expressed. We wish to develop the ability to use this language in *making* music. They have within them a potential musical instrument—the voice. They have an interest in and are intrigued by sound. We wish them to have the opportunity to experiment with sound, to make up their own patterns with their voices, on drums, on sticks, on pianos, on flutes, on stringed instruments, on glasses, on bells. *That* includes composing songs and music. Does that mean composing a symphony? No, it does not. The first attempts at self-expression through music are just as far removed from a symphony as the initial efforts at writing in the vernacular are from the "great American novel." The first four-measure song is comparable to the first planned oral language effort. Each is a small beginning, but each is a necessary step in growth. When the children grow up, they are not all going to write "the great American novel" or a symphony, but attempts at expression in each of these two media are valuable aids to understanding and appreciating the novel and a symphony.

We wish children to have the opportunity to react emotionally to the art that is music. Music—great music—is the expression of feeling, of emotions and ideas through the medium of tone. It must be heard before it can reach the inner self, before its full beauty and charm and message can be savored. Unfortunately, there is little testing one can do to determine whether or not music has reached children (or adults) and whether it has been more than tasted. Probably, the only evidence that can be accepted as proof is the way music effects behavior—for example, if children are more than willing to listen or more than willing to sing, or if a child cannot resist moving his body to the rhythm of music, it can be assumed that he has been "reached." This idea will be repeated often in this book: the only evidence that music has reached the child is the observable evidence of his behavior in relation to music.

Music also makes an appeal to the intellect. There is a mass of information to be gained *about* music. We want children to become acquainted with some of the terms used in music— organ, *largo*, Bach, *pizzicato, finale,* Toscanini, *suite, crescendo,* Steinway, march, Ole Bull—but all those are labels, not music. There are a number of ways to test ability to fit appropriate labels to music, but remember, when you find a child knows the name of a composition, you know only *that* and still know nothing about his emotional reaction to it.

The intellectual and the emotional enjoyments that result from music and making music are many and complex. Some of these are: (1) the feeling of security engendered by hearing familiar compositions; (2) the emotional release that comes with performing; (3) the recognition of the accuracy with which a picture is painted, an idea portrayed, or a story told; (4) the emotional appeal of certain melodies; (5) an awareness of the techniques necessary for the satisfactory interpretation of a composition; (6) a realization of the effective use of instruments; and (7) a comprehension of the perfection of form. We wish to guide *all* children in those experiences that will lead to the understanding and enjoyment of the art of music.

We wish children to know something of the science of music, too—those items they need in the pursuit of their ordinary course of learning, with first things coming first. Such is the procedure in teaching mathematics. Addition is taught first because it is fundamental to further operations. Multiplication is taught before division because one must be able to multiply numbers before he can divide. The idea of teaching first things first and the next step only when and because it is needed applies equally well to the science of music.

The study of the science of music can be compared to the study of English grammar, too. The study of grammar is delayed until correct forms have been established by usage, and *then* rules are learned and technical names or labels are applied. "I would-a went" is changed early in a child's life, and the correct form is established through using it. Later, in studying grammar, he learns the rules governing the correct form and learns the related technical names. In music, the correct sounds (forms) of certain fundamental groups of tones are established by using them over and over again in song material. It is *then* that technical labels and rules are learned—and learned in relation to what the child already knows.

It is *easy* to discover children's knowledge of the science of music. Just give a test: Where is *do* in the key of D? What is the letter name of the fifth line? What does ⁴₄ mean? Write a major scale on F sharp. Each child's answers tell their own story. The child can or cannot fit the appropriate labels.

It is easy to discover whether or not he knows but judgment must be used in deciding when he *should* know. Actually, when does he *need* to know the answers to those questions? He *needs* to know only when further growth is impossible without them. And a *thorough* study of the science of music should be reserved for those who have a need for it, who show an interest in it, and who have the prerequisite skills.

For Discussion

1. Compare the old type music program with the type found in today's schools. Do you agree that a rich musical program will result in lasting knowledge and far-reaching interests? Why? On what basis do you make your judgment? Cite examples to prove your point.

2. Consider your own elementary school experiences in music. How do they compare with the classroom situations described in this chapter?

3. If you are one of the many who took piano lessons at one time and who now says, "I just can't play a note," analyze the reasons for your present lack of skill. Be honest; don't try to fix the blame on someone else without considering your part. What would have stimulated you, if it was stimulation you needed? [2]

4. What basic skill do those second-grade children who play the Autoharp need? How is it developed?

5. What experiences have you had with the language of music? How have you used it? If you have had no experiences, do you think you would enjoy expressing yourself through its medium?

6. After you have listened to a composition or some singing or playing yourself, analyze your reactions: Why did you enjoy the experience? What was the high point? The low point? Why? If you heard or performed your "favorite" music, why is it your favorite? Think about your reactions and try to discuss them. It may be difficult but try to avoid general statements. Be specific.

7. List all the specific activities in this chapter that can be included as part of the music program. Group them under the following headings: singing, playing, moving, creating, listening, and reading.

8. Make a list of the first ten technical facts a child needs to know in the science of music. After each fact state "After *that* then he needs to know _____ because _____."

9. Observe children and present facts to the class proving "Children are *not* naturally musical."

[2] Incidentally, you don't play *notes*, you play keys and *read* notes.

10. Give some instances of children's "easily observable behavior" in relation to music. Justify their behavior.

11. Is the music program described here too ambitious? What are the delimiting factors? Which activity would you omit? Which did the author omit?

12. Do you like or dislike music? Why?

13. After each "being that is a child," list the music activities through which each of those beings can be attracted and developed.

14. Write a three-hundred word summary of this chapter.

2

Appreciation

It is the hope of those who plan the music program for the elementary schools that all phases of the program will lead to greater appreciation of music on the part of the children in these schools. What is "appreciation"? How is it brought about? What can the activities of listening, singing, rhythms, and creating music contribute?

WHAT IS "APPRECIATION"?

The automobile mechanic has definite reactions when he lifts the hood of an obviously expensive car after he has finished working on a series of broken-down "jalopies." The mechanical perfection of the high-powered motor excites him, and its potentialities arouse his imagination. Conditioning these reactions is his understanding of motors.

The detail and style of the hand-knit garments in the window of a shop arouse the interest of a woman who has just finished knitting her second sweater. The flare of a skirt, the manner in which the pockets are set in a sweater, the complicated pattern of a blouse, stimulate her interest, and she is aware of a desire to make similar garments. Her knowledge of the first principles of knitting give her sufficient understanding of the skill neces- sary for this more intricate work, but she likes to knit and is willing to gain greater skill in order to be able to make the things she would like to have.

· The reactions of the mechanic and the knitter were condi- tioned by their understanding of the processes involved. Indi- vidual skills and individual backgrounds made it possible for each to estimate perfection in certain areas that others might acknowledge with a cursory glance, if they notice it at all. There was more to the reaction of each person than a mere estimate of perfection. A feeling of joy, of satisfaction, of compelling interest was coupled with his understanding. The result was *appreciation*. The background of an individual and his accumu- lated knowledge of relative facts give point to an experience that results in appreciation. Interest leads to ascertaining in- formation. Interest must be there, or there can be no receptive- ness that will make possible understanding with enjoyment. Appreciation is enjoyment with understanding; appreciation is understanding with enjoyment.

WHAT IS "MUSIC APPRECIATION"?

Appreciation of music is the hoped for outcome of all the activity that is the music program in our schools. It results from the fusing of experiences—some, almost incidental; others, de- liberately planned. "Association with" is implied because with- out contact there can be no understanding.

A sensitiveness to the aesthetic quality of music is present in appreciation. Music is the language of feeling and emotion as well as a language couched in tone. In order that it be fully understood, its translation must affect feeling and emotion.

Understanding is implicit in appreciation. One phase of this understanding is an awareness of the interplay of the many elements of which music is the result. Another is knowledge of the "labels" used in talking about music—*coda,* pipe, *suite,* down beat, harmony, *allegro.* Understanding includes the knowledge of the meaning of the "labels," too.

A real acquaintance with music results in a true appreciation in which there is both an emotional response and an intellectual response. Yes, there is a higher level of reaction to music than tapping rhythm or humming a pretty tune.

The commonly heard remark, "I just love music, but I don't know anything about it," gives terse recognition to the fact of two possible responses. Those people who are interested in music for *children* want them to "love" it (emotional response), *and* to "know something about it" (intellectual response). The emotional response is evidence that music has reached the inner self—the real self. The intellectual response implies ability to estimate worth, implies an awareness of the aims of the composer and the performer, and implies an understanding of the medium of music—tone.

The fine line that sometimes separates the emotional response from the intellectual response will be left for the philosopher to define. In many instances, the point where one leaves off and the other begins is difficult to mark. The point for present consideration is that recognition be given to the fact that there are *two* responses implied in the appreciation of music, the emotional and the intellectual.

HOW IS APPRECIATION BROUGHT ABOUT?

Two closely related ideas are important in carrying out a program designed to bring about an enjoyment and understanding of music. The first is that *every music lesson is an appreciation lesson.* This may have been said so many times it fails to create interest, although too often it has been ignored in practice. The second idea is that *the procedure when teaching for appreciation differs from the method used when teaching facts.* This concept is not widespread and has not become so hackneyed a statement as has the former.

The wording of the statement, "Every music lesson is an appreciation lesson," shows it to be a relic of the day when *children* came in contact with music only during the fifteen- or twenty-minute daily music period. If that statement were changed to "each *experience with music* makes its contribution toward appreciation, whether it be a positive or a negative contribution," it would better express the actual truth. Unfortunately, too little attention has been paid to the negative influence of some experiences.

All people who hope to guide children toward an appreciation of the arts would do well to consider the differences in procedure and method between teaching for appreciation and teaching for the retention and use of facts. The need for variation may be shown by this illustration: Little Franklin may be kept in after school until he learns how to spell a given list of words, but you cannot keep him until he learns to "love" a song —or a poem or a picture. Franklin might stay until he could sing the song, tell the occupation of the composer's grandfather, or account for all his progeny, but he can't be kept there long enough to make him love the song. He might stay there until he could repeat the poem, but the possibilities of making him "love" the poem decrease with every moment of his enforced stay. He might stay in until he could paint an exact reproduction of a picture from memory, but the chances are that his love for art would fly farther out the window with every stroke of his brush. Little Franklin's favorable emotional responses are not so engendered. High-handed measures and pedantic techniques have no place in teaching for appreciation.

It is a readily observable fact that people learn what they want to, what attracts them and what interests them. For that reason, teachers should bring children and music together gently and artfully. The procedure resembles somewhat "throwing out bait"—"bait" to attract attention, "bait" to attract interest," "bait" to bring about understanding and enjoyment, "bait" to stimulate the desire to learn. Since the direction of throwing is toward the whole area of music, the lures don't have to be of the fanciest kind, just the plain, substantial kind that are manageable, efficient, and satisfying—satisfying to all the beings that is a child. And who can tell *what* will be caught: undiscovered talent? a means of enjoyment? a satisfying hobby? a way of life?

The attractive materials of music available for today's children, a consciousness of desirable procedures, and the program itself are the means of bringing about appreciation. The materials and procedures and the program plus the hoped-for results and a realistic appraisal of the aims make "teaching *for* appreciation" a more appropriate name for the activity than "teaching appreciation."

TEACHING FOR APPRECIATION

The realm of music is far-reaching. It has many ramifications. This fact is recognized by including all its areas in the program so that children will become aware of its various phases. It is hoped that understanding with enjoyment will result from this awareness and association. Making music, rhythms, listening, creating—all these conjoin and are a part of music. All have their important contribution to make. All have their individual appeal. Some children will find their greatest satisfaction in one area, others in a different area.

It is recognized, too, that actual experience in these areas is more important than the tangible results. The impulse and desire to create, for example, are much more important than the results. After having had a successful, happy experience in creating, children can easily be guided to improve their efforts. What if these efforts do not approximate the results of Brahms? Very few adult efforts do, either—but what greater awareness children have of Brahms' excellence after they, too, have created. The impulse and the act are more important than the result.

The most delighted folks at a "concert" given by children in the elementary grades should be the singers themselves. Satisfaction on their part is more important than satisfaction on the part of those who listen. *You* may delight in their interpretation and the loveliness of their singing, but theirs should be the greater delight.

Making music, rhythms, listening, creating—all these give the background and experience so necessary for understanding. They *can* give enjoyment. The acceptance of these activities on the part of children is an indication that these experiences have been enjoyed. The demand for more such activity shows that these experiences have been satisfying.

Today's manners, mores, and methods are tied up with an awareness of child nature and with child interests. In teaching *for* appreciation there is stress on learning to do *this* in order to do *that* in carrying out a child's project. Drill has an immediate purpose and does not seem to go on and on. The purpose is in sight. .

Pleasure in gaining skill is one of the desirable attributes of teaching *for* appreciation. Skills are used immediately to provide enjoyment—enjoyment for today as well as tomorrow.

The enjoyment and understanding of music is the end and aim of all experiences in the music program. Teaching *for* appreciation is the means by which it is attained.

For Discussion

1. How can a period devoted entirely to finding *do* or singing the tonic chord bring about "appreciation"?
2. Discuss the story of Franklin. Is it overdrawn?
3. What about "making" children practice their piano lessons? Before answering this question, consider your friends who have said, "I'd give anything to be able to play the piano."
4. What are some of the related learnings involved in learning to read a song in order to be able to sing it?
5. What more important outcome can result from learning music and learning about music other than personal satisfaction? In

place of music, consider that question in relation to art, drama, baseball, literature, and swimming.

6. What skill or art do you feel you "appreciate"? Analyze your feeling.

7. Individuals have been observed reading or studying while radio music fills the room. What purpose does music serve in this situation? Does such music indicate that those persons "just love music"? Are they likely to "learn anything about it"? What important aspect of "association" is lacking.

8. Discuss a Music Memory Contest as a means of building appreciation.

9. Has radio—the nation's "11 million sets in working order"—contributed to "appreciation"?

10. What can television contribute to "understanding"? Is it? Discuss some music programs you have seen on educational television. How did they contribute to "understanding"?

11. Write a two-hundred word summary of this chapter.

12. If you don't like the "bait throwing" idea, discuss the teacher as a "super-salesman."

3

Making Music—

Singing and Playing

To children, music is something to do, something they like and enjoy doing, something satisfying. And, because it is satisfying, they learn music and learn about music while making it. They make music by singing and by playing instruments.

SINGING

It was three o'clock on the last day of school before the Christmas holidays. The afternoon was given to plays and parties in the City and Country School. The six-, seven-, and eight-year-old children were in the gymnasium, sitting on the floor and singing after the conclusion of their afternoon program. As other groups of children completed their planned activities for the day, they too rushed up to the gymnasium because word had spread through the school that there was singing upstairs. Soon the room was filled with singing children. What did they sing? Carols, folk songs they had learned in school, and those of a semi-popular type—songs they loved. Was there repetition of songs? Of course there was, because the teacher knew that singing *Silent Night* or *Joy to the World* only once would not be sufficient for a group thrilled with the holiday spirit. Three-thirty came and went. Finally, some time after four, the teacher suggested that waiting parents and previously made plans should be given some consideration.

An unlikely story? It happens to be true. But why did these children want to remain in school an hour and fifteen minutes after the scheduled session was over? And the last session of school before a greatly anticipated holiday! Consider your own experience. The day before a holiday in your school was probably a "special" day, but the chances are that, as soon as the bell sounded, you were on your way for fun. Why did the children in the City and Country School stay? Primarily because they were enjoying themselves and getting satisfaction out of staying. Some may have remained because other children were staying, but an hour and a quarter is a long time to a six-year-old, or even to an eleven-year-old.

They just sat there and sang? Yes, just that. Each child knew he would have the opportunity to sing his favorite song, and, if it were sung several times, he would be all the more delighted. And that is what singing time should be—a time for experiencing inner joy and satisfaction.

One of the reasons singing is so satisfying is that it is an excellent means of self-expression, for emotional release, for identifying one's self with people, places, things, and ideas. All of us do not have the ability to record our emotions in music, but certain songs of others seem to crystallize our own feelings. As we sing them we have a feeling of satisfaction. We become close associates of the people of whom we sing, whether they be "cowboys" or "The Carpenter," sailors' chanteys, work songs, or great love songs. We lose our own identity and become the character in the song. At the same time we are members of a group pervaded by a spirit of unity. Singing sweeps, fuses, and unites. You have enjoyed the experience. Think about it and see if you can analyze your feelings and reactions.

Groups of people have crystallized their deepest emotions and keenest interests in songs. We can sing those songs and better understand the particular group. The song of the Russian peasant may mirror despair or picture his hope for joy. The fun-loving Irish have transferred their gaiety to rollicking tunes. A picture of the plantation slave—his hopes, his fears, his ambitions, and his daily life—has been portrayed in his song. Replete with facts concerning any of these groups, children can vicariously, but understandingly, experience the same emotions that are expressed in the songs of the people. As Jonny Engles, a ten-year-old, watched a weary pedlar push his cart down the street, he said, "Why, that man walks just like I felt today when I sang *The Volga Boatmen*." Singing is not only the means of expressing individual emotion but also the means of experiencing the emotions and feeling of others.

Singing is the most important phase of music in the elementary school, not only because it is personally satisfying, but also because a wide musical experience can be gained through it. By using material children can read themselves or learn by rote, a rather complete understanding of music can be experienced. Actually, the instrumental forms—rondo, symphony, overture, and so forth—can be learned by singing the various themes. This is not a plea for teaching these forms in this way since the tone color and effects of orchestral instruments are lacking. But the themes can be taught. Examine the objectives for the elementary school child in music as set up in various courses of study. You will find that most of them can be attained through singing.

Singing is the most important part of the music program for still another reason: songs children sing contain the basic groups of tones fundamental to our music. These groups, repeated time after time, are absorbed. Common patterns of rhythm are absorbed, too. Reading music, then, becomes a matter of identifying these groups and these patterns. It should be pointed out that children of India or Ethiopia would not absorb the fundamental patterns of *their* music by singing the songs our children sing—*their* music is based on different fundamentals.

Since children come into the world equipped with a musical instrument, it would be an unforgivable waste not to make use of the voice and develop it. Between the singer and his song there is no artificial barrier (a violin, a clarinet, for example) that requires practice for manipulation. He can learn to sing—and sing beautifully—Brahms' *Lullaby* after hearing it several times. *If* he had a violin, *if* he had a teacher, several years of practice would be necessary before he could *play* it beautifully.

THE CHILD VOICE

A child appears to have three voices: a speaking voice, a "play" voice, and a singing voice. The variation in the range of sounds and in the quality of sounds he makes is amazing. His voice is flexible. It is this pliancy that challenges the teacher's skill.

The ordinary speaking voice of the pre-primary and primary school child is characteristically soft, clear, and high pitched. His singing voice should be of the same quality. His play voice is essentially strident, harsh, and forced. It is the result of necessity and excitement. Should the child's singing voice be projected a great distance, or should he become excited while singing, his singing voice will take on the undesirable qualities of his play voice. If he has to make the people in the last row of the auditorium hear his vocal efforts, undoubtedly his voice will be forced and strident. If he becomes excited while singing and playing a game at the same time, an undesirable change will take place in the nature of his singing.

The voice of the intermediate grade child is fuller and has

a greater range than that of the primary grade child. His clear, high, flute-like head tone is more beautiful than that of smaller children. The majority of the boys in the finest boys choirs come from this group. Many people think the singing of the children in this age group, and those two or three years older, is the most beautiful of all singing, not excepting the great voices of opera and the concert stage.

Although the changing voice of the adolescent does not often require attention in the elementary school, it is well for teachers to be able to recognize it and understand its cause. The period of adolescence is a period of rapid physical growth. Vocal chords, the vibration of which produces sound, change in size as do the controlling muscles. Those of girls grow in thickness and produce a fuller, richer tone; those of boys lengthen, thereby producing a deeper, lower tone. While this change in size is taking place, the controlling muscles should gradually grow in strength to compensate for the added strain. Sometimes, however, these muscles seem to tire or lose control. This lack of control often results unexpectedly and embarrassingly in a too-high or too-low pitch in the voice.

The inherent quality and the range of a child's voice are the result of his physical structure. The quality we hear, though, is the result of his effort to copy a model. It is the responsibility of his teacher to be certain he has a *good* model—and it is the responsibility of his teacher to guide his development intelligently. Such guidance includes making certain he sings within the proper range. How is this done? By selecting songs with the proper range and by making certain the pitch of the singing is correct. Unless the teacher has absolute pitch, a pitch pipe is essential equipment.

SONGS FOR CHILDREN

Selecting children's songs is a process requiring the most careful consideration. The "song on the next page" is not often the one that will bring about a better understanding of the area or the center of interest that engages the group. It may not extend their musical growth. Perhaps it is fundamentally a scale song when the last eight songs they have learned have been of this type. No, the "song on the next page" is probably one that the group should learn at another time, if at all. The next song to be chosen should be considered most carefully. A generous variety is available in song literature. The songs children learn should represent variety in form, mood, and melodic and rhythm pattern.

In deciding whether or not to use your time and energy to learn a certain song, study it. *If* the song is of the proper range and difficulty; *if* it remains in the memory after a little study; *if* its rhythm is smooth and flowing, interesting, and vital; *if* it is the proper length; *if* the text is proper and worthy; *if* the words are easily sung; *if* the words and music agree; *if* other children liked to sing the song; *if* the song has permanent value; and *if* you, the teacher, enjoy hearing it again and again, *it is a good song.* Start teaching it.

Incidentally, very, very few of the so-called "popular" songs of the day meet those requirements of a good song.

Range

The correct range of a song is that which permits a vocalist to sing easily and lightly without forcing his tones. The range of songs in children's books of the current song series has been carefully checked so that little children will not sing too low too long. The material in other books should be studied. For example, songs in the key of C hover in range around middle C. Too many tones around middle C may force little children (their natural voice quality being high pitched) to use their "play" voice in singing.

Phrases

For those to whom singing is a new experience, phrases (sections to be sung in one breath) should be short. Artistic singing demands that a phrase be sung in one breath. The phrases, but not the words, should be short. Consider:

> Three blind mice, three blind mice,
> See how they run, see how they run!

Children *can* sing each line as a phrase, but they will mimic their model. If the teacher gasps for breath after the first three words, each line will probably be sung as two sections. Even so, the words should be long and should be sung their full note value, as:

> Thre-e-e bli-i-ind mi-i-ice, thre-e-e bli-i-ind mi-i-ice,

This emphasis on the vowels must be made without distorting or slowing the tempo. All that happens is that the sound of the words is prolonged. Just try prolonging the *d* in "blind," or the *ce* in "mice." It can't be done. This emphasis on vowels demands a bit more control of the breath than does chopping the words short. Longer phrases can be sung easily and naturally with practice.

> "Believe me, if all those endearing young charms
> Which I gaze on so fondly today"

is a long phrase. Artistic singing demands that it be sung in one breath. Awareness of the meaning of the words demands that it be sung in one breath. By the time children are ready to understand the meaning of the song, they will have sufficient control of breath and voice to sing it with one breath. (Perhaps some time children will sing "My country, 'tis of thee, Sweet land of liberty" without gasping for breath and pausing after the word "thee." The same *may* be true of "Oh say, can you see by the dawn's early light. . . .")

Rhythm Pattern

The rhythm pattern of a rote song is not a particular problem for children—they learn songs with intricate patterns, for example, in listening to the radio—but it can be a problem for their teachers! When children "tip" (see page 41) or clap (see

Chapter 4) as they listen, they have no difficulty in learning to sing "in time." Physical response of some sort to the beat of music (clapping, tapping, or tipping) as they listen to learn makes both simple and complicated patterns easy.

Words

Words of songs are so important that they have a claim to the most careful attention. They should be of interest to the children. If a twelve-year-old is excited about boats, music is likely to lose a lover if he has to sing, "I want to be a daisy with a white and yellow hat." If he is a five-year-old, he is not curious about the "goodness of great men." Words of the poem that children are expected to sing should be at their level of understanding. The classic translation of the words of the hymn ". . . my cross I'd bear" into ". . . my cross-eyed bear" *is* funny, but, at the same time, it proves that there is an utter lack of understanding on the part of the singer. The last part of the first stanza of *America* is given an unusual turn of meaning when sung, "Land where my fathers died, land where the pilgrims cried." Such distortions indicate that the picture suggested by the words is nonexistent. Children's enjoyment of singing will be enhanced if they know the meanings of the words they are expected to sing.

"How many stanzas of the song shall I teach?" All the stanzas should be taught if the poem that has been set to music is a good poem, a complete poetic idea. The exceptions to this general statement are certain patriotic songs, certain community songs, and certain songs for special days. Because it is desirable to have the whole school know a list of songs for assembly singing, little children are often required to learn songs the words of which are beyond their comprehension. *The Star-Spangled Banner* is one of these. They should know this song, but, until they have a conception of the meaning of the words, they should not be required to learn all of it. This song has a taxing range. When it is sung in the approved key of A flat, many people find it easier to sing than when it is sung in the key of B flat, the key in which it is usually notated.

The function of the tune is to enhance the beauty of the words. If it does not do that, enjoy the poem as a poem.

Subject Matter

As was stated before, there is variety in songs available for children. Some can contribute to the understanding of an area of interest. Songs can be the reason for investigating: *Why* would a group of American Indians have a *Corn Grinding Song?* a *Horse Dance? Why* are there so many songs about widows in the folk songs from Spain?

Some songs can enlarge concepts. Each ethnic group, each national and cultural group has its own songs. The various periods in the history of the United States, the people in each section of our country, most of our occupational groups—each has contributed its own songs through which we can learn. When these become the subject of study and investigation, another medium of understanding is at hand.

Much of the material related to the contribution of recorded music (Chapter 6) is relevant to songs children sing.

Accompaniment

An accompaniment should heighten the effect of the words and melody. Fortunately many of the accompaniments that are found in the music textbooks are simple but interesting harmonically. The accompaniment requires comparatively little technical facility, but the accompanist needs a genuine respect for the significance of printed symbols and a musicianly manner of interpretation. Moreover, an accompaniment has an important role in promoting musical growth. Its use accustoms the children to hearing tones other than those they are singing. Listening while singing is excellent preparation for singing part-songs.

To "accompany" means to "go along with." Thus, an accompaniment should "go along with" the voices. It does not drown them, nor does it blot them out by the volume of its tone.

GOOD SINGING

Miss Watson was a teacher in the first grade of a school in the poorest district of a small city. Without kindergarten training, her class had come to her with as meager a background as would appear possible. The children had had no desirable pre-school musical experiences. Today, second- or third-hand radios may be found in that district, but when Miss Watson started teaching there, radios were scarce. Young, full of enthusiasm, and possessing a small, high, clear, pleasing voice and a love for singing, she gathered her brood about her and began one of her jobs, which was to teach them to sing.

Slowly and steadily their efforts became simple songs distinguished for the clarity of the melodic line. By the end of the year each child could sing fifty songs by himself, and the group knew about a hundred full-page songs.

The ensemble had the high, clear quality of Miss Watson's voice. The children dramatized, not actually, but with facial expressions, every song they sang. The picture of the song was mirrored in their faces and voices. Lively, gay songs brought a sparkle to their eyes. The pathos of voice and expression when they sang about the little kittens losing their mittens (a tragedy the children could well understand) was a revelation. Because they had a clear conception of the idea to be expressed, they phrased correctly; their enunciation was good because they wanted to convey the meaning of the story to others; their pronunciation was a bit provincial at times, but with every new song and every passing day their twang diminished. The mothers who came for their children after school got in the habit of coming early and enjoyed the last ten minutes of the day with them—always a period spent in singing.

The class received an extraordinarily well-rounded musical experience in spite of a complete lack of equipment except for a pitch pipe. The piano in the gymnasium was scorned by the teacher because of its lack of tone and tune. Yet the children had a meaningful rhythmic program, they learned melodies sung by the teacher, and they made their own tunes to poems. All this was accomplished by a skillful, resourceful teacher. Miss Watson's class exemplifies good singing.

What *is* good singing? Perhaps by describing what it is *not*— the antithesis of the picture just given—will help clarify what it is.

A group of fifth-grade children was contributing to a program that the fourth grade had planned for the auditorium period. The older group decided that its part in the program would be a dramatization of one of its favorite poems while the class recited it; after that, the group would sing the poem. The poem for the choral speech and dramatization was the old English verse:

> There was an old woman as I've heard tell,
> Fa, la, la-la-la-la-la (after each line)
> She went to the market, her eggs for to sell,
> She went to market, as I've heard say,
> She fell asleep on the King's highway.
> There came by a pedlar whose name was Stout,
> He cut her petticoats round about,
> He cut her petticoats up to her knees!
> Which made the old woman to shiver and sneeze!
> When this little woman did first awake
> She began to shiver and began to shake!
> She began to wonder, she began to cry,
> "Lawk-a-mercy me, this is none of I!
> But if it be I and I hope it be
> I've a doggie at home that I'm sure knows me;
> And if it be I, he will wag his tail
> But if it be not, he will bark and wail,"
> Home went the old woman all in the dark,
> Then up got her dog and began to bark!
> He began to bark and she began to cry,
> "Lawk-a-mercy me, this is none of I!" [1]

[1] Copyright 1932 by E. C. Schirmer Music Co. Used by permission. The melody may be found in Louise Kifer Myers, *Music Fundamentals Through Song*. Englewood Cliffs, N. J.: Prentice-Hall, Inc., 1954.

At the appointed time on the program, the fifth grade gave its performance. In a crepe-paper skirt that surrendered unresistingly to the pedlar's huge shears, the "old woman" acted her part perfectly. The "dog" behind a chair cavorted and barked realistically. The dramatization was excellent. The choral speech accompaniment would have inspired even the most miserable actors. As a matter of fact, the face of each child reciting the poem showed that *he* was fully aware of the dramatics of the situation. Especially interesting was the interpretation of the mood of the moment as portrayed by the manner in which the children said, "Fa, la, la-la-la-la-la." Interest, sympathy, horror, pathos, excitement, and finally, feverish excitement—all were indicated in the interpretation of those lines. The whole poem was given in a superlative manner. The audience waited, with the keenest anticipation, for the poem to be sung.

During the singing it did not seem possible that the same group was performing. They mumbled their words, they breathed when they wanted to, their faces were blank, and the charming "Fa, la, la-la-la-la-la's" had no character. The song had no lilt, no verve. The tempo was less than half as fast as the spoken words. It was flat, uninteresting, and uninspired. The consensus was that it was simply not "good singing."

Good singing is characterized by the following:

1. Good tone quality. It should be musical and produced without effort.

2. Correct tempo. The words and music of a song call for a tempo that enhances the mood. "There was an old woman" is imaginative and gay. The moments of pathos and excitement require treatment different from that of the light parts.

3. Correct rendition of the symbols on the printed page. In the Middle West in the early 1920's there was a group of itinerant band leaders who made their living by directing village bands. On appointed nights during the week they scheduled and conducted band rehearsals in various towns. One of these leaders, whose lack of training and skill was compensated for by enthusiasm and a desire to serve those who hired him, had a constant admonition for the members of his bands. It was: "Play it as she's wrote, boys, play it as she's wrote." Excellent advice. Shakespeare was concerned with this same matter. In *Richard III*, he said,

> Ha, ha! Keep time.
> How sour sweet music is
> When time is broke and no proportion kept.

Changes in dynamics and rhythms are relative. Marked gradations between contrasts in dynamics and rhythms are desirable, but exaggerations are not. In this aspect of interpretation there is need for good judgment.

4. *Correct phrasing.* A good singer sings as a good reader reads. When a good reader reads poetry, he does not stop and gasp for breath at the end of the line unless stopping is indicated by the punctuation or the idea. The meaning of the words suggests certain accents. In choral music these accents take precedence over measure accents. Words in phrases are grouped together. The reader reads ". . . in-the-house." Too often the phrase is sung ". . . in . . . the . . . house."

5. *Obvious emotional response.* The expressions of singing children will show whether or not they are feeling the "picture" suggested by the words. Their faces mirror their inner responses.

6. *Good enunciation.* Enunciation means "distinct articulation." Vowels carry the vocal sound, whereas consonants shape it. Correct vowel sounds insure good tone quality. Meticulous attention to consonants, especially final consonants, insures audience understanding.

7. *Good pronunciation.* Pronunciation is concerned with the stress and sound given the parts of words or the whole word. When "elephant" is called "el-le-funt," it is mispronounced. Words are important in a song, and the true identity of each must be preserved.

TEACHING SINGING

Singing is a skill. Vocal control and aural exactness are necessary for its development. Although the road from the nursery school to the concert stage is long, every singer who travels that route has to have those faculties upon which to build. Without the ability to produce specific tones at the proper time there can be no vocal music. It makes no difference if a person can sing the most beautiful tone imaginable on high G; he must be able to sing it every time that note appears in the score, or the ability is worth nothing. Producing specific tones at an exact time is the result of vocal control and aural exactness.

This section of the book is concerned with teaching those who have fair vocal control and aural exactness. Under the title *The Poor Singer,* which appears later in this chapter, plans will be suggested for guiding the development of those who seem to lack oral control and aural exactness. (See page 48.)

A treatise on the "Teaching of Reading" would discuss thoroughly the importance of readiness for reading. In a like manner, it is well to consider "singing readiness."

Singing Readiness

A total unawareness of music and singing is hard to imagine. Because this unawareness is more likely to occur in very young children, plans will be suggested for stimulating them to want to sing. Should a teacher of older children realize their need for this same definite stimulation, she can adapt these suggestions to meet the needs of her class.

A singing teacher—not a teacher of singing, but a teacher who sings—is one of the best means of acquainting children with singing and awakening in them the desire to sing.

This teacher might well do as Miss Watson did—gather her brood around her and sing to them. Three or four well-chosen songs—chosen because of the appeal of their subject matter and because they fitted the musical experience of the children—

sung enthusiastically and well will serve as an introduction to the art of singing. If, after singing them, the teacher asks such questions as "Which song did you like best?" "Would you like to hear it again?" the enterprise is well under way. After the children have heard the song of their choice several times, the teacher can suggest that perhaps the group would like to sing it—if a child has not already made the suggestion.

This approach to singing is good for three reasons: (1) the children get the same kind of satisfaction and enjoyment from it as they do from hearing the teacher tell an interesting story; (2) it gives the opportunity for choices to be made, and (3) it promotes attentiveness because of the necessity of making a choice. And it *may* introduce the children to the activity of singing!

How much better Miss Watson's introduction was than the way another teacher began her first music class. She said to the children: "I am going to sing you a song. I want you to learn it. Everyone should learn to sing. Your mothers and fathers know how to sing. They like to sing. It is fun." A song could have been sung during the time it took to say those words, and the children could have formed their own ideas as to whether or not singing might be fun.

Teaching Rote Songs

A song that is learned by "ear" is a rote song. In connection with school music, this type of song is thought of as one that contains melodic and rhythmic patterns too difficult for children to read. They learn to sing it by hearing it sung by the teacher or on a phonograph record or sometimes by another child or adult. In general, there are three ways of teaching rote songs, *the phrase method, the whole method,* and *the part method.*

The Phrase Method. In the phrase method, the teacher sings the complete song. Then she sings the first phrase; the children sing the first phrase. The teacher sings the second phrase; the children sing the second phrase, and so on through the first stanza. The process of teacher singing and children echoing is continued as phrases are combined. There are variations in the method, but essentially all are the same. The song is learned bit by bit.

Many wrong tonal combinations result when children are taught by this method. The mistakes occur most often at the beginning of phrases. Often just the first tone is wrong; sometimes the entire phrase is in another key. These mistakes are heard in the simplest songs. Close examination of what the children hear when songs are taught by this procedure will disclose the difficulty. For example, in this song:

> I saw an airplane flying by,
> Oh, so high! oh, so high!

> *Teacher sings:* I saw an airplane flying by,
> *Children sing:* I saw an airplane flying by,
> *Teacher sings:* Oh, so high! oh, so high!
> *Children sing:* Oh, so high! oh, so high!

Consider the last word in each line. As the children hear and repeat these lines, the last word in the teacher's line, "by," is more closely connected melodically with "I" than it is with "Oh," which really follows "by" in the melody. The melodic connection desired is between "by" and "Oh," but this is heard only when the song is sung in its entirety. If the song is broken into larger pieces, misconception of tonal and melodic relationships can result wherever the break is made. Moreover, the less musically certain the teacher and the more complicated the melody, the greater the opportunity for mistakes.

The Whole Method. In this method of teaching the whole song is taught at once—the children hearing it over and over again in its entirety. Songs that people learn by listening to the radio are learned in this manner. Radio singers do not break them into small bits and repeat these parts. Music teachers can learn a valuable lesson from this observation—valuable because it saves much time and effort, and valuable because it lessens the likelihood of wrong tones.

Miss Jackson, a second grade teacher, often found herself explaining why her class could sing so many songs and sing them well. Her method of teaching was the reason *why*. While the children were deciding what investigations and activities would engage them in a new area of study, Miss Jackson sang eight or ten songs for them, the subject matter of which centered around the new theme. The children decided which songs they would like to learn, and the teacher listed them. Miss Jackson sang those songs several times for the children. One day, after having sung the first song on the list, she directed discussion around it. The next day the discussion centered around the second song, and so on. By doing this she made certain that the children had a concept of the sequence of meanings (knew about what they were singing) so necessary for complete understanding. Listening to these songs would sometimes be "incidental" to other activities during the day.

After the children had heard the songs for several days, Miss Jackson invited them to join her in singing the one they had heard most often. Frequently she found that they knew it quite well. If certain phrases needed attention, these were practiced. Segregation of parts at that time and for that purpose is entirely different from teaching the whole song phrase by phrase—the melodic connections of the parts had first been established. The remaining songs were taught in the same way.

In this class there were always (1) songs with which children were becoming acquainted, (2) songs that they were about to start singing, (3) songs that they were in the process of learning, and (4) songs that they knew.

Miss Jackson believed that one of the reasons her class learned songs accurately and easily was that they "tipped" as they listened and learned. "Tipping" is about the same as clapping the meter of the music, not the rhythm of the words, with the important difference that the fingertips are used instead of the palms of the hands. There is no sound as a result of the activity. Phrases that could prove rhythmically difficult seem to be simplified by this constant muscular association with the meter. "Tipping" provides for more activity than a single gingerly moving finger. Rests are actually felt and are not slighted when associated with "tipping." Moreover, the children become used to keeping time together while singing, which will be necessary later in reading music in the classroom. As Miss Jackson sang to the children, she "tipped" with them. While they were learning the songs, all "tipped." When a song was learned, "tipping" had served its purpose and was discontinued.

Toward the end of the year, a first-grade teacher decided to experiment and see how many songs her children could learn in one week by using Miss Jackson's plan. The songs were selected by the children before the week of experimentation. During the period of selection, the children heard each song once or twice. On Monday, the actual listening and learning process started. On Friday, the class knew and sang well nine new full-page songs.

The Part Method. This is actually the "chime-in" method. The reference, of course, is to an invitation to sing simple oft-repeated phrases or words when they occur in a song. Since they *are* simple and *are* repeated, children learn these before the remainder of the song is registered by the musical memory. The "chime-in" method consists, actually, of the teacher's permission to sing when a section or phrase is learned.

Teachers sometimes say they do not have time to teach many songs—as many as Miss Jackson did, for example. If you will take a stop watch with a second hand, you will find it takes but a short time to sing a song. How short is "short"? Twenty-two seconds for one stanza of *Three Little Kittens Who Lost Their Mittens;* thirty-seven seconds for one stanza and the chorus of *Dixie;* and sixty-two seconds for one stanza of *The Star-Spangled Banner.*

Should the teacher sing with the class? Many writers say very definitely that she should not. The theory on which this statement is based is that a teacher who is singing cannot listen carefully to the children. Therefore, she does not notice incorrect tones, mispronounced words, or bad tone quality. In addition, if she sings constantly, the children will come to depend upon her, and there will be a lack of growth in independence among them, and lack of opportunity for the musical memory to develop. The musical memory is developed by remembering —and with the teacher singing, children don't have to remember: they follow along less than a split second behind and *appear* to be remembering. There is probably another reason, too. Many teachers have become so habituated to singing with the class that this activity, plus an equal amount of talking during the remainder of the day, results in their being unnecessarily tired at the end of each day's session.

However, there are times when it is desirable for the teacher to sing with the class. For example, if songs are taught the way Miss Jackson taught hers, the teacher invites the children to sing with her to give them confidence in singing a song for the first time. Or, when singing for fun is the activity of the moment—singing the old favorites and the recently learned ones— a teacher who does not sing is conspicuous. A child said to his teacher one day, "We sing because we're happy and like to sing. Don't you like to sing or aren't you happy?" She sang with her children after that.

Some unfortunate children have teachers who limit their development in ways other than teaching them only a few songs a year or singing with them constantly. Their teachers sit at the piano, with their backs to the class, awkwardly pick out a tune or pound out the melody and its accompaniment, and call *that* teaching a song! Let those in that first group pick out and learn their songs in private. Let those in that second group (1) read again what an accompaniment is supposed to do and be, and (2) save the accompaniment to enhance the finished song, the song that is learned. Inexperienced children hear a melody as a mass of tone, not as individual tones, so they cannot identify the melody in the welter of sound resulting from a loud rendition of tune with accompaniment.

In other words, teach children songs by *singing* them and singing with good tone quality, in the correct tempo, accurate

as to tones, with correct phrasing, correct enunciation and pronunciation, as if a gem or jewel were being presented. *If* this
presentation can be *accompanied* (not drowned out) by an
autoharp or other chording instrument, the "gem" is enhanced.
Because the tone quality of a chording instrument is different
from that of the voice, the melody is not buried in sound.

Piano accompaniments can make a valuable contribution to
musical development—*but not in the song-learning stage.*

Teaching Part Singing

Ability to sing parts—ability to harmonize—is the result of
aural development. Eye recognition of symbols is not a problem, although one must become aware of the position of the
notes on the staff. Developing necessary aural power is the
problem.

Just as children vary in their natural ability to remember
tones, in their natural rhythmic sense, in their natural sense
of tone, they vary in their natural ability to sing tones that harmonize with the melody. To be able to harmonize is a source of
satisfaction for adults as well as children. It is a skill resulting
from a feeling for relationships between tones. It is a skill resulting from practice. As a skill, it can be developed by activity
calculated to improve aural power and the sense of tonal relationship.

There is a collection of fact called "harmony." What is included in "harmony" is well standardized—the rules governing
the relationships between the alto, tenor, and bass parts gen-
erated by a melody (soprano) tone or a group of melody tones.
We have heard the results of the rules so often that some of us
supply a missing or needed harmony tone *by ear.* We have
heard tones in correct relationships so many times that our ears
are alerted and sometimes disturbed by a tone foreign to the
pattern. Our ears know, even though we do not know the technical names for the combinations or the rules that apply.

We all have this *feeling* for relationships, more or less, and
children have it, more or less. One boy in the first grade had

it more! His teacher was singing the descant Row (1), Row (8), Row (5) as the class tried to sing *Row, Row, Row Your Boat* without her voice. At the end, the children were singing *her* part. The boy said: "You sing with the kids and I'll sing *that*." She did and he did. He had a good ear!

What experiences can aid the development of children's 'ear" so they learn to harmonize? So they can sing two-, then three-, and four-part music? What experiences can develop the feeling for relationships among tones heard simultaneously? Children get acquainted with chord tones in melodies by hearing and singing them—one at a time in broken chords, in a horizontal relation. They need ear acquaintance with those same tones sounded simultaneously in a vertical relation. How can they get it? By directing conscious attention and by hearing it. Just as simple as that.

The teacher can provide an opportunity for developing aural power and for cementing relationships that exist between a tone and the others in the same triad by furnishing an accompaniment to songs by:

1. Playing the *root* [2] of the triad to which the melody-tone-on-the-measure-accent belongs. It can be played on melody bells, tone blocks, and/or the piano. For example, in accompanying *America,* key of F

Play		F	C	F	F	C	F	and so on
In other keys								
	play	1	5	1	1	5	1	and so on

For *The Deaf Woman's Courtship* (key of E flat)

Play		E flat	E flat	B flat	E flat	E flat	E flat	B flat	E flat
In other keys									
	play	1	1	5	1	1	1	5	1

A repeated root, played an octave higher, adds variety—and aural experience.

2. Playing on a chording instrument the triad to which the

[2] Triads are explained on page 184.

melody-tone-on-the-measure-accent belongs. Just the fundamental chord is sufficient—nothing fancy to show skill, no
melody tones—just the chord tones. The piano, autoharp, harmolin, guitar, or ukelele accompaniment to a song may add interest, may be "pretty," may be easy to learn, may be a source
of satisfaction in making music—such accompaniment may be
all or do all of these things—but its greatest contribution is to
children's aural development in familiarizing them with the
fundamental relationships existing between a melody tone and
the other tones of its triad. That is the important contribution
of the so-called "chording" or "strumming" or "social" instruments. Their contribution is so important to children's development that one person (Guess who?) would require teachers to
be able to play and to *use daily* one of these instruments, or
the piano. The maximum requirement for piano playing: ability
to play just the fundamental triads at the proper places. It
would be "all right" with *that person* if a tone in a triad were
doubled (chord of four tones) or if the chord were "broken"
every once in a while—it would be "all right," but not necessary
to meet the requirement.

A child in the first grade, sitting on the floor with an autoharp in his lap, or a sixth-grader with an autoharp on a table,
can strum chords F, C, F, F, or E flat, E flat, B flat, E flat with
ease and aplomb—playing by ear or reading the chord letter
name.

The following activities provide an opportunity for developing aural power and for cementing vertical tonal relationships:

1. *Singing descants.* The two tunes—melody and descant—
are learned by rote. After they are learned, they must be sung
in such a manner that the two tones produced simultaneously
can be "savored," absorbed, and enjoyed. A descant must not
be allowed to become an *opponent* of a melody—nor should
those singing the melody and those singing the descant engage
in a vocal bout, each group trying to best the other in volume.
Instead, each group should consider the other as the more im-

portant—to be listened to with pleasure. These same comments also relate to singing rounds.

Experience in singing descants can be followed by making up descants. Some of the facts that aid harmonizing by ear can be used in this creative effort.

2. *Harmonizing.* These facts will aid the teacher in harmonizing—harmonizing by fact and by ear. "By ear" is the initial approach for children.

(a) Except in rare instances, the melody-tone-on-the-measure-accent determines the accompanying chord.

(b) The root of a triad harmonizes with the tones of a triad. *1* and *5* belong to two triads. A song always ends on *1*—and the ear must decide about the other places to use 1 and V. (Remember: this is what children have heard in those suggested accompaniments.)

(c) The third tone below and the sixth tone below a melody tone make pleasant combinations. When used, this is known as "harmonizing in 3rds and 6ths." For example, the first two measures of *Silent Night* are in 3rds, the next two in 6ths; and, much of the first section of *Joy to the World* is in 3rds.

(d) Not every tone needs to be harmonized. For example, in *Down in the Valley,* several tones are not harmonized:

```
sol do re | mi mi mi mi sol sol | re sol ti re | sol sol fa mi re | do
          | do — — — — mi      | ti           | ti  -  la sol fa |
```

And, *Long, Long Ago* is in 3rds all the way through, except at *do* at the end of phrases and low *sol*—where each part sings the melody tone.

Here are several ways to proceed:

(1) Harmonize *Three Blind Mice:* The teacher plays the following, musically, but with more emphasis on the second part:

```
3 2 1 : | | : 5 4 3 : | | : 8 8767 8 55 5 : | | 8 8767 8555 4 3 2 1 | |
1 7 1 : | | : 3 2 1 : | | : 3  4   3  -  : | | 3 4  -3  2   1 7 1  | |
```

The children listen several times, then *hum* the second part, and sing. The children play the harmony part on song bells while singing. Learn other songs this way. *Stars of the Summer Night* is good.

(2) Sing the root of the triad to which the melody-tone-on-the-accent belongs. *God Bless America* is good.

(3) Use an instrument for a harmony part or use it for the melody while the group sings the harmony part.

The following are ideas for making descants and harmony:

(1) when the melody starts *low,* start the new part high; (2) when melody starts high, start the harmony or descant *low;* and (3) use scale tones between roots, instead of I-V-I-V try I $_7$ $_6$ V, I $_7$ $_6$ V, and so on. The ear will have to be the guide in using this idea.

Children learn to sing parts by hearing and by singing them. Children learn to harmonize by harmonizing. If they can sing a tune, sufficient aural power can be developed to enable them to sing a part other than the tune. When they can learn to read a melody, they can certainly read another part.

THE POOR SINGER

People vary in their ability to sing just as they vary in other respects. Singing *My Old Kentucky Home* may be as signal an achievement for one person, as singing the leading role in the college operetta is for another. As in all curves of distribution taking into consideration large numbers, the extremes of a curve of singing ability have relatively few persons at either end. In school the children who constantly challenge the resources of the teacher are those who have to work more diligently and to concentrate more closely in order that their singing approximate that of the children with average ability. Those children are the ones who will be called "poor singers" for the purpose of this discussion. The following material relates equally well to adults who do not sing accurately and easily. Such adults have the same fundamental problems as children.

The inability to sing a song—and by "sing" is meant only "carry a tune"—is manifest in several degrees. It has nothing to do with the quality of a phrase accurately reproduced; it has to do only with the ability to produce tones accurately and in the designated sequence. There are those children—and adults —who can sing (1) a single tone with a group but not alone; (2) a single phrase with a group but not alone, and (3) a short song with a group but not alone. At each level of ability, singing with a group is the greatest achievement. Progression from one level to the next represents progress—not only encouraging but exciting progress for the person who has always wanted to sing and has never had anyone to help him learn.

Analysis of the Poor Singer's Difficulties

A person who cannot sing lacks completely or partially one of the following, or, as is most often the case, is weak in a combination of several of them. This makes diagnosis of his trouble more difficult.

1. Oral power. Almost every child in the public schools has the power of speech, but often impediments to speech are present. Adenoids and enlarged tonsils interfere with singing as they do with speech.

2. Aural power. The aspect of aural power important here is the power to differentiate between pitches of various levels. "Pitch perception"—the ability to perceive pitch—is the term used in describing this ability.

The ability to hear differences and likenesses in tones and intervals varies between the person who cannot tell *God Save the Queen* from *The Star-Spangled Banner,* and the person who has absolute pitch. (Absolute pitch is the ability to identify by name any musical pitch.) But without the ability to hear differences in pitch there can be little singing. The lack of aural power is not nearly so prevalent as the number of nonsingers would indicate. It is a lack of *training* for individual growth in pitch perception that is so prevalent. It is easy to dismiss with a wave of the hand a person who cannot immediately sing a tune he hears. All too often those who can sing are taught to sing better, while others with poor pitch perception powers are not even allowed to try.

3. *Tonal memory.* Although some people may be able to reproduce accurately a small group of two or three tones, they seem to lack the power to remember phrases three or four measures long.

4. *Musical experience.* There are many adults who are sure they cannot sing. Usually it develops that as children they had been told not to try because they "could never learn to sing." As a result, they have been segregated and silent for years during periods when others were singing. Little children, even though they lack experience in music and in singing, seem perfectly willing to try time and time again. A common difficulty with these folk is being unable to "find" their "singing" voices. They try to make their "speaking" voices "sing."

5. *Self-confidence.* Ridicule or an unsympathetic reception of his vocal efforts has silenced many a would-be singer. The more sensitive he is, the more determined he is never to try again. Little children seem to have unquestioned confidence in their ability to learn to sing—until the sad day when they realize that others are making fun of them, or that the teacher is annoyed because their efforts appear to be unsuccessful. Older people who cannot sing not only have a feeling of inferiority to overcome when they start to learn, but they also have to overcome an extreme lack of confidence in their ability to do anything about it.

Sometimes with these ineptitudes there is an accompanying inability to "find" the singing voice, as was suggested above. Another aspect of this is the failure to conceive of a singing tone outside the normal range of the speaking voice. It seems impossible for people with this difficulty to sing "up in the head," their placement of tones being confined wholly to the chest register.

Meeting the Needs of the Poor Singer

A person cannot learn to swim by sitting on the bank and watching others. He cannot learn to run a mile in record time by viewing the races in a track meet. He cannot learn to drive a car by sitting in the back seat and watching the driver. Watching others swim, run, or drive a car, however, may inspire him to hope to do these things. So it is with learning to sing. A person cannot learn to sing by hearing others sing or seeing others sing. Observing their habits may help him, but the actual earning takes place inside him as the result of his own efforts. The way to learn to sing is to practice singing. Guidance is desirable if growth is to result, but all the guidance and observation possible will avail nothing without individual activity.

From this, then, it may be deduced that the person who cannot sing nor distinguish *God Save the Queen* from *The Star-Spangled Banner* needs not only practice but also a great amount of help in gaining this skill. The individual who cannot "carry a tune" needs practice for the development of his pitch perception powers.

Since the number of children in the public schools who lack oral power is negligible, no special attention will be given to their problems here. However, those with speech difficulties should be considered. As a rule, those who stammer sing well with the group and often sing well alone. Sometimes adenoids and enlarged tonsils cause the same difficulty in singing as they do in speech. As far as the teacher is concerned, her only recourse is to recommend the removal of these obstacles if they affect singing ability. Although this is obviously not the most important reason for giving them attention, it might be further substantiation of need for their removal.

Aural power and tonal memory are closely related. In most cases, it is not easy to distinguish between the two. It requires no unusual ability, though, to decide that Tom, who can sing an eight-measure melody after hearing it once, has a better tonal memory than Jan, who can sing only half of the melody after hearing it once. On the other hand, it is difficult to make a diagnosis of Alice's particular disability when she cannot sing the two tones she is supposed to reproduce. It is not evident whether she cannot match the tones because she is unable to hear them as definite tones or because she cannot remember them long enough to sing them. Fortunately for Alice and her teacher, regardless of which of these faculties is weak, both will improve with the regular systematic treatment that will be suggested.

Levels of Ability. Individuals vary in their ability to hear differences in tones and to remember tones. Levels of this ability are listed below—the lowest level first. Each level must be attained before the next is possible. Each level is characterized by ability to:

1. *Differentiate between high and low tones.* Tones far apart should be used for testing—for example, C, second line above the treble staff, and C, two lines below the bass staff. If these cannot be produced on an instrument, extremely high and low tones produced vocally by the teacher will suffice. Adjacent tones should not be used because of their similarity, which sometimes confuses even those with good pitch perception powers.

2. *Differentiate sufficiently well between tones within an octave, centered around the treble staff, to be able to tell which of two tones is the lower, or which of three tones is the highest,* and so forth. This is a step a bit more advanced than the level of hearing listed above because of the more limited range and less exaggerated intervals. A greater power of tonal memory is necessary because three tones have to be remembered in order to compare the level of tone.

3. *Match a specific tone.* ("Match" means to reproduce vocally the pitch indicated.) This one tone should be within the ordinary vocal range of the individual. For those who lack or nearly lack aural power, matching a single tone is a notable achievement. Once this initial step is gained, desirable growth in singing is possible. A person whose ear enables him to sing

an eight-measure phrase after hearing it once has little comprehension, and too often, little sympathy, for the effort required
by some people to match one single tone.

4. *Match two and then three successive tones.* A young man
spent ten minutes of every school day practicing with the music
instructor in college. He had never sung and seemed to lack
completely the necessary powers. At the end of two weeks of
concentrated practice he was able to sing the G below middle
C. At the end of another week he was able to sing the E and
C below that G. He called those tones *sol-mi-do.* He was
pleased beyond words when he discovered that, by putting
those three tones together, he was able to sing the first three
tones of *Dixie* and *The Star-Spangled Banner.* In another week
he could sing the tones in reverse order, and was happy to know
that he had learned the first measure of *The Blue Danube.*

5. *Sing a short phrase.* To continue the story of the college
student, although he knew the *sol-mi-do* and, finally, the *do-mi-
sol* combinations, it required a week's practice for him to sing
the following:

He did not become certain of the last two notes for several
days because of their proximity to G. Incidentally, his class was
as pleased with his progress as he was and insisted on singing
"Ray's piece" at each meeting in order that Ray might sing with
them.

In a two-week Music Education Workshop planned for in-
service teachers, the activities included learning to play by ear
1-3-5 on the piano from each key in an octave. One student
could not always sing the combination correctly nor could she
hear whether or not she played the correct keys. Her assignment was changed to playing 5-3-1 since the instructor thought
the student must have heard that combination many times—
the first three tones in *Dixie, The Star-Spangled Banner, Come
Thou Almighty King* and *Pussy Cat, Pussy Cat, Where Have*

You Been? The student may have heard those first three songs but she could not remember the sound of the first three tones— it was the sound of the first three tones in *Pussy Cat* she remembered. Soon, she was "Pussy Cat-ting" down the keyboard. She could *sing* it, too!

6. *Sing two short phrases, and then three, or one long phrase.* Ability to sing this amount means that the individual can sing longer songs that are built on a pattern of phrase repetition. For example, in the music notated on page 53, measures, five and six are exact repetitions of measures one and two. Measures three and seven are alike except for one tone. Repetition of melodic patterns is a fundamental practice in musical form. This repetition offers extra opportunities for singing without too much effort for the person with limited aural power.

Ability on each of these levels is a definite improvement over the preceding one.

A word of caution must be added: This section on *Levels of Ability* considered only *two* of the possible *five* reasons a person cannot sing easily or well. Refer again to the analysis of the poor singer's difficulties.

Activities for the Poor Singer. The most important activity for those who do not sing well is to practice singing. If they do not sing well because they cannot distinguish the difference between tones or cannot remember tonal groups, they need practice in distinguishing tones and in remembering tonal groups. Do you think that those statements are meant to be facetious? That they are too obvious? Indeed, they are probably the most important statements in this book. The fact is that too many teachers have not permitted poor or uncertain singers to sing at all!

If an individual is weak in his ability to remember tones, he needs practice in remembering. This means he must have occasion *to hear* and then to sing. Singing constantly *with* the class or *with* the piano or *with* the teacher will not help. He can sing along a fraction of a second behind the leaders and will seemingly be doing well. Actually, he has to remember only one tone at a time as he sings in this manner. Singing *with* the piano might be doing him some good, but it is not developing his musical memory. He needs opportunities for hearing and then singing alone if growth is to result.

SUGGESTIONS. Some devices that can be used to promote the desired growth in imitating tones or groups of tones are the following:

1. Imitating a siren sound on the neutral syllable "loo" will help a child find his singing voice or head tone. Prolonging one of the higher tones will help fix the head tone. If the child is not able to match the teacher's beginning tone, the teacher should match the tone she hears and proceed upward from that. When the upper tones are reached, practice should always start there, and descending melodies used. This helps carry the desired head tone quality to the lower tones, eradicates forced singing, and helps "keep" the singing voice.

The idea of "lifting" the tone can be developed by having the child imitate or answer a call by the teacher. One teacher calls the roll by using the tones of the tonic chord, and each child answers on the same tone. In this way the child gets the idea of "calling over" to the teacher, and through the power of suggestion the tones are lifted up and over.

Giving the child a definite call to sing in a song that is to be dramatized has proved successful. The interval of the call should be easy and wide. For example, in the song, *The Little Red Hen,* the answer, "Not I!" to the oft-repeated question of who will help the Little Hen, sung on *do-mi,* or *do-sol,* in the key of C, D, or E, would result in the use of the head tone. Songs that could be adapted to this purpose are found in most books of children's songs.

2. For a child who has difficulty in finding his singing voice, either one or both of the following suggestions may help: (*a*) On a tone a little higher than his speaking voice, ask him to prolong the last syllable of a spoken word—*echo* and *papa* are

good words to use because of the final vowel sound. The sustained *o* or *ah* is made with the *singing* voice. (*b*) Sing short sentences on the tone of his speaking voice (usually middle C or D flat above), and then start a familiar song on that pitch and sing along with him so he gets the "feeling" of singing.

3. Repeated phrases in songs the class knows offer interesting sources of material for practice. These bits of songs have two advantages as material: (*a*) Additional opportunities for *hearing* are offered every time the group sings the songs, and (*b*) when the individual learns to sing them, he can join the class in singing the parts he knows. People with poor pitch perception powers require many more repetitions of a tune before it makes an impression; therefore, working on phrases of favorite songs—songs likely to be sung quite often—insures frequent, more or less incidental opportunities for hearing.

4. Pitch and differences in pitches, objectified and associated with definite objects, help some children. For example, singing (or trying to sing) 3-2-1 while playing or watching someone play 3-2-1 on a keyboard instrument; or, "climbing a ladder" of tone; or "going up steps." Little children can dramatize height by singing on tiptoe, trying to reach the ceiling, or imitating a bird while sitting on a perch (the teacher's desk). The next suggestion is an extension of this one.

5. Fixing certain combinations of tones in the minds of the individual and learning other tones in relation to these is of definite value. Older children and adults have been taught to sing the tonic chord and "fix" it in their memory by diligent and systematic practice. Further practice is related to that chord. *Do-sol-mi-do* acts as a "handle" that objectifies certain tonal relationships in the whole realm of tone. Once the concept of this fundamental relationship is a part of the student's equipment, he has a fixed point from which to measure the positions of other tones.

The teacher must keep in mind the following facts relative to these suggestions and their purpose:

1. They offer simple *singing* and *listening* experiences on the level of the individual's abilities, with the idea of providing for the release and growth of his powers, regardless of how limited they seem to be.

2. Objectifying tonal relationships has proved to be of value in teaching these relationships.

3. Where there is no aural power there is no singing power. Therefore, opportunities for developing aural power *by listening* and then reproducing are necessary.

4. The ability to match *one* tone correctly is sufficient basis upon which to build for singing power.

5. Finally, and most important, the way to learn to sing is to practice singing with help and under guidance.

RESPONSIBILITY FOR GROWTH. To aid a child in finding his singing voice, is the responsibility of *all* his teachers, not just that of the first-grade teacher. It often happens that the patience and skill of his fifth-grade teacher or a suggestion made by his high school teacher will result in definite improvement, even though previous help was not effective. Because the first-grade teacher is accustomed to spending much time and effort in helping the individual child to sing, she accepts the challenge of these uncertain singers as a regular part of her work. The second-grade teacher more or less expects to do this kind of remedial work with a few boys and girls. These teachers are usually so successful that few children fail to respond, but if a child does not learn to sing in the lower grades, *it is the duty of every teacher with whom he comes in contact to work conscientiously in aiding him.* Mrs. "Pussy Cat" learned after she had been out of college several years.

DURING SINGING TIME. What shall we do with these uncertain singers during singing time? What can *they* do during singing time?

1. They should sit so that they can hear the good singers in the group—in front of good singers or in the midst of good singers.

2. These children should *sing* during singing time except (*a*) When the class is learning a new song, those who do not have fairly accurate aural power should remain silent because the incorrect tones they sing may be incorporated into the tune the class is learning. However, as soon as the melody is learned, an occasional incorrect tone will not distract those who know the tune. (*b*) The children who have not found their singing voices and, because of this, drone along on one unrelated pitch should be asked to confine their efforts to their individual singing time for the sake of the class.

3. Enlist the aid of the class in helping them learn. Children are not in school long before they discover there is variation in ability among them—so "We'll all help them learn to sing." For example, the class can sing prolonged vowel sounds to be imitated; or it can repeat three or four tones of a song for the poor singer to imitate; or individuals can play 3-2-1 on various instruments for the poor singer to match.

4. Sometimes uncertain singers have difficulty in registering the starting pitch of a song, in getting it started correctly—but once started, they can sing along. To help them get started, ask the class to sing the first word and prolong the tone while "everybody tunes in."

5. Learning to sing repeated phrases in songs can be the basis for individual growth.

6. These children can play repeated groups of melody tones on melody bells or the xylophone or a single tone on a tone block, or they can strum chords on a chording instrument.

These uncertain singers must not be alienated from music or ignored during music-making time just because the guidance and help they require differs from the needs of the remainder of the group. It has not been proved that average or below-average singing ability is an indication of a lack of power for understanding and enjoying other phases of music. The fact that singing familiar songs with a group may represent the height of these singers' vocal prowess should not preclude the opportunities for their most extensive development. No one has the right to deprive these would-be choristers of this source of fun and enjoyment.

USING SONGS

It has been stated that singing is the basic activity in the program described. Singing what? Songs. These songs are "children making music" and, aside from their beauty, aside from the enjoyment they provide, they have an utilitarian purpose. They can become the means for gaining skills. They can become the source of information. They can become the basis for learning about music. The more dearly they are held in the heart of the singer, the more likely the facts of music (or basic skills) learned from them or through them will function in subsequent learnings.

Here are some of the ways songs may be *used* (actually, it is "must" be used!) after they have been learned: as a "harness" for acquiring the habitual use of the conductor's beat, for counting aloud, for walking in time or all three simultaneously; as a means of gaining awareness of patterns in rhythm and patterns in tone and their notation—the same or different patterns; as a source of common groups of tones for which the correct syllable or number names must be learned.

PLAYING

There is an ever-increasing group of instruments on which children can make music—instruments that are easy to learn and easy to play—since little time is needed to acquire technique for personal satisfaction and for the enjoyment of others. These are the reasons children like them. Teachers like them, too, not only because they are easy to teach and easy to learn but because they are excellent "lures" for furthering learning in music. Also, through their use, (1) concepts applying to ensemble playing can be gained, (2) concepts necessary in reading can be established, (3) skill in reading duration values of notes can be developed, and (4) another means of learning, rich in satisfaction, is made available.

PRE-ORCHESTRAL INSTRUMENTS

These instruments can be grouped as melody-makers, chord-makers and percussion, which are used to mark the accent and pulse of music. A list of the more common instruments, grouped according to their usual function, follows. Although the xylophone and melody bells usually play a melody, when two or three tones are sounded simultaneously, they play a chord. Therefore, they have been listed under chord-makers as well.

Melody-makers	*Chord-makers*	*Percussion*
tonette	Autoharp	drums
ocarina	harmolin	rattles, gong
song flute	(xylophone)	tambourine
flutophone	(melody bells)	rhythm sticks
recorder	(sets of bells or	scrapers
symphonette	tone blocks)	claves
melody bells		
psaltery		
xylophone		
tone blocks		

And in addition to all these, there is the most important—the piano. Children can learn to play chords on it without "taking lessons" and use them in the same manner as chords on the Autoharp are used. They can play melodies the way they do on melody or song bells. Of course, this use of the piano and this way of playing it differ from the conventional concept of "piano playing"—but it is eminently satisfying and "educational."

Reason for Using These Instruments

The great advantage of these instruments is the variety of purposes they can serve, the variety of possible combinations, and the variety of ways in which they can be used. As to purposes: to learn music, to learn to play, and to have fun. As to combinations: all percussion or all chording or all melody; percussion and chording or percussion and melody; chording and melody; and all or any with *real* instruments (violin, piano, guitar, ukelele, clarinet) some children can play. As to variety of ways in which they can be used; alone or with other instruments; with singing, with records, with piano; as accompaniment to heighten the effect of dramatic play or a poem or as accompaniment for movement. Actually, it seems as though their use is limited only by the lack of ingenuity on the part of teachers and children.

It could be that these instruments are the most attractive means currently available for furthering interest in music and music-making—with the possible exception of moving to music or rhythms.

Various aspects of learning to play pre-orchestral instruments and ways of using them are discussed in Chapter 4, "Rhythms." Facts related to and suggestions for teaching instrumentalists to read may be found in Chapter 7, "Reading Music."

CONDUCTING

There must be a means of communication between the person who makes a group of musicians perform as one and the individuals who comprise the group. This means of communication is known as "conducting."

About Conducting

The conductor of a chorus or instrumental group has much the same relation to the ensemble as an organist has to his instrument. The conductor "plays" on the individuals just as the organist plays on the keys, utilizing the stops of the organ. The aims of the conductor and the organist are the same—the best possible interpretation of the music at hand. Fortunately for the organist, the stops of the organ are manipulated mechanically—they have no minds or impulses of their own. They obey automatically. The conductor is not so fortunate. His "instrument" is not so docile. It is made up of twenty, or sixty, or three hundred "parts" that are distinctly individual, each having its own will and whim. For the conductor to accomplish his aim there must be the clearest understanding between him and the various "parts" of his "instrument." Complete and absolute coordination of "parts" is necessary.

Down through the ages there has evolved a pattern of symbols that has served conductors in their attempt to gain this desirable coordination without having to strive for results verbally. In addition to this pattern of motions (symbols), each conductor has his own individual variations and signs that must be understood by members of his group. Conducting could be called a "sign language" to be used in a particular situation. Like all languages, it must be understood in order to be effective.

Down through the ages a pattern of motions has evolved for conducting. The pattern of motion developed for conducting is known as the "conductor's beat." Each segment of the pattern has a definite meaning. For example, the term "downbeat" and its meaning are generally familiar. The conventional "conductor's beat" is a series of motions that has a definite meaning. The term "downbeat" and its meaning are generally familiar.

The question that is of immediate concern is: How much in the field of conducting has a place in the classroom? Should we adopt the methods of the leader of the dance band in starting a selection and pat a measure of the desired rhythm with our foot? Or, should we adopt the methods of the symphony orchestra leader who sometimes gets a glorious burst of music by a slight movement of his baton?

The technique of the dance band leader fits his purpose admirably. The "thump, thump, thump" of his foot sets the tempo of the music. Dynamics, harmony, or melody may be changed as the selection proceeds, but the very purpose of the music precludes variation in speed. There is no identity of purpose in conducting in that situation and in conducting in the classroom.

Moreover, the technique of the symphony conductor would result in an interesting cacophony. At the signal to start, bedlam would result. Each child would have his idea of the pitch for the first word. Each child would have his idea of the tempo. The players in an orchestra are trained to watch the conductor closely in the matter of the starting tempo and are responsive to every signal he gives, or, because of training and experience, they can remember various speeds. Also, their tones are fixed by their instruments or are relative to fixed tones; therefore, their tones at the beginning of the selection are not the result of imitation or luck but are the result of the players' skill.

When a group of any size starts singing, each member of that group must have a definite conception of the exact pitch and tempo of the song to be sung. The more experienced and better trained the chorus, the less help it needs in using this important information. For example, each section of an eight-part chorus, with its ability to remember a tempo and to respond to the slightest variation suggested by the conductor, gets its pitch from one tone. The average group of children in a classroom needs more help than this.

The size of the motions used by the leader varies with the number in the group. Because of the distance between the leader and many of the five hundred children in a large group, the signals and directions of the leader must be large and away from his body if they are to be seen. Directions should be clear-cut and simple with all unnecessary motions eliminated. The style of conducting groups of ten, thirty, or fifty children is quite different from that of directing large groups. The problem of seeing the teacher is eliminated. Many of the cues and suggestions for interpretation can be given by means of facial expressions. There is no necessity for full-armed sweeping motions that are obvious enough for hundreds to see. There is need only for small, well-defined motions, visible to the group.

It is desirable for *all* conductors to see themselves in action in a full-length mirror. If this is not possible, each should "pretend" to conduct in front of a small mirror. Certainly, many of the contortions through which conductors go are the result of habit, and they themselves would frown upon their actions if aware of the fantastic bodily motions involved in some of their conducting. Many musical programs have not been enjoyed because of the antics of the conductors. These antics, not the music and not the children, have been the show.

The Conductor's Beat

The pattern of symbols used by conductors is one of simple motions for the arm and hand, or for arms and hands, or the baton. All conductors use this same basic pattern although variations of many kinds are common.

For music that has two pulses or beats in a measure—$\frac{2}{4}$, $\frac{2}{8}$, $\frac{2}{2}$—the pattern for the right hand is:

```
Beat - - - - down      up      down      up
Count - - - - -1        2        1         2
```

For music that has three pulses or beats in a measure—$\frac{3}{8}$, $\frac{3}{4}$, $\frac{3}{2}$—the pattern for the right hand is:

```
Beat - - - - down    out     up    down    out    up
Count - - - - -1       2       3      1       2      3
```

For music that has four pulses or beats in a measure—$\frac{4}{8}$, $\frac{4}{4}$, $\frac{4}{2}$—the pattern for the right hand is:

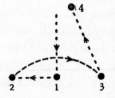

```
Beat - - - - down    across    out    up
Count - - - - -1        2         3      4
```

For music that has six pulses or beats in a measure—
$^6_8$, $^6_4$—the pattern for the right hand is:

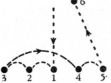

Beat - - - -down	across	across	out	out	up
Count- - - - -1	·2	3	4	5	6

For music that has nine pulses or beats in a measure—
$^9_8$, $^9_4$—the pattern for the right hand is:

Beat - - - - down	out	up
Count- - - -1-2-3	4-5-6	7-8-9
(1)	(2)	(3)

For music that has twelve pulses or beats in a measure—
$^{12}_8$, $^{12}_4$—the pattern for the right hand is:

Beat - - - - down	across	out	up
Count - - - -1-2-3	4-5-6	7-8-9	10-11-12
(1)	(2)	(3)	(4)

For a fast $^6_8$ measure, most conductors prefer a more simple beat:

Beat - - - - down	up
Count- - - -1-2-3	4-5-6
(1)	(2)

(Most children's songs written in six-pulse measure are
sung with two beats to the measure.)

This same idea of consolidating beats is sometimes used in
a quick three-pulse measure:

Beat - - - - down	down	down
Count- - - -1-2-3	1-2-3	1-2-3
(1)	(1)	(1)

This is just a series of down beats.

(Most children's songs written in three-pulse measure are
sung with one beat to the measure — waltz tempo.)

The sequence of movements in the conductor's beat is logical.[2] The downbeat (beat 1) is the most important of all and is always the same. The next most important movement is the one *preceding* the first beat; therefore, for this approach to the down beat, the arm and hand are away from the body in full view of those who are following the conductor. The dots are pausing or directional points for the hands even though motion is continuous.

It is from these basic patterns of the conductor's beat that deviations are made. The teacher need not be concerned about variations. The most simple small motions will suffice for the classroom. A downbeat of about six inches can be seen by all the children and can be copied by them when they need to beat.

Reasons for Learning the Conductor's Beat

There are three reasons children and their teacher need to learn the conductor's beat: (1) An awareness of its function in music-making by groups is part of a general background in music; (2) It can become an easily observable "tool" in the development and evaluation of the rhythmic sense of both instrumentalists and singers, and (3) It can become a "tool" in learning to read music.

The conductor's beat as an easily observable means by which the sense of rhythm can be developed and evaluated and its use as an aid in learning to read music and in reading music is the substance of Chapter 4, "Rhythms." Therefore, it will not be discussed here.

[2] Beat 1 starts at the *end* of the downbeat——on the dot. It lasts until the second dot. Beat 2 starts on the second dot, ending on the third dot. Beat 3 starts on the third dot, ending on the next dot. All the tones or notes on beat 1 come on or between the first and second dot. Beat 1 lasts or continues to the instant of the second dot. All the tones or notes on beat 2 come on or between the second and third dot. Beat 2 lasts or continues to the instant of the third dot. And so it is with each beat of the measure. In other words, the *beat note* (or the unit of measure, whether it be a half, a quarter, or an eighth note) starts on the dot and is given its full value only if it lasts to the next dot. If it were prolonged only half-way to the next dot, it would not be interpreted accurately. It would have only half the value it is supposed to have.

Conducting in the Classroom

What are the implications of the comments about conducting for the classroom teacher? Since the teacher becomes the person who must make a group of musicians sound as one, since each group has its particular needs, and since each conductor must make a realistic appraisal of these needs, let's consider what children who are makers of music need.

Children *need to know* before starting to play—as do the members of a dance band—how fast or in what tempo to start. They *need to know* so that their music on the first two beats will be "in time," as well as the music in the middle or at the end of the piece.

Singers *need to know* on which tone to start, as well as knowing the tempo; otherwise chaotic sound will result should each one start on the tone he thinks is correct. What satisfies these needs? An introduction. An introduction supplies *a* tempo from all possible tempi and supplies singers with *a* tonality in which to sing.

A piano introduction for inexperienced singers should end on the tone with which the song starts. Experienced singers can learn "to think" a starting tone, relating it to the final tone of the introduction.

A vocal introduction by the teacher not only furnishes tone and tempo but can also set a mood. Just as the piano introduction, it should be tempered to suit the needs of the particular group. After singing the introduction, the teacher prolongs the starting tone and invites the children to sing by an "understood" motion of the hand, a signal.

When using a chording instrument for an introduction, the teacher must sing the first melody tone for inexperienced singers.

Instrumentalists *need* an idea of tempo. For the inexperienced, the teacher can say, while beating a measure, "One-two-ready-play" and so on. The experienced can register the tempo by watching the teacher beat a measure in the conventional way and start playing at a signal.

Since it is important that the "language" of conducting be understood, practice in making signals (the teacher's signals must be consistent) and practice in interpreting signals is necessary.

The following signals are suggested: attention, starting, stopping, louder, softer, accent, slower, faster. Children can learn the conventional signals as easily as any other signals.

EVALUATING GROWTH IN MAKING MUSIC

Although it is believed that the act of making music is more important than the result of the activity, it is also believed that growth should result from repeated activity: Children should make better music this month than they did last; they should learn the second ten songs more easily than they did the first ten, and their efforts at playing pre-orchestral instruments should more nearly approximate an ensemble after playing together for three weeks than it did the first week. No matter how low the level of a first endeavor, improvement should be apparent in the sixth or seventh attempt. Growth is the basis for evaluation.

The more nearly singing meets the standards of "good" singing, the better it is—and accuracy is the basic qualifying requirement. If singing is not accurate as to time and tone, it cannot be considered "good." The more nearly singing meets the standards of "artistic" singing, the better it is. (See the definition of "artistic" on page 217.) Children's singing, unfortunately, can be only as "good" as is its model.

Growth may also be judged by the number of repetitions required for learning a song. A decrease in the number is evidence of growth in aural power and musical memory. But, some songs are easy and some are difficult. "Difficult" really means "requires more repetition." An analysis of melodies from simple to complex, and, accordingly, from easy to difficult follows:

(1) Short scale passages, tones of I, IV, and V triads in one or two short musical ideas (2-4 measures) with repetition of ideas and repetition of rhythm pattern, as in *Here We Go Round the Mulberry Bush;*

(2) Same as (1) but with long musical ideas, as *Old Woman* and *All Through the Night;*

(3) No repetition of short musical ideas (groups of tones) but with repetition of rhythm pattern, as in *Pussy Cat, Pussy Cat, Where Have You Been?;*

(4) No repetition of long musical ideas but with repetition of rhythm pattern, as in *America,* and,

(5) Some repetition of long musical ideas (eight measures), as in *The Star-Spangled Banner.*

In addition, growth and development in aural power and musical memory can be evaluated in terms of the number of repetitions required for learning songs of various levels or degrees of difficulty.

Growth in making music by playing can be evaluated in much the same way. The more nearly the results approximate "good," "artistic," and "ensemble," the better they are. When recognition of like melodies and like sections of melody and like rhythm patterns is apparent, growth is evident. Accuracy, again, is fundamental. As in singing, tone quality, dynamics, tempo, and phrasing are essential parts of "accuracy." In ensemble playing, playing as *one* (instead of three or thirty) is basic. Ensemble playing can be evaluated by the same qualifications as "good" singing with the added specific "as one."

It is difficult—"impossible" is a better word—to say by what standards children's music-making activities in any grade should be judged. Growth is the basis for evaluating, and growth results from experience in making music. Results do not accrue automatically from being in a grade.

For Discussion

1. Check through the songs on thirty consecutive pages of a song book for children to see if they conform to the suggestions re-

lating to range of melody, length of phrase, word interest, and variety in rhythm pattern. Check these songs for "level of difficulty."

2. By what criteria should songs for children be selected? Should children sing songs that do not meet these requirements?

3. What is good singing? Evaluate the singing of a group in terms of the specifics of "good singing."

4. At what age do people stop learning songs by rote?

5. Try "tipping" while listening-to-learn a song.

6. Since a physical response while listening-to-learn is an invaluable aid to learning, get clues for such responses from the subject matter of ten songs.

7. Should or should not a teacher sing with the class? Why?

8. Why can't some people sing?

9. What does "individual growth in pitch perception" mean?

10. List the levels of singing ability, beginning with the lowest level.

11. Evaluate the singing ability of four people you know. (You may include yourself.)

12. Learn to play 1-3-5 from each key between middle C and the next C on the piano, melody bells, or xylophone.

13. Which instruments on the list of pre-orchestral instruments can you play? The criterion should be ability to play 1-3-5 and 8-5-3-1 on six keys of a keyboard instrument and 5-4-3-2-1 on any of the flute-like instruments.

14. Determine what to do about the word "Christmas" in a song. The accent is on the first syllable. The second syllable is likely to become "-mahs," "-muss," "-miss," or "-mass." None of these sounds any better when sung by one hundred voices than it does when you sing it alone.

15. Beat vigorously and count aloud while music with the following measures signatures is played:

$$\frac{4}{2} \quad \frac{2}{4} \quad \frac{4}{4} \quad \frac{6}{8} \quad \frac{12}{8} \quad \frac{3}{2} \quad \frac{3}{4}$$

16. Can you justify singing popular songs in school? Teaching them?

17. Teach a song by the phrase method; the whole method. Select ten songs peculiarly adapted for the part method.

18. Plan a simple dramatization or a "production" of *There Was an Old Woman.* The action suggested by the words can be accompanied by any or all of the following: singing the words and melody; singing or chanting *la-la* (or other nonsense syllables) on I, IV, and V; percussion, chording and/or melody instruments; patterns of movement: same pattern throughout or pattern suggested by words (on "lawk-a-mercy," body bent, palms of hands on thighs; on "me," hands thrown in the air, high above the head) and so on. The "production" can be lengthened by an instrumental and/or movement interlude between stanzas.

19. What activities bring about readiness for singing two-part songs? for harmonizing? What does each activity do that the others do not?

20. Under what conditions do rounds contribute to gaining skill?

21. Plan a harmonizing part for four songs. Sing the songs. Add a third part to be played on song bells. Perform. No song bells? *Sing* three parts.

22. Sing and play the "activities" for developing readiness for harmonizing. Plan and sing parts for some of your favorite songs. Add a descant—and sing.

23. Defend the point of view expressed in the last paragraph in "Evaluating Growth in Making Music" (page 69). Defend the *opposite* point of view.

24. "Grade" the first ten songs in each of three books according to the analysis on page 69.

25. Discuss what is meant by "tones in a horizontal and in a vertical relationship."

26. Write a summary of the section Making Music-Singing.

27. Write a summary of the section Making Music-Playing.

Suggestions for Teachers

1. Using the conductor's beat, check the songs your class sings—including patriotic and community songs—for errors in rhythm. *Danger points:*
   (a) Rests at the end of phrases or sections (for example, the measures at the end of the second and third lines of *Old Folks at Home* have four beats, not three).
   (b) The last measure of a song has the same number of beats as the third or sixth measure (except when the first meas-

ure starts on a beat other than the first). Watch this point carefully when starting the second or third stanza.

(c) Each measure of *America,* including the sixth measure, has three beats.

(d) *Juanita,* the folk-tune, is probably the most often incorrectly sung song. It is written in $\frac{3}{4}$ time. Beat three beats to the measure and sing it. Sing the way you beat—do not beat the way you sing! None of the measures has four beats.

The best way to eradicate such inaccuracies once they have been discovered is to call attention to them and to have every child (*and* the teacher) use the conductor's beat vigorously while singing.

2. The words of a song make pictures—at least they should, if the child understands the meaning of the words. Use these suggestions to discover how well your class understands the following songs. Many children from the second grade to the seventh grade can sing any or all of the stanzas. Does your class know what it is singing about?

America, the Beautiful recalls episodes in our country's past, describes its physical features, and offers prayers for its future. What pictures are sketched in the first sentence? Why is our country beautiful? What scenes or episodes are described in the first sentences of the second, third, and fourth stanzas? For what blessing do we pray in the last sentence of each stanza? What is alabaster? In the last stanza, what does "alabaster" include?

America is a song of joy and praise and prayer. Who and what should join in the song? What does ". . . like that above," at the end of the second stanza, mean? For what do we pray?

The Star-Spangled Banner recounts the thoughts of Francis Scott Key as he watched our flag throughout a battle. Tell your class the story of the circumstances under which the song was written. Read the poem to the class. Talk about the pictures. What does "spangled" mean? "Foe's haughty host"? "Rockets"?

3. To develop the idea that words make pictures, ask the class to collect pictures for each of the series of word pictures in a song. A photomontage made of the collection would be excellent for display purposes.

4. To teach children the patterns for the conductor's beat, draw the pattern on the blackboard as you explain the beats. For

practice, ask them to trace the pattern in the air (while counting aloud with you) as you trace it on the blackboard. Remember, if you are facing the class when you ask the children to
follow your hand in practicing, you will have to change the direction of your second beat and those coming after it in order
for them to make the pattern correctly.

5. Spend ten minutes practicing "starting" songs the children know
according to the suggestions given under *The Conductor's Beat*
(page 67).

Suggestions for starting songs that begin on other than the
first beat in a measure: For a song with three pulses in measure,
starting on beat 2, say "one-two-three, sing"; starting on beat 3,
say "one-two-three-one, sing."

"Sing" is said on beat before song starts.

6. Do *you* sing with your class all the time? Why?

Things to Do

NOTE: This listing of specifics is offered as an aid in starting activities. Once started, the suggestions throughout this chapter will
point the way further. Notice that singing and building a song
repertoire are suggested first for each group. There *must be* a
common background of song material for accompanying group
movement and to which the facts of music can be related.

First Grade

Start singing some songs to class immediately. Start "tipping" and
making motions suggested by words. Vary this listening-to-learn
with activities designed to help the poor singer. During these
"games" (activities) listen for those who may need help even after
becoming accustomed to the program in music. After children have
heard your songs ten or fifteen times, ask them to sing repeated
phrases with you or sing softly with you as you listen. Until you are
certain they *do* know, sing the complete song as an introduction.

Other Grades

Start singing and teaching songs immediately. Ascertain songs
they know and like—folk songs currently "popular," songs learned
in other grades. *These* will become the accompaniment to movement until new songs are learned. Direct activity toward learning
the conductor's beat. At first, in grades two and three, it will be
marking beat 1 (clapping, bowing, swaying); in other grades it

will be learning to beat. Sing the *count* to melodies instead of the words.

CAUTION: Do not ask children if they *know* a song because to them "know" generally means "is familiar." Find out if they really know by asking them to join in singing.

Prospective and In-Service Teachers

Start singing: the songs mentioned in this chapter and those mentioned on pages 186-187 are excellent. After finding five or six songs the group knows, *use* them while learning others by rote. *Use* them for learning the conductor's beat and while walking and clapping and in all the ways suggested in this and other chapters.

All Groups

As soon as the group sings several songs easily and accurately, selected activities suggested in Chapter IV, *Things to Do,* may be started.

4

Rhythms

Rhythms are generally considered to be the combination of music and bodily movement in pattern. In some instances, movement is motivated, directed, or controlled by music. Tapping a glass with a spoon is a physical response to music—a response motivated by music. Waltzing is a physical response to music—a response controlled by music and, many times, motivated by music. Interpreting the story or the idea of a musical composition through movement is a physical response to music, a response motivated, directed, and controlled by music. In other instances, movement suggests music. Walking like an elephant or moving like falling leaves while an accompaniment is "fitted" to the activity is an example of movement suggesting the music. All these activities are rhythms.

Rhythms have a natural place in a music program based on the nature of children. They are an extension of children's need for, and love of, motion. They can satisfy the creative being, the intellectual being, the social being, and the emotional being, as well as the physical being that is a child.

Rhythms have a natural place in a program designed to teach children to make music. They can develop and refine the sense of rhythm without which music cannot be made. They can aid children in gaining the muscular control and coordination without which music cannot be made.

Rhythms have a natural place in a music program because they can be used to acquaint children with music and to direct conscious attention to the music itself. Concentrated listening is necessary before music can direct and control activity.

Rhythms are a most important phase of music in the elementary school.

THE PLACE OF RHYTHMS IN THE MUSIC PROGRAMS

Rhythms are the valuable means by which the active or dormant rhythmic sense is developed; they can aid in singing songs correctly; they can provide another medium of expression for use in dramatic play; they can become a means for learning musical compositions; they can become an invaluable aid in learning to read music, and, they can provide a socially acceptable means for the release of physical energy and emotional tensions. Although all the reasons for including rhythms in the music program are important, the most important is that of developing the active or dormant rhythmic sense.

Developing the Sense of Rhythm

A sense of rhythm, a feeling for rhythm—just what is it, what does it enable one to do? It seems to be an inner compulsion for order or pattern in sound. It is a sensitivity to pattern in sound. It enables one to make regular, recurring patterns of sound. It enables one to adapt and relate his movements to regular patterns of sound.

It is your inner compulsion for pattern or order in sound that causes you to group the endless "ticks" of the clock into a pattern. The clock doesn't "say": "*Tick*-tock, *tick*-tock, *tick*-tock, *tick*-tock." It "says": "Tick-tick-tick-tick-tick-tick." The proof that there is no real pattern is that you can count "*1*-2-3, *1*-2-3, *1*-2-3" and "*1*-2-3-4, *1*-2-3-4, *1*-2-3-4" just as readily and easily as "*1*-2, *1*-2" as the clock ticks. Nor does the automobile in which you are riding "say": "*Get*-me-there, *get*-me-there, *get*-me-there" as it passes over the tar-filled spaces between the areas of concrete that make the road. The car doesn't say anything—but it is the inner compulsion to put sounds in order or to arrange sounds in a pattern that makes you group them so there seems to be a regular recurring pulsation in the sounds.

Those who are sensitive to pattern in sound would be startled and annoyed if the orchestra interpolated a four-beat measure in the middle of a waltz. And, if the band left out a beat in one of the measures, every one of the marchers, with the possible exception of Jim, would be out-of-step and confused. Sensitivity to regular pulsation can be developed and refined.

Notice again the specific items in the material explaining what the sense of rhythm is and what it enables one to do. Notice that two of the specifics—inner compulsion and sensitivity—are *within* the individual and in the realm of feeling.

The only way you and I can tell what an individual feels is by what he says and by what he does. And in relation to his rhythmic sense, the way he behaves is by far the more revealing.

When I say, "What a beautiful flowing waltz!" and the person to whom I am talking says "Yes, isn't it?"—nodding his head or moving his hands in time to the music as he answers—I know he feels the regular recurring pulsation in the music. His action tells me so. But if his movements bear no relation to the beat or flow of the music, I can only conclude that he does not feel or is not sensitive to the general pattern of accent in the music.

If, on the other hand, instead of nodding or moving his hands, I had expected the following response

| 1 | 2 | 3 | 1 | 2 | 3 | 1 2 3 | 1 2 3 |
| run | run | run | run | run | run | leap | down |

and he did not respond in that manner, I would be in a quandary: "Can he not hear or feel the pulse or does he not have the necessary muscular control and coordination to execute that pattern of motion?" Before deciding that he has an undeveloped sense of rhythm or that he is not sensitive to the regular flow of the music, I must consider the nature of the expected response: it is not a simple one but requires a considerable degree of muscular control and coordination to fit the movements exactly to the beat of the music. Therefore, I shall ask him to clap the pattern: if he can clap it, he hears and feels it. He can clap it. What he needs, therefore, is experience designed to gain greater control and coordination of movement.

The problem and the challenge is to use the general enjoyment of rhythm and the sensitivity to it as the basis or point of departure for providing experiences that will enable children (and adults) to *make* music that flows regularly, moves evenly, and progresses unfalteringly at the indicated rate.

Physical response of some kind is necessary in guiding development. As one person expressed it: "I hope these activities (physical responses) will cement a little metronome inside children so they will make each measure exactly the same length, and make it impossible for them to deviate from a regular pattern."

Not only can those with a well-developed sense of rhythm set and maintain a pattern of regular pulsation in music, but they can also adapt their own feeling so that the music they make is regulated by another person's rhythmic feeling. You can sing *America* alone so that the accent, the pulsation, recurs regularly but, when you sing with a group, you can adapt your feeling for rhythm so that it conforms to or is regulated by the conductor's feeling as indicated by his beat. Or, if you are the drummer in the band, you subordinate for the moment your own concept of a march rhythm as you concentrate on the leader's concept of "march," indicated by the agreed-upon cue —his beat—and adjust your own feeling and your own movement to dovetail with his feeling and his movement. One of the disciplines to which a member of a chorus or a band or an orchestra is subjected is that of subordinating first, then adapting and adjusting his own concept of pulsation and beat to the leader's concept of pulsation and beat.

The facet of the sense of rhythm that enables an individual to make a pattern in movement can also be subordinated momentarily as it adjusts to a cue for motion—a cue outside himself. You can step-step-step-step evenly, regularly, but when you march to band music you subordinate your own sense of "march" and adjust your stepping so that it dovetails with the band leader's sense of "march." You can show me how an elephant moves lumberingly along, but when I play "elephant" music, you adjust your sense of "elephant" to my music. In social dancing, the moment you become sensitive to or register the pulsation of dance music, you adjust your movement to the waltz or foxtrot time of the music. The sublimation of individual feeling and adjusting to an external pattern is an important and necessary skill.

And, what if there are no rhythms, no opportunities for physical responses to music in the music program? Are they necessary? Does the sense of rhythm *have* to be developed?

Of course it is true that many children of another day did not have opportunity for engaging in rhythms, and yet we had makers of fine music and makers of beautiful patterns of motion. And we saw many examples of excellent muscular control and coordination. But in that day, the opportunity for participating in musical organization was generally limited to those who were born with a relatively high level of sensitivity to rhythm and a high level of muscular coordination. It was comparable to what happened in singing—those children who sang easily and well *naturally* were encouraged to sing better, whereas those who couldn't were neglected. Today we are challenged not only by those with an undeveloped sense of tone but also by those with an undeveloped sense of rhythm. We know the lack of rhythmic sense limits participation in music-making with a group, limits making music others enjoy, and limits participation in dancing. Today we accept the challenge and provide the opportunity for physical response to music—the generally approved activity for developing the sense of rhythm.

A man who is acknowledged to be a most skillful teacher and director of elementary and junior high school orchestras was asked what instrument a child without a sense of rhythm could play. He thought a moment and then said: "I don't encourage a child with a poor ear to try to play a string instrument as his first instrument—and that's about the only restriction in choice as far as ear is concerned. But what instrument can he play if he has an undeveloped sense of rhythm?" He stopped. Then, in a questioning, hopeful tone: "He can always hold the flag."

Dramatic Play

Dramatic play aids in developing the imagination, in expressing ideas and emotions, and in objectifying understanding. "Play like . . ." is used by children as they grow up. Play that is identified with the environment or play that interprets ideas reveals many things to an expert. Even the non-expert can gain a comprehension of a child's previous experiences, his ideas, his emotions, and his understanding by observing his play. When music and/or movement become accessories to dramatic play, its positive values are enhanced.

Rhythms can become another medium for self-expression. Instead of the water colors used in making a picture, the body becomes the medium of expression. Instead of painting an "old man," the body can be used to portray an old man. It can picture an old man walking with his dog. It can picture an old man walking with his dog past the church where he feels perhaps he should be, but is not. And it can show what his wife says when he arrives home. The body can express hope and fear, black and white, tall and short, and washing machine and steam shovel, as well as Rip Van Winkle and Robinson Crusoe. When accompanied by appropriate music, the use of the body as a means of self-expression becomes even more enjoyable—and more revealing. A musical accompaniment to bodily movement also appears to free children from their inhibitions.

Learning Musical Compositions

For "doing what the music says," concentrated listening is necessary. In interpreting or dramatizing the story told by a particular selection, concentrated listening is necessary. Before showing that certain aspects of music have registered, concentrated listening is necessary. For example, conscious attention must be directed to the music to indicate the duration of a phrase with a predetermined movement, changes in tempo, the repetition of a melody, the rise and fall of a melody line, or the change of mood.

In the activities mentioned above, music itself determines or circumscribes movement. But movement can be fitted to music —and it can be fitted to music we hope children will become familiar with and enjoy for years to come. Muscular control and coordination can be gained just as well by fitting movement to the music of Copland or Mozart as it can by fitting motion to music designed *too* specifically, such as the "Push, push, fall" music. A vocabulary of movement [1] can be acquired just as well by fitting movement to the music of Brahms or Strauss or Sousa as it can by fitting movement to Miss Improvisor's composition *The Big Black Bear Walked Across the Street—Sideways.*

When children and the world's great music meet, and the physical being—as well as the emotional and intellectual being that is a child—is permitted to respond, the meeting is likely to be a pleasant one.

Aid in Singing Songs Correctly

You will remember that Miss Jackson (page 41) suggested that the children in her second grade "tip" while they listened to and learned songs. "Tipping" is "rhythms," and using the conductor's beat or moving the arm on each down beat or gently

[1] See page 88-96.

swaying the body while listening and learning and singing songs is rhythms.

There is one simple test that can be made to show the value of even a limited physical response. The teacher asks the children to sing the first stanza of *Way Down Upon the Swanee River*. After getting the children started, the teacher makes no effort to conduct, but as inconspicuously as possible (for her own enlightenment, as it were) she beats time, using the conventional conductor's beat. The chances are that the children will slight the note values in measures one and eight; they will hold the dotted half note only two beats, gasp for breath on the third beat, and proceed immediately to the next full measure. After the children have sung the stanza, the teacher should suggest that they sing again. This time she asks each child to do his own beating (using the conductor's beat), as she sets the tempo by saying, "Beat, beat, ready, sing"; then the children beat and sing. Notice the values that were slighted before. During the repetition each measure, in all probability, was given its full value.

A "new" music teacher found that the *Marines' Hymn* was a favorite song of the children in her classes. Each group wanted to sing this song whenever the "new" teacher asked for a choice. The first time each class sang it, the fourth beat in the fourth measure, after ". . . on the shores of Tripoli," was omitted. At the conclusion of the singing, the teacher discussed the conventional way to beat time for songs having $\frac{4}{4}$ as a measure signature. She showed them how to do this, first while standing in front of the group, and then by outlining the beat on the blackboard. She invited each child to draw the same pattern in the air with his forearm while resting his elbow on his desk. After some few minutes of practice, the children were asked to beat while singing the *Marines' Hymn. Not one group failed to give four beats to each measure of the song.*[2] It would seem that, if

---

[2] The children in the sixth grade, incidentally, did not know the significance of "Tripoli," or the "Halls of Montezuma," nor the meaning of "caissons" even though they knew the song well.

a response with only the forearm could cause those changes, response with the whole body might affect the children's whole concept of rhythms.

Aid in Physical Development

Rhythms is the part of the music program that can aid in the physical development of children. Moving to music provides opportunity for developing muscular control and coordination. Wanting the body to carry out definite prescribed activities is one thing; having the power to carry out these activities is another. One of the reasons for including rhythms is to aid children in gaining control of movement.

Control of big movements must be developed before muscles can control small movements. Big movements—swinging, swaying, clapping, bending, walking—involve the big muscles of the body. After there is command of the big muscles, certain of the large movements can be combined: walking and/or swaying and/or clapping. Then, smaller movements, made by smaller muscles, are attempted: playing the beats of a melody on a tambourine, then, the rhythm of a melody; stepping the beat for one measure and walking twice as fast during the next; or, beating time with small or short motions, and, finally, controlling the small movements of wrists and fingers in playing musical instruments.

When muscular control is gained and muscles can be made to do *what* the individual wants *when* he wants, it almost appears as if the sense of rhythm were imbedded or situated in muscles. Or, as if a separate pendulum for each muscle, swinging back-and-forth, back-and-forth—evenly and at a steady pace—dictated the length of the step or the length of the swing of the arm or body and the length of the measure.

Imagine a heavy metal ball about the size of a small orange suspended in front of you. Set it in motion. It makes an arc of about two feet. Follow its motion with your arm. Pat your foot on the floor when your arm reaches the highest points of the arc. Real pendulums suspended in this way would slow down

—their arcs would become smaller—but your pendulum is different. The arc *it* makes remains the same size.

As your arm follows the pendulum and your foot pats at the highest point of the arc, count 1-2-3-4 evenly. Count 1 comes where and when the pendulum changes direction, as it starts swinging back. Swing your body and count. Now, as the pendulum moves at this same pace, count 1-2-3-4-5-6. Swing and count. This time, swing, count, and beat 1-2-3. Each full swing of the pendulum (and *you*) is equivalent to a measure of music.

Imagine a smaller pendulum moving in a smaller arc. Count and beat 1–2–3 with each full arc. Count 1 comes more quickly, more frequently than before. Therefore, your counting is faster and your motions are faster.

When movement is fitted to music, the music with its steady even flow becomes or has the effect of an *external* pendulum, a real and not an imaginative one. As the music goes, so goes the pendulum: fast music means a small arc with count 1 coming quickly; slow music means a large arc with a longer time between each count 1. Control and coordination is a fact when the individual can make his body do what he wants it to do in a given arc or arcs, whether it be in one measure or four measures. By helping children gain control over their bodies, rhythms can aid in developing the physical being that is a child.

Percy C. Buck,[3] the eminent organist and teacher, says that when action has become automatic and has earned the title of "Habit," the muscles have fallen into a rut or created a rut. Rhythms can establish a rut for each set of muscles that controls any "pendulum" made by any part of the body: when the arms swing, the swing will be free and regular as the arms travel a well-worn and familiar pattern; when the legs move, they will fit into the groove of equal full steps; and, when the body moves, it will be controlled by muscles that automatically swing freely and fully, regularly and evenly.

[3] Percy C. Buck, *Psychology for Musicians*. London: Oxford University Press, 1949.

Aid in Music Reading

Music is a combination of tones of different pitch and different length. Notes are the symbols for tones. One aspect of a
note—its place on a staff—represents its pitch or level of sound;
the other aspect—the kind (quarter, half, and so forth)—represents its length, its duration in time.

For all practical purposes an 88-key piano (the regulation
size) can produce most of the tones used in our music. Each of
these tones can be represented on a staff by a note showing its
exact pitch or level. And, conversely, that note is a symbol for
that specific pitch, that exact tone.

The aspect of a note that represents the length of a tone—
its duration—is fixed and exact, too, but not in quite the same
degree as the level aspect. For example, a note on the third
line of the treble staff is always a B—B natural, B sharp or B
flat depending on the symbol or lack of symbol at the beginning
of the staff or accidentals—it is *always* the symbol for the same
tone. But, a dotted half note does not *always* represent the same
duration in time. The dotted half notes in *On Top of Old
Smoky* [4] *and Jacob's Ladder,* for example, represent longer
sounds than do the dotted half notes in *Little Annie Rooney* or
Wait for the Wagon. Moreover, the eighth notes in *Rig-A-Jig-Jig*
represent *shorter* sounds than do the eighth notes in *Down in
the Valley.* But, all the dotted half notes in *On Top of Old
Smoky* are of exactly the same duration, and all the dotted half
notes in *Little Annie Rooney* are of equal length. Similarly, the
eighth notes in *Down in the Valley* are all the same length as
are those in *Rig-A-Jig-Jig.*

A whole note, or a dotted half note or an eighth note has no
exact duration. It does not, for example, always last through
so many ticks of the clock. But, in any song in which a whole
note lasts while the clock ticks eight times, a half note will last

[4] These songs and others mentioned in this chapter are found in *Music Fundamentals Through Song* by Louise Kifer Myers, published by Prentice-Hall,
Inc. 1954.

through four ticks, a quarter note through two ticks, and an eighth note through one tick. The measure signature of a song says: "The duration aspect or time values of the notes of this song are written in terms of a quarter note, each of which receives one beat. Therefore, each half note lasts for two beats, each eighth note a half beat, and each dotted quarter lasts for a beat and a half." *But* the measure signature does not and cannot say how long a beat is.

Sometimes, too, the measure signature says that a half note or an eighth note is the unit of measure. It can and often does say that. It cannot and does not indicate how long a half note is nor how long an eighth note is. Regardless of individual length, though, a whole note is *always* twice as long as a half note and a quarter note twice as long as an eighth. The length of any kind of note arises from its exact and fixed relation to the kind of note used as the beat note. The relation is fixed—a whole note = two half notes = four quarter notes = eight eighth notes = sixteen sixteenth notes. Those *relative* values are exact. They are constant. They have the same relevance for the first cellist in the New York Philharmonic Symphony Orchestra as they have for the second violinist in the elementary school orchestra.

Count aloud and clap the following:

(1) $\frac{3}{2}$ ♩ ♩ ♩ | ♩. ♩ ♩ | ♩ ♩ ♩ | ♩. ♩ ♩ |

(2) $\frac{3}{4}$ ♩ ♩ ♩ | ♩. ♪ ♩ | ♩ ♩ ♩ | ♩. ♪ ♩ |

(3) $\frac{3}{8}$ ♪ ♪ ♪ | ♪. ♪ ♪ | ♪ ♪ ♪ | ♪. ♪ ♪ |

Because the relationship between the notes is exact, each line of notes sounds the same even though each is written in terms of a different beat note.

The above discussion of relative time values is meant for the enlightenment of teachers; it is not meant to be the "subject" of a lesson in the third grade or the second. Under certain circumstances, it might be used as a "lesson" for upper elementary grade children who have had considerable experience in rhythms and in other phases of a music program designed to promote reading readiness.

Rhythms can be a most important phase of pre-music-reading experiences. They can lead to an awareness of differences in the length of notes and to the recognition of the symbols of these differences (the relative time values of notes) without becoming involved in the level or pitch aspect of notes. Although rhythms are fun and can appeal particularly to the physical and to the creative being that is a child, the appeal to the intellectual being can be enhanced by learning these symbols as symbols for movement. Specific suggestions for translating movement into symbols and symbols into movement will be given later in the section "From Movement to Symbol," page 103.

Release of Physical Energy

Pushing, hitting, punching, running, jumping, bumping, sliding—any of these is "bad" behavior when a group is supposed to be working quietly or moving from one place to another in a more or less sedate manner. Such activity is engaged in rather widely and surreptitiously—so widely, in fact, it appears that physical energy must be released surreptitiously if opportunity for approved activity is not provided. Interestingly enough, pushing, hitting, punching, and so on, are some of the movements used in dramatic or rhythmic play and rhythms.

Experts tell us a change of pace is good. After an extended period of using the mind, use the muscles; after sitting, move; and, after moving, sit. We know this is true for adults and we must suspect it is true for children—they just can't sit still for long periods, they *must* move. Forewarned is forearmed. Let's act as if we knew these facts and provide opportunity for moving.

Preparations need not be elaborate for these incidental "Change-of-pace" activities. Children can engage in them while sitting in their seats or standing near them. Here are some examples of what they can do:

1. While sitting and singing *I've Been Workin' on de Railroad*, reach down to the floor and lift an imaginary railroad tie and place it on the desk in time to the singing or push a big rock out of the way in time to the song.

2. Climb with long hard pulls of the arms while singing *Jacob's Ladder*.

3. On tiptoes and in one place, take a waist-high step on each beat of *America;* then, beat time with the conductor's beat, exaggerating the size of the down beat; and, then combine the stepping and beating.

4. Tuck a violin under the chin and play the down beat of a waltz with long, sweeping strokes, swinging the whole body.

5. While singing a favorite song, one half of the group claps on the down beat while the other half snaps fingers on remaining beats.

6. Play a singing game children have made up for one of their songs—a game that can be played in rows or in aisles.

These change-of-pace activities are fun; they release tensions and energy and help establish the feeling for and muscular reaction to the down beat, just as certainly and as surely as can a longer session of rhythms. These activities have purpose and are socially acceptable and respectable.

GUIDING PHYSICAL AND MUSICAL GROWTH
THROUGH MOVEMENT

While a certain kind of growth is taking place during the process of gaining skill in response, the muscular coordination necessary to express the *feeling for rhythm* is fixed as skills are used. Just as one acquires a vocabulary of words so that he can express himself or understand the meaning of others, so he acquires *a vocabulary of movement* for expression through this medium. It is through use that relationships are fixed. Adults do not immediately stop using a particular dance step after successfully executing it *once*. The joy in dancing comes when the dancers know the step. And so it is with rhythms. The skills developed through rhythmic activities are to be used either as a means of self-expression or because they make possible another means of enjoyment.

Although activities will be suggested (1) to develop a feeling for music through rhythms, and (2) to guide creative responses, each of these phases is tied up with, and closely related to, the other. For example, a child skips or throws a ball or pushes a wagon (muscular coordination) in time to music (feeling for rhythm) in a pattern he has devised (creative rhythms). Since these activities *are* so closely related there will be, of necessity, some over-lapping in the discussion of each phase. It is difficult to discuss these two phases separately and more difficult to teach them separately. The best thing to do is to teach the two phases together.

About Movement

The hoped-for result of experience in rhythms is free motion, relaxed motion, swinging, smooth motion, controlled by the big muscles and controlled by the pattern of motion and/or controlled by the beat of the accompaniment. There is no contradiction inherent in the idea of free, relaxed, swinging, smooth motion being "controlled." Controls are necessary for the development of the rhythmic sense and for muscular coordination.

Not all "movement," however, is *rhythms*. To justify using music time for "movement," there must be the attempt *to fit* motion into a pattern or *to fit* it to the regular recurring pulsation of an accompaniment. Hopefully, the fit becomes more precise with practice.

Movements that swing rather than jerk are desired. For example, a person who skips with his head held high, his arms swinging back and forth, and who covers ground with each step is relaxed. A person who skips up and down in almost the same spot, with his head bent forward on a stiff neck and with a rigid bend in his elbows, is tense.

An emphasis on *big* movements cannot be reiterated too often. Coordination of big muscles has to be developed before coordination of the small muscles is possible. Big movements are important. Vigorous movements are important. In clapping a rhythmic pattern or the beats in a measure, a big swing of the arms is desirable. If a resounding noise results, it may be hard on the teacher's nerves, but the noise was produced in a good cause—freedom of motion. Judicious guidance will eliminate some of the effect, but it should not be allowed to eliminate the cause. Little puny claps resulting from hands on rigid wrists indicate a lack of freedom and have no place in a program designed to release muscular and emotional tensions and inhibitions.

The movements listed in the vocabulary are fundamental and natural. The evidence of growth is greater control of movement, in making the body do what the mind wills and when the mind wills.

Children will probably use these movements early in their dramatic play experiences. It is the responsibility of the teacher to provide opportunity for refining movement and for adjusting it more precisely into a pattern or to the accent of music. It is the responsibility of the teacher to note particulars in the need for improvement, to give suggestions likely to result in improvement, and to make certain children have the opportunity to develop skill in all the movements listed. They are the means available in the music program for acquiring muscular coordination and control without which music cannot be made and for developing the sense of rhythm without which music cannot be made. "Holding a flag" is *not* "making music." Rhythms can be one of the most satisfying and enjoyable parts of the music program.

The eleven movements constituting a *vocabulary* follow. Like movements are grouped and discussed in terms of purpose and with suggestions for teaching. Group A includes big movements in which the whole body is used; in Group B, the whole body is used, but the emphasis is on "getting some place" or changing place in the room, with motion somewhat refined, and the activity in Groups C and D refines motion for a specific purpose.

A Vocabulary of Movement

A. 1. Swinging, swaying and bending
   2. Pushing and pulling
   3. Crawling, stretching and twisting

These are big movements and can involve the whole body. They can be combined and varied in many ways and to such a degree that sometimes an observer finds it difficult to decide just which of the movements is involved. Actually, naming them is not important—moving is important. And these big movements help establish the feeling for the downbeat and the measure accent. Hopefully, too, they help establish that pendulum mentioned earlier in this chapter.

In terms of a familiar song, these big movements might be made in the following manner to music written in fours and played or sung at a moderate tempo:

Oh,	beau – ti – ful for	spa – cious skies for	am–ber waves of
	1 2 3 4	1 2 3 4	1 2 3 4
	sway back sway	back sway	back
	push pull push	pull push	pull
	bend stretch bend	stretch bend	stretch

Two motions are made in each measure; the first with vigor and the second with a release of energy—force-release, force-release or accent-release, accent-release.

Four movements might be made in a measure (the motions illustrating dramatic play):

		1 2 3 4	1 2 3 4
	Oh,	beau– ti– ful for	spa– cious skies for

Making	scoop						
snow balls	up pat pat pat			scoop pat pat pat			
	snow						

Raking leaves	big pull	little pull	pull	pull		big	little	little	little
Playing drums	big	small	small	small		big	small	small	small

Movements to music written in three (slow waltz tempo) might be made like this:

	1 2 3 She's	1 2 3 my	1 2 3 sweet-	1 2 3 heart
Making snow man	push	push	push	push *or* pat pat pat
Playing drums or violins	big	big	big	big
Trees in the wind	sway	back	sway	back

B. 4. Walking or marching
   5. Jumping
   6. Hopping
   7. Skipping
   8. Galloping
   9. Running

These are the natural ways children "get places." They are easy, although some children have to be taught how to skip. They are easy especially when a person can execute them at his own natural speed or pace. But when he tries to fit his motions precisely with the accent of an accompaniment that proceeds at an unnatural pace, he needs considerable control in order to perform. This is particularly true when trying to move more slowly than at a natural pace.

The ability to walk or march in time to music is less wide spread than you might think. When next you see a parade notice the number of marchers whose steps do not exactly dovetail with the accent of the music. Remember rehearsals fo baccalaureate and commencement? The number of times you went up and down the aisle as you practiced walking in time to the music? The major cause of difficulty during those rehearsals was that those occasions call for a "processional"—a slow, almost twice-as-slow-as-normal walk. A considerable degree of control is required to manage the body during the interval between accents.

Jumping, hopping, skipping, galloping and running—natural, easy but not always easy to fit to the accent of music.

A small jump or hop at first—the space covered in each jump or hop should be between one and a half and two times as long as the feet. The speed of moving is likely to be two jumps or hops to a measure of a military march.

Children have been observed racing pell-mell around the room when hearing what they called "running music." It was evident, since they had started to run, they had caught the *mood* of the music, and they were *motivated* by the music. It was also evident they were not *controlled* or *directed* by the music in any way except that most of them tried to stop when the music stopped. Had that particular composition been played to give them an opportunity for sensing mood, their response would have been admirable. However, since they were supposed to show a controlled response to the rhythm of the music, their responses were a farce. Some teachers express the opinion that really rhythmic running requires great coordination.

C. 10. Clapping

Clapping and any of its variations—tipping, tapping, patting —are probably the most simple observable physical reactions to the pulsation in music. And, its very simplicity results in its being the most important. The question of muscular control and coordination does not arise—children learned these motions long before they came to school.

Remembering that the only way we can make an objective judgment about another person's sense of rhythm (and the only way he can judge ours!) is by the way he acts, the simple motion of clapping becomes an uncomplicated, easy to read barometer. When he is asked to clap four measures of quarter notes in $\frac{3}{4}$ time and it does not sound like this:

but sounds instead like this:

we can be relatively certain he needs some help in developing his sense of rhythm and in getting his muscles set in a "rhythmic" rut. And, we know too, that he wouldn't make an especially good drummer or violinist or pianist.

Clapping is an excellent means of determining whether the duration aspect of a group of notes is comprehended. When the relative note values of a song are clapped, the clapper can direct all his conscious attention to the *kind* of note, ignoring for the moment its level aspect.

Clapping can also be used in making a sound (or "percussion") accompaniment to songs. For example (clap on quarter notes):

I've   been   work-in' on   de | rail   road. ..

or (clap on eighth notes):

I'm goin' to |leave   Ol' Tex - as |now

Clapping, tapping with pencils, patting the feet, and so on can be combined for interesting and enjoyable accompaniments.

D. 11. The conductor's beat

The conductor's beat can be used by others than those by whom and for whom it was developed—conductors. The fact that it, too, frames a measure of music just as measure bars frame a "complete pattern of accented and unaccented pulses" (a measure) makes it an excellent tool for singers in reading music. The range of experiences leading up to the almost unconscious automatic use of this pattern of motion is just as important for the instrumentalist. He, however, cannot use it in playing or reading because his hands are busy with his instrument. It is hoped that his foot (or big toe) will pat with unusual regularity as the result of efforts to develop his rhythmic sense.

A group of teachers asked a visiting music consultant in what grade music-reading should be started (a perennial question!), and the visitor answered: "In nursery school or kindergarten— but if you say I said so, I shall deny it!" Then she explained what she meant. The singing and other music-making activities and the listening and the moving to music *all* combine to instill in children the patterns of tone and the patterns of rhythm common to our music. Later, children learn to recognize the symbols of these patterns, and still later, to recognize and interpret them in unfamiliar music.

The basic pattern of pulsation in our music is accent-soft or accent-soft-soft (1–2 or 1–2–3). This, then, is the basis upon which development of the sense of rhythm starts. Early efforts are made to implant in the muscles, in the senses, and in the mind a positive reaction to and a feeling for 1–2 and 1–2–3 and, finally for groupings of 1–2 and 1–2–3. When the music consultant said she started teaching music-reading in nursery school or kindergarten, she meant she started activities there designed to establish the feeling for the down beat and designed to establish the feeling for the measure—the smallest complete unit of which our music is made.

After a positive reaction to, a feeling for, and a recognition of, a succession of downbeats has been established in the muscles, in the senses, and in the mind, then comes the effort to establish awareness of what goes on between one downbeat and the next. What goes on can be illustrated in the dramatic play of making snowballs and raking leaves (see page 91-92).

While the feeling for the measure is being established, identification or marking off a measure by counting is introduced. Later, the patterns of motion known as the conductor's beat are learned.

Sing the counts 1–2–3 in the appropriate places in the tune *Oh, My Darling Clementine,* use the conductor's beat, and pat your foot on each count, accenting count 1. Such activity will almost certainly establish the feeling for and the identity of "measure." It will almost certainly establish the fact that "downbeat," "count 1," and "accent" are synonymous.

There is one teacher who would be pleased if an additional "stanza" were added to nearly all the songs children in the first and second grades know—the stanza being a mixture of singing the counts, marking the downbeats with big vigorous flowing motions of the arms, and patting the beats with the feet. Children beyond the second grade would use the pattern of the conductor's beat or clap the melody notes ("pushing" dotted quarters and "bouncing" the pulse of longer notes) and step the beats instead of patting them. Other teachers might object— it isn't "artistic." Maybe not—but it is a convenient and easy way to tie together movement and music. The teacher who approves of this added stanza would sacrifice some "artistic" for the sake of instilling in children an accurate sense of rhythm and of providing them with a tool that makes music-reading easier.

In summary, these are the movements that constitute the vocabulary of physical responses to music:

Group A. Those natural movements involving the big muscles of the body: swinging, swaying, bending, pushing, pulling, crawling, stretching, twisting;

Group B. Those usual and natural ways of covering distance: walking (marching), jumping, hopping, skipping, galloping, running;

Group C. The refining of what is one of children's first "learned" motions—clapping—important not only because it is easily observable and makes "good" sound, but because the manner of playing many musical instruments is but an extension of clapping; and,

Group D. The Conductor's beat—a pattern of motion—valuable as a tool in learning and valuable in evaluating learning.

Using the Vocabulary

The various movements listed and discussed in the vocabulary become the means by which the potential results of the rhythms program become actual results. They become another medium for developing an awareness of music and through which an awareness of music can be demonstrated; they become another medium through which creativity can be developed, and they become the medium for learning the relative duration value of notes.

Activities for Developing an Awareness of Music. During the first and second grades, rhythms should be completely within the realm of feeling and response. Later, after feeling and response are established, symbols to call forth a certain response will then have meaning—a meaning rooted in the child's being. The symbols for certain patterns should then be placed on the board in connection with certain activities listed below, but *not* in the first and second grades.

The following activities help bring about an awareness of some of the essential qualities of music itself. The first activity in each group is the most simple; the last the most difficult.

A. Activities for response to measure
  1. Class listens to music to discover whether it swings in groups of two's or three's.
  2. Teach conventional conductor's beat.
  3. Class beats and steps at the same time.
  4. Class listens to music to discover measure and beats time while music is played—one measure with the right hand, the next with the left.
  5. Class listens to the pattern of a measure and then interprets the pattern with physical responses.
B. Activities for response to the pulsation
  1. Comparison of slow and fast motion.
    (a) Children walk as teacher sets tempo by beating percussion instrument by saying, "Walk, walk, walk, walk." The children walk twice as fast, then three

times as fast. The teacher places rhythm pattern on the blackboard:

The walk at double and triple tempi would be a *run*.

(b) Children walk four steps and run eight steps. Teacher places pattern on the blackboard:

(c) Children walk four steps and run three times as fast. Teacher places pattern on the blackboard:

C. Activities contributing to the understanding of form and to to the interpretation of music

1. Discover definite and indefinite endings in music (cadences).
2. Mark one phrase with an arc in the air with right hand, the next phrase with the left hand, and so forth.
3. Adapt the style of conducting to changes in tempo and dynamics.
4. Walk in one direction when music ascends, in another direction when it descends.
5. Walk with steps that are suggested by the inherent

characteristics of *legato, staccato, portamento, piano,* and *forte.*

6. In short compositions or songs written in AB (binary) and ABA (ternary) forms, conduct one part with right hand, next part with left, and so forth.

Creative Activities. The vocabulary of movement becomes another means of self-expression for children. Through movement they can express ideas, what they know and think, what they hear and see, and how they feel. The combination of dramatic play plus movement plus music is a readily understood medium of expression. Just as in using words as a medium of expression, skill comes with practice, preciseness comes with practice.

MOVEMENT AS A MEANS OF EXPRESSION. What can be expressed in movement? Ideas of the following:

(a) Any animal (including man)

(b) Natural activities (pushing, throwing, swinging)

(c) Life and things (airplanes, automobiles, fire engines, tops, chairs, people building a road or a house, scissors, egg beaters)

(d) Toys, puppets, circus, farm life, city life

(e) Characterizations of pirates, witches, scarecrows, firemen, postmen, milkmen, and so forth

(f) Ideas that grow out of schoolroom activities, a summary of things learned

What can be expressed in movement? An awareness of technical terms and the technical aspects of music itself:

(a) Tempo

(b) Measure

(c) Notes of various duration

(d) Phrases, cadences

(e) Dynamics

(f) Musical terms (*legato, staccato, portamento, piano, forte*) *(g)* Form (repetition rhythm pattern, repetition of melody, A B A, A A B B, A B A C A D A)

(h) Mood

When children say or do any of the following in their rhythmic expression, awareness of a technical aspect of music is indicated: change rate of movement when *tempo* changes; emphasize in some manner count 1; change direction with repetition of phrase or at a cadence; use big movement with loud music, little with soft; move smoothly in *legato* sections, jerk in *staccato,* and so on; and, plan movement on the basis of the form of a song or instrumental composition.

> *Note 1:* Awareness of the technical aspects of music is as likely to be indicated simultaneously with expressing ideas listed previously as it is in an attempt to show what is heard in a particular selection.
>
> *Note 2:* Remember the only way we can actually know what a person hears is by what he *does.*

What can be expressed in movement? Stories—stories about anything and everything:

(a) Stories in music—Dukas' *Sorcerer's Apprentice,* Paul White's *The Mosquito, Little Orley's Big Concert, Peter and the Wolf, The Hunters of the Sea.*

(b) Stories or poems children read or write.

(c) *The* story of "what we learned about" India, China, wood, transportation, our city government—the summary of a study (or a part of it).

In "telling" the story of a specific musical composition, the music is the accompaniment, of course. The accompaniment for the dramatization of other ideas must be chosen from available material—and selected by the children. They may choose from the recorded music they know or from "live" music the teacher or a member of the class can play. Or, they may choose to make their own "percussion" accompaniment.

Planning accompaniments and making up singing games are other "uses" for rhythms.

PERCUSSION ACCOMPANIMENT. "Percussion" is used to denote

a rhythmic, nontonal, nonchordal accompaniment. Probably the most simple "percussion" accompaniment is made by clapping the hands, snapping the fingers, and/or tapping objects made of different materials. The instruments commonly found in a rhythm band, played by the tapping, clapping, or scraping technique, add more color in accompaniments for movement or singing.

Children for whom moving in patterns is a relatively new activity are likely to make their accompaniment fit the beat and pulse of the measure. Skill in listening and greater control of small muscles can result in the tambourine playing all the melody tones, the triangle coming in on an "off" beat, while the claves and small drum share the honors of marking the beats.

After playing "by ear" and "by feeling," the next step in development is planning a score and playing by note with a violin, piano, Autoharp or harmolin.

SINGING GAMES. Today many of the well-known singing games—*Farmer in the Dell, London Bridge,* and so on—are almost the exclusive property of little children. Children of all ages enjoy them—and, so, in the absence of an extensive repertoire from which to choose, let's make up some. And, since a large floor space is not always readily available for the whole group to move about in a circle, let's plan activities that can be carried on in the aisles, in straight lines. For that same reason (limitations of space), the feet should not try to cover a lot of ground quickly.

What motions can be made in a singing game? Some few general suggestions follow—you and the children can think of many more:

1. In the aisles (with a row of seats between) one can face a partner, turn his back to him and face another partner, move forward, move backward, and step in place. (If there are vacant spaces other than aisles in which a few children can move, the first or last person in each row can occupy that space.)

2. Facing partner, one can take four (or more or less) sliding

steps to the right or to the left, he can stomp-step in place, he can step-bend-the-knee in a slow promenade (walk), turn and retrace his steps, turn completely around or halfway around in place.

3. Hands and arms may be on hips, thrown in the air, touching partner's hands over seats or those of the person in front or back.

As for the pattern or form of action in games:

1. One bit of action for a phrase of the song, repeated in the opposite direction for the next phrase; new pattern, repeat.
2. One pattern for the verse and a simple repeated pattern or action for the chorus.
3. Nonsense syllables can be a signal for an individual to make his own pattern, to be copied later by the group.

EXAMPLE (1): At the end of the first verse of *Looby Loo*— "I put my right hand in, I put my right hand out, I put my left hand in *and shake my-self about*"—on those last words, a designated individual makes up his own pattern while others watch. This pattern then becomes the pattern for the interlude between verses "Here we go Looby Loo. . . ."
EXAMPLE 2: In *Skip to My Lou*, everyone sings the verse, clapping the accent and snapping fingers up to the last phrase before the chorus—"Skip to my Lou, my dar-ling," where one person makes up a pattern of motion. This pattern is carried on by the whole group while singing the chorus.

Here is a "made-up" singing game for *Pop! Goes the Weasel:* Directions and specifics: face partners in rows; (1) "step" means a step to the right with right foot, bringing up left; (2) "stop" means an uncompleted slide in which the remaining time is used to get mentally prepared and physically balanced for changing direction. On "Pop," jump into the air, and clap hands; touch the floor on "goes." Second part: make a right quarter-turn in place on each step.

step				step			
right	right	right	stop	left	left	left	stop
right	right	right	right	jump	down	clap	clap
				clap			

(I've no time . . .)

right				left			
step	step	step	step	step	step	step	step
turn							
touch	clap	repeat	clap	jump	down	clap	clap
partner's			face	clap			
hands			front				

(Steps become slides when the game is learned.)
Accompaniment: singing, percussion, or chords on piano or Autoharp.

From Movement into Symbol. Attention is now directed to statements made earlier in this chapter: (1) ". . . rhythms can be an invaluable aid in learning to read music" and (2) children can learn the "symbols of relative note values without becoming involved in the level or pitch aspect of notes."

Much of the "movement" in which children have engaged is in relation to songs—songs well known to them through frequent singing and listening; songs they have often walked, stepping on each beat, or patting each beat with a foot while using the conductor's beat or while clapping or tipping each melody tone; songs which, almost unconsciously, almost automatically, they "accompany," beating time as they sing. These songs become the medium for transferring feeling into symbol and translating movement into symbol.

Thus, in terms of "learning *new* things in relation to *old*," symbols (new) are related to feeling (old) and to what the body has done (old) and can do.

In these songs children know so well (another "old") are all the combinations of relative note values they are likely to interpret by singing or playing. In these combinations are tones of equal duration, tones that receive one beat, two or three or four beats, two tones to a beat, three tones to a beat, tones shorter than a beat, and tones longer than a beat. When children are accustomed to walking to the beats of a song and clapping its notes, it is easy for conscious attention to be directed toward the duration values in terms of beats or steps. Singing the counts and clapping notes, too, have the advantages of being objective—something we can hear and do and something we can see—nothing in the realm of speculation or remembering. Counting, beating, clapping and stepping are *basic* to translating movement into symbols.

Suggestions for Teaching

1. To establish recognition of the symbols for the fundamental beats in the measure:

TEACHER: "Children, sing *America, the Beautiful* while walking (stepping beats) and beating time" (these children have done this many times—they move and beat precisely while singing this and other songs). After a few measures, the teacher says: "These are the notes that represent your walking (teacher writes on blackboard):

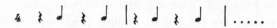

The 4 is there because the music is written in 4's and you were beating 4."

TEACHER: "Sing words and clap on beats 2 and 4." . . . "This is what you clapped:

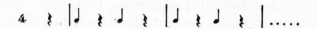

TEACHER: "Sing 4–1–2–3 to melody and clap on counts 1 and 3." . . . "This is what you clapped:

TEACHER: "Sing 4–1–2–3 to melody and clap on counts 2, 3, and 4." . . . "This is what you clapped:

Number each line of notes. Clap each line. Divide the class into four parts. Each responds simultaneously: Group 1 taps pencils for notes in the first line; Group 2 claps notes in the second line; Group 3 snaps fingers for notes in the third line; and, Group 4 taps desks for notes in the fourth line while singing softly.

Repeat this procedure using a song written in 3's—*America*, for example. The lines of notes would be:

Continue this "idea" of symbols-for-sound by planning percussion or sound accompaniment for a song by relating the pattern of movement (clapping) to symbols.

After five or six songs have been used in this way (1) *name* the symbol (if no one has been curious enough to ask its name before) and place the 4 in the measure signature to indicate that the quarter note is the unit of measure; (2) vary the line each group reads and interprets, and finally, (3) place a mixture of patterns from a song in one line and ask the group to read and clap it. Call attention to these patterns when they are clapped in other songs.

To the teacher:
> Look through ten pages of songs in a children's song book and count the number of measures containing only quarter notes. This is a common pattern. After children can react correctly to similar symbols on the blackboard, direct their attention to sections of a song containing mostly quarter notes. While chil-

dren beat the designated 2, 3, or 4, ask them to read the words under those notes in the time of the melody notes. Direct attention to their *likeness:* "The first three notes in *America* are like '. . . say can you.' . . ."

2. To establish recognition of symbols for tones longer than one beat (♩., ♩, ♩., ○ and corresponding rests):

While the teacher sings *America,* giving an exaggerated vocal punch on the dot after the quarter notes and three punches (or "bounces," if you prefer) on the dotted half note, the children pat the beats and clap melody notes.

The children sing the song in the same manner while beating time, and, sing again, clapping melody notes and making obvious physical bounces with the hands on the prolonged notes.

The teacher places on the blackboard the pattern of the melody notes in first six measures. The children sing the counts (1-2-3) and clap the notes while the teacher points to them.

TEACHER: "This is a dotted quarter followed by an eighth. Is the eighth longer or shorter? . . . This is a dotted half note. How many beats did you give it?"

The children watch the board while singing counts and clapping melody notes to discover if the rhythm pattern is repeated. (The pattern is repeated once, and then new material is added. If the children are curious as to what the new material looks like, their questions should be answered.)

The children sing 4-1-2-3 to the melody of *America, the Beautiful* and clap the melody notes, pushing or bouncing the longer-than-one-beat-notes. This pattern is placed on the board:

$$\frac{4}{4} \quad \texttt{♩ | ♩. ♪♩ ♩ | ♩. ♪♩ ♩ | ♩ ♩ ♩ ♩ | ♩.}$$

and the children clap and sing it. "Is it consistent throughout the song?"

Children may wish to make a percussion accompaniment again and see it in place under these notes in order to read and "play" them.

These songs are particularly good for identifying quarter notes and notes longer than one beat:

> *A Prayer of Thanksgiving* (Netherlands Hymn)
> *On Top of Old Smoky*
> *Little Annie Rooney*
> *She'll Be Comin' 'Round the Mountain*

To test for skill in recognition of symbols, select from a children's book an unfamiliar song containing the symbols studied so far. Discuss the measure signature, and direct their thinking, thus: "Count measures filled with four (or three or two) quarter notes." "How many dotted quarter or half or dotted half notes are there in the song?" "Read words under the dotted quarter and eighth notes, or dotted half or half." Finally, read the words of the song in the time of the melody notes. *This is the aim* of all this activity—ability to interpret the symbols for duration by reading the words in the time of melody notes.

To the teacher:

> After children can react correctly to dotted quarter notes, half notes and dotted half notes on the blackboard, direct their attention to songs containing these symbols and have children beat and read words in time. Direct attention to their *likeness:* "This dotted quarter followed by an eighth in *America* . . . 'Tis of thee' is like the ones in *A Prayer for Thanksgiving* . . . 'gathered to-geth-er to' . . ."

3. To establish recognition of the symbols for two even tones to a beat, ♫ ♫ and three even tones to a beat, ♫♩ :

Proceed as in the previous suggestions for establishing recognition of symbols by choosing a song children know well in which there are examples of two even tones to a beat. After stepping and beating and clapping melody tones, write the symbols for melody tones and then direct conscious attention to tones for which symbols are to be learned. The following songs are good choices:

Long, Long Ago
There Was a Little Woman
The Volga Boatmen
Joy to the World

The Deaf Woman's Courtship
Old Folks at Home
Sweetheart Out a-Hunting

To the teacher:

Direct attention to the *likeness* of patterns in these songs and others in children's books.

In the following examples from familiar songs, the words *after* the two sixteenths (and those before, too) are important and must come on an accented beat so there is a need to "hurry up" the relatively unimportant words:

♪	♪	
Where	the	buffaloes
Where	the	deer and the
And	the	skies
And	we'll	all feel gay
At	the	silent break of dawn
There	I	found
When	I	begged
Which	I	gazed on so
Were	to	fade

Recognition of the less frequently used symbols is established by directing conscious attention to their relation with words.

In the triplet, the 3 under or over the curve is the signal for interpreting those three tones in the time of two. Usually, the words offer a clue. Songs in which the triplet occurs are:

Rig A Jig Jig (chorus)
Waters Ripple and Flow
Juanita (chorus)

4. To establish recognition for two uneven tones to a beat ♩. ♪ :

This common pattern occurs several times in *The Star-Spangled Banner* and *Dixie*. The combination is found often in the following:

Dinah, Won't You Blow Your Horn?   *London Bridge*
"Bridal Chorus" from *Lohengrin*   *Dance Song*
I've Been Workin' on de Railroad   *Oh, My Darling Clementine*
Love's Old Sweet Song (chorus)   *Viennese Popular Song*
Taps   *Rig-a-Jig-Jig* (verse)

To the teacher:

Direct attention to the *likeness* in clapping and in the notation.

5. To establish awareness of the eighth note as the beat note:

Consider the notation of two or three songs written in $\frac{3}{4}$ or $\frac{4}{4}$ and re-write in $\frac{3}{8}$ or $\frac{4}{8}$.

(The half note is rarely used as the beat note. If children should need to read music in which the half note is the beat note, discuss its implications, clap the values, and read the words in terms of these values.)

6. To establish recognition of the symbols of three pulses or tones to a beat ($\frac{6}{8}$ or $\frac{2}{4}$. or $\frac{9}{8}$ or $\frac{3}{4}$.).

The symbols used in the notation of three pulses or tones to a beat are not new—it is the grouping, the emphasis, the accent, that is different. The former procedure for recognizing symbols *may* be used, but the suggestions that follow this song list have particular merit.

Songs in $\frac{6}{8}$:

> *When Johnny Comes Marching Home*
> *Believe Me, If All Those Endearing Young Charms*
> *Charlie Is My Darlin'*
> *Rice Pudding*
> *Home on the Range*
> *Pop! Goes the Weasel*
> *Silent Night*

Since it is the grouping and not the symbols that is "new" in $\frac{8}{6}$ and $\frac{9}{8}$ measure, the following suggestions are made:

(a) *Think* of these songs as being in "two's" or "three's," and when placing the relative time values in any song on the blackboard, place them in easily discernible groups of two's and three's.

(b) Place several different measures of a familiar song on the blackboard (Examples from *When Johnny Comes Marching Home*):

(*c*) Ask the children to sing counts (1-2-3-4-5-6) to *When Johnny Comes Marching Home* while stepping and beating 1-2.

(*d*) Have the children pat 1-2 with feet and clap notes as they sing and look at the board for the purpose of identifying some of the measures they clap. "What words go with measure 4? Sing and clap the song again and count how many times you sing measure 4."

(*e*) "Some of these same groups are in *Pop! Goes the Weasel.* Sing it. When you recognize on the board a measure you have clapped, put your hand up."

(*f*) Another approach: Place on the blackboard two or three measures from different songs that have identical patterns:

John - ny	comes	march	- ing	home	a - gain	Hur -
Give	him	a	heart	- y	wel - come	then	Hur -
cob - (ob)	bler's	bench	the	all	a - round	the
all ____	in	fun ____	mon - key	chased	the
pa - tience	to	wait	till	mon - key	tho't	'twas

Ask children to clap notes and read words.

Select other patterns common to two or three songs and proceed in the same manner.

In following these suggestions, the feeling for and the awareness of relative time values as demonstrated objectively in clapping, patting, walking, and beating are translated into symbols. In turn, then, these symbols can become symbols for movement, for action. In the early stages of gaining skill, recognition is in terms of simple physical response—clapping; later, it is in terms approximating the ultimate use, interpreting in singing and playing, by giving words the values indicated.

Suggestions for Testing Skill in Symbol Recognition

1. After children have become aware of some of the symbols, select an unfamiliar song containing these symbols. Prepare them or direct their conscious attention to these symbols for relative time values: "What is the beat note? How many dotted quarter notes (or half notes) are in the first line? the second line? How many measures contain only . . . ?" and so on. Then, "While counting aloud, clap or tap pencils for notes. Read words in time."

After more experience, eliminate any physical response except beating and *read* words after preparation.

2. A more advanced test is writing the notation of the relative time values of a simple familiar song without referring to a song book. Suggest each person beat time and sing softly *to himself* while writing. This is quite difficult without the definite preparation suggested in this chapter. It is a skill teachers need in recording songs children create.

The aim of all this activity is to learn to read the symbols for the duration aspect of notes. The only necessities: a teacher who knows what she is trying to do and children who can beat time and clap and step while singing many songs. The way to learn any and all of these common patterns in notation is to (1) direct conscious attention to a pattern in a well-known song by clapping pattern while counting aloud and by beating time while saying the words; (2) discover the same pattern in several other songs; (3) learn the symbol for the pattern from the blackboard; (4) find the symbol in music (song) notation; and, (5) interpret it by reading words in the time of melody notes. The way of learning might be summed up (always emphasizing *likeness*): by-ear-and-muscle to symbol-on-blackboard to symbol-in-notation-of-song.

Accompaniments and Accompanying

Accompaniments for rhythms can be furnished by percussion instruments (tom-tom,[5] claves[6]), pianos, phonograph records, or by the singing of children not taking part in the activity. For less vigorous, simple activities, such as rocking a baby to sleep, children may sing their own accompaniment.

The music used to motivate, control, and direct the children's physical responses should be simple; that is, it should have an uncomplicated rhythm pattern. If the music is used for stepping, the accent to direct stepping should be clear cut, easy to find, and not hidden by an assortment of complex rhythms superimposed upon the *stepping* rhythm. A *simple* pattern is ♩ ♩ ♩ ♩. It is *possible* to walk to a Brazilian samba, but the complexity resulting from the various rhythms being superimposed one on the other is a deterring, rather than a helpful, factor for the inexperienced.

Because the accents must be clearly indicated, many teachers find a percussion instrument one of the most desirable in providing accompaniments for rhythms. These are the reasons they give: (1) The teacher is able to move around the room while playing; (2) children can easily learn to use them; and (3) they are inexpensive to buy or can be made easily.

When the piano is used in connection with rhythms—whether it directs movement or accompanies it—the playing must be rhythmical. Not only must it have a swing, but its style should enhance the idea behind movement: The music for skipping should be light, airy and graceful; music for pushing, ponderous; and music for marching, crisp and peppy.

Where should the piano be placed in the room? It should

[5] See directions for making a tom-tom in the section "Homemade Instruments."

[6] Two sticks of hard wood (eight inches long and an inch or less in diameter), tapped against each other, make an acceptable substitute for a tom-tom. The stick in the left hand should be held in place by the fleshy lower part of the thumb and the tips of the four fingers. Held in this position, there is a pocket of air under the stick that gives resonance to the sound. As used in South American music, these sticks are known as *claves*.

be placed so the teacher can see the children as they move. If it is true, as some children have suspected, that a teacher has a second pair of eyes in the back of her head, then the teacher can have the piano placed flat against a wall, sit with her back toward the group of moving youngsters, and watch them while playing. If it is not true, then the piano should jut out from the wall at an angle so the teacher can see them over her shoulder. If the piano is small and the teacher can see over it while seated, then the back of the piano can face the moving children.

A teacher accompanist is a busy person—she has to play and observe children at the same time. If she has to play, look at a page of printed music, look at her hands, *and* look at the children—all at the same time—she truly needs that extra pair of eyes. *She* is moving—head up, head down—but are the children? She'll never know. Some one or two of these looking-activities is likely to be neglected. Let it not be looking-at-the-children.

Fortunately, accompaniments, simple as to harmony, and swinging along in the appropriate style are more than adequate. An expert in the area of little children and movement guided such a group's rhythms on a program of the Music Educators National Conference—guided the children by playing the piano and played only C (below middle C) and the next E with her left hand and the C and E above with her right. Taking direction from the style of playing these four keys, the children ran, twirled, picked a heavy load off the floor, chased butterflies in a kind of a skip, and rested on the floor, soothed by the identical tones.

If you are a look-at-the-notes and a look-at-the-keys but not a look-at-the-children pianist, try this: With your hands in front of you, pat in the air the rhythm pattern of *America* (fingers only, no thumbs); pat again, alternating hands; and, now, at the piano press down the sustaining pedal and pat the black keys in front of you in the same pattern. Go up and down the piano. Make a skipping pattern

♩ ♪ or ♩. ♪

up and down the keyboard. On the low keys make heavy, slow "swing-a-swing-a-swing." If that last "piece" is rhythmical, it is likely to be as good "elephant" music or "push" or "pull" music as you will find in books of music or on records. If you play "high-low-high-low" slowly and with a swing, it can be a wonderful accompaniment for movements involving the whole body—an exaggerated bounce and catch or turning a jumping rope or a skating motion. You have been playing *tone clusters*.

A child says: "I'm an airplane—play some airplane music, please." His feet take short fast steps, his body is low for the take off and is raised in flight and settles back to earth again. The accompaniment: the pattern made by the child's feet is played in tone clusters low on the piano, then up and up the keyboard—and, finally, down, down, down.

Such accompaniments are more musical than are those made by the tom-tom, but they have the same advantage for freeing the eyes of the pianist. Such accompaniments are likely to be more free and swinging than are those of a look-at-the-notes and look-at-the-keys pianist.

Miss Dorward lists and grades accompaniments according to the type of rhythmic pattern involved: [7]

1. Accompaniments in which the rhythmic pattern is the same as the pattern to be stepped, for example:

| Children: | step step | run run run run |
| Accompaniment: | ♩ ♩ | ♫♫ ♪ ♪ |

2. Accompaniments in which the beats only are tapped or played, even though children move to a variety of rhythmic patterns. For example:

| Children: | step | run run step | run run |
| Accompaniment: | ♩ | ♩ | ♩ | ♩ |

[7] E. Marion Dorward *Music Education through Rhythmic Activity for Elementary and Junior High School Teachers.* Unpublished thesis, School of Education, New York University, 1940.

3. Accompaniments in which the rhythmic scheme is the same as one of two patterns that children are performing simultaneously. For example:

First group:	step	run run	run run	step	run run	run run
Second group:	step	step	step	step	step	step
Accompaniment:	♩	♩	♩	♩	♩	♩

4. Accompaniments that have additional or conflicting rhythmic patterns, or in which the underlying pulsation is temporarily obscured or omitted. For example:

(a.) Popular dance music (preferably without vocalist)
(b.) Standard "popular" classics
(c.) Standard classics recorded in steady tempo for rhythm bands
(d.) Songs with simple rhythmic patterns
(e.) Folk dances

5. Accompaniments for activities requiring special music. For example:

(a.) Virginia reel
(b.) Minuet
(c.) Folk dances

Accessories

Scarves, jumping ropes, and balls are the more common accessories to rhythms. There are several reasons for their use: (1) They are fun to use; (2) they are easy to obtain; (3) they are familiar objects; (4) they give the self-conscious child something else besides himself upon which to concentrate; (5) they are likely to result in big, free movements; and (6) the motions resulting from manipulating these accessories can serve as patterns for other responses. For example, children can regulate the motions of *imaginary* throwing by remembering the actual motion involved in throwing a ball.

Tempo

Probably the most important aid to a satisfactory and developmental experience in rhythms is the proper tempo. What is the proper tempo? *It is the rate of speed at which a particular activity can be carried on freely and vigorously.*

The muscular control and the coordination of those who are attempting to respond are the factors that determine the proper tempo of a response.

The tempo of a particular activity is set either by the accompaniment or by the children. In the latter case, the accompaniment is adapted to the tempo set by the children. Obviously, if the tempo is set by the children, it is an indication that they *can* carry out the responses they have in mind. On the other hand, when the tempo is set by the accompaniment, it should be considered carefully. If it is too fast, the responses are not with the beat, and fumbling and awkwardness result. Perhaps they do not have sufficient skill and coordination to perform at this rate; perhaps not even the most finished dancer could accomplish what the children are attempting. If the tempo is too slow, the motivation and propulsion that should come from the accent and swing of the music are lacking. The space of time between starting and finishing a response is too long. There is too much opportunity to lose balance and control.

How can the proper tempo be determined? The most simple way is by observing the results of effort. A tempo that is too quick is easier to notice than one that is too slow. If results are unsatisfactory, the teacher should try out the tempo and analyze *her* reaction in terms of what the children have been doing.

Rhythms for Primary Children

Those who are charged with the responsibility for guiding the growth of children through rhythms do not have to resort to any degree of artificial stimulation. This is an activity that teachers and children enjoy wholeheartedly. Because it is so enjoyable, the teacher must be on the alert to make certain that growth as well as enjoyment is taking place.

As in all other phases of teaching music, the teacher must "take children from where they are." In children's initial school experiences the teacher can assume that they are untutored in the *formal* aspects of rhythms—formal in that responses are motivated, directed, and controlled by a force other than the will to move. If children are in the third grade rather than in kindergarten or the first grade when the first attempt is made to mold their physical responses in conformity to an external stimulus, their teachers will no doubt find that some of the activities listed as promoting muscular control and coordination are physically easy. In such instances, emphasis should be placed on the rhythmic aspect of the performance, on listening to the music for direction, and on having a satisfying experience in the expression of self.

Suggestions for Initiating Activity. The best approach for initiating rhythmic activities is to relate action to a song or to the dramatization of a character or idea recently mentioned in a story. If the idea of moving to music is completely new, it is best to have children move while seated in their chairs—they can move and move vigorously their bodies, heads, arms, feet, and legs—the mere fact that they are sitting produces some degree of control. An experienced teacher may be able to guide a large group in its first moving-whole-body experience with results other than chaos, but the inexperienced teacher with inexperienced children had best make use of the control imposed by sitting.

Statements such as these will set minds and bodies to moving: "Show with your arms how Trinkle Pete climbed the tree"; "The old man was tired. Show how very tired he was while I play some *tired* music"; "Push the heavy wheelbarrow"; "Alice heard her neighbor playing the violin last night—let's play violins as we sing. . . ."

In only two of the activities suggested above was music the starting point or the inspiration for movement—in clapping and in playing violins. Presumably, the accent in the music was the guide for motion. In the other activities, if there was an accompaniment, it was adapted to movement. After the accompaniment was fitted to the motions, it could then effect some control in making and refining the pattern.

Suggestions Related to Teaching

1. Remember that the purpose of rhythms is to convert the natural love of and need for releasing physical energy into controlled motion—controlled by mind, by muscles, and by music—thereby developing the sense of rhythm. The ideal is completely free motion within prescribed limits; and/or satisfyingly free movement within a pattern; and/or moving with abandon within controls. "Going off in all directions at once" is fun, it releases tensions and energy, and it is the basis upon which controls are gradually imposed—but until there is some degree of control by mind, by muscles, and by music, it is not "rhythms." It is "free play."

2. The ideal place for rhythms is in the classroom—a classroom that is sufficiently large to accommodate all the necessary chairs, tables, and other equipment, with enough space left over for a group of children to move freely in a circle, to run and jump with controlled abandon without endangering their lives and their limbs. This ideal, like so many others, is often difficult to attain. Some substitutes: auditorium stage, gymnasium, halls, basement, school yard and the space left vacant in the classroom when furniture has been moved. There are the aisles, narrow though they might be, and the seats—the "place" it was suggested the inexperienced start.

Some teachers have successfully used the playground for rhythms. This place is excellent for gaining the controls necessary to "run-run-run-jump or leap"—a pattern using the whole body. There the teacher plays "run-run-run-leap" on the tom-tom, the children clap that pattern, step it in place several times and, then, execute it.

The opportunity presented by the need to go from one room

to another in the building has been used by some teachers. There are other ways than marching or strolling to get places. You can arrive by "step-step-step-step-stop-2-3-4" or "hut-2-3-4-stop-2 step-4." And, there is the "step-bend-the knee" suggested by the dotted quarter note in *I've Been Workin' in de Classroom*. Some principals like the efficiency as well as the obvious enjoyment of children who move in these different ways.

"Marching" from place to place in school is sometimes frowned upon. *These* steps are not marching, they are moving.

When space is limited and the activities require space, a half or a third of the group can move while the remainder furnishes a percussion accompaniment.

Teachers know that children do not find their regular classroom seats restricting all movement. Some of that movement incorporated into a pattern will develop muscular controls and the sense of rhythm just as surely as movement in the music activities room with its soundproof walls, its large uncluttered floor space, its piano, phonograph, special accompanist, and supply of percussion instruments.

3. There is a definite relation between children's size and their natural rate of movement. Small children make smaller, faster movements than do large children. For this reason, the teacher must get the concept of correct tempo from the movements of children themselves. When little children swing their bodies back and forth, the arc so made is smaller than the arc made by a taller person—the arc is smaller, therefore, the high points of their natural swing occur more frequently and, therefore, the accent in the accompanying music must occur more frequently. Because of all this, the tempo must be faster for them than it would be for larger children. After they register the idea of coordination between their natural movement and the accent, the rate of accent can be changed and their attempts to fit movement to accent can result in gaining control.

4. When the beat or accent of the music is supposed to control movement, it is a good practice for children to clap the accent in order to demonstrate that they hear it. For example,

in order to skip to music, two things are necessary: (1) children must know how to skip and (2) they must hear and recognize the pattern in the music that will direct and control their response of skipping. In order to play in a rhythm band, they should demonstrate by clapping that they hear the accent that will control their playing. If the dramatic play upon which they decide involves "bend-pull-pull," children need the opportunity to concentrate on the music they have chosen for an accompaniment by clapping "loud-soft-soft" as it is played.

If those mentioned earlier, who had to practice so long to master the slow march used in processions, had spent some time just clapping the accent to demonstrate that they could hear it, practice time would have been shortened considerably.

5. Children need experience not only in adapting movement to music (a pattern of sound) but also in setting and maintaining a pattern by themselves. This is the skill they need when they play a musical instrument by themselves. And this is the circumstance that too often reveals the real lack of rhythmic sense. Adapting movement to a pattern and getting muscles set in a rut help, but there are other more directly related, helpful activities: deciding on and then playing a pattern of soft and loud beats on a drum or tom-tom, playing melodies on melody bells or tone blocks, playing chords for accompaniments on the Autoharp, and clapping a pattern for other children to interpret or use. These activities are setting and maintaining a *design in accent*, and are directly related to gaining skill in the specific where skill is generally lacking.

6. A signal for stopping movement is necessary—one more socially acceptable than a yell from the teacher. It could be something like this:

Notice that it is a signal *for* a stop. Excellent control is required to stop *on* a signal. The signal prepares one mentally for stopping and gives one time physically *to* stop. Thirty bucking broncos need time to register "stop" before they can actually do it.

A few moments of practice in recognizing the signal, before an activity begins, is sufficient: "Let's find out if you can recognize the stop-sign—put your hand up when you hear it"—the teacher then plays on drum or piano or other accompanying instrument

7. In early experiences in rhythms children may pattern all their activities along the same line—they may twirl in every effort at dramatization or wave their arms or take little running steps. The teacher should enlarge their concept of movement and see to it that they get experience in using the whole vocabulary.

8. Children in the primary grades engage in the beating-time activities (generally using only the down beat), in clapping and walking beats, and the clapping-melody-tones activities, but they do *not* generally engage in translating their motions into symbols except in rare instances. They make percussion accompaniments but they do it by ear and by feeling. Their activity is concerned with developing the rhythmic sense and muscular coordination and control and with inculcating a *feeling* for the duration values of notes. Symbols for these values are learned after feeling is established. Feeling is established when children can adapt movement to a pattern of accent in music, when they show they can sense accent in music, and when they can produce regular patterns of accent in a series of sounds. The last item is the test. A few, a very few, groups will be able to pass the test in the last part of the third grade. Some individuals are born able to make a pattern of sound in rhythm, but just a few—a very few.

Rhythm Bands. "Rhythm bands" or "rhythm orchestras" are

the names usually applied to groups of children playing percussion instruments. Some of the instruments used are those of the percussion section of a modern symphony orchestra—tambourines, cymbals, drums, triangles, and castanets; others are percussion instruments that make musical sounds of indefinite pitch (bells); still others are those that make their own peculiar individual sounds that defy classification—sticks and bird whistles. The music that is interpreted or accompanied is either a phonograph record, piano music, or the singing of children.

Participation in rhythm bands can be of educational value to children *if* the musical accompaniment is a motivating or controlling force. If all the activities concerning playing in a rhythm band are judged by whether or not they contribute to the development of the rhythmic sense and to the *understanding* and *interpretation* of a composition, certain practices will follow, and certain other practices will be eliminated.

JUSTIFICATION. Obviously, participation in rhythm bands is a delightful means of developing a sense of rhythm. If developing a sense of rhythm were the only reason for providing this additional experience, there would be little point in expending all the time and energy necessary for acquiring and distributing the essential materials because the rhythmic sense can be developed equally well by clapping. There must be some learning. It is through listening, which enables children to make suggestions for interpretations of compositions, and carrying out those suggestions that musical growth results. *Growth in musical taste and judgment,* resulting from planning the scores of compositions and the concentrated listening, justifies a rhythm band. Further justification is possible when it can be shown that participation in the rhythm band leads directly to participation in elementary school bands or orchestras.

ACCOMPANYING MUSIC. The music to be used as an accompaniment should be given careful consideration, especially in initial attempts. The fundamental rhythmic pattern should be well defined. There should be contrasts in style, melody, and mood. The tempi of the different sections can be varied, but there should be no great variation in the tempo of a particular section.

Children must be thoroughly familiar with the music they intend to interpret before attempting to make the "score" or the pattern for playing. They must also be familiar with the sounds produced by their instruments. Familiarity with the composition comes with hearing it many times. Familiarity with the instruments is gained by using them and discussing the quality of the sounds they make. Children must know the selection and know their instruments so that the *music itself can suggest the use of certain instruments.*

THE SCORE. The score may either approximate an orchestral score in that a part is planned for each group of instruments throughout the whole composition, or each group of instruments may be assigned to play a certain section or sections of the composition. Many teachers feel that the latter type is more satisfactory. When the decision is made as to which group of instruments is to play a section, this information is written on the blackboard as a reminder for the conductor.

The type of score inherent in the informal "by ear" and "by feeling" percussion accompaniment discussed earlier is excellent and is sufficient for most "playing" sessions.

CONDUCTORS. Children will enjoy conducting the band. The leaders give directions for groups to start and stop playing and indicate changes in dynamics. The conductors should do more than beat the time; they should give directions so that the children playing in the band will play more artistically than they would if there were no conductor.

POOR PRACTICES. Attention is directed again to a statement made earlier in this section: "If all the activities relative to playing in a rhythm band are judged by whether or not they contribute to the understanding and interpretation of a composition, certain practices will follow and certain others will be eliminated." One of the practices to be eliminated is that of exploiting the children in those bands. There is one primary group that spends all its music time practicing the rhythm band because it is expected to perform at every meeting of the PTA. In another city, there is an annual rhythm band concert for which literally hundreds of children are drilled for hours in their parts.

In the first instance, the "concerts" occur so frequently that the children do not have time to study each composition or to plan the score. Planning is the responsibility of the teacher alone. In the second instance, the score is planned by one teacher and distributed to the other teachers and the children. Admittedly, parents and other friends of the school enjoy the programs—the children are so cute! But this is hardly adequate reason for robbing children of their sleep, their opportunity for growth in other areas of music, or for wearing them out physically with long sessions of drill.

THE IDEAL PRACTICE. The ideal practice is implicit in the idea that one of the usual things we do is making and planning and playing accompaniments for songs or for records or for movement. Some of us can play melody bells or the Autoharp, the flutophone or the tone blocks, the piano, the violin, the clarinet, or the drums, the cymbals, the triangle or the tambourine—and so we do. Some of us can clap and snap our fingers in time to the music—and so we do. Some of us can play instruments making specific tones and we'll all learn the same piece to play while others sing it—so we all perform together. If not, some of us will play while others sing and move and play percussion instruments. It is from the natural, everyday, simple use of these instruments that the greatest growth results. Nothing fancy—an extension of clapping or of patting the feet, which makes "good" sound but is too rarely used—but fun and so educational!

HOMEMADE INSTRUMENTS. Instruments for the rhythm band can be either purchased or made. Many music publishing and band instrument companies have a complete line of such instruments, and musical scores are available. However, the homemade variety can be a satisfactory substitute if money is not available for the purchase of manufactured ones. When children make their own percussion instruments, they get additional fun out of using them. The following suggestions will help assemble instruments for a rhythm band:

1. A long nail suspended on a string and struck by another nail will produce a sound similar to a triangle.

2. Metal discs an inch or so in diameter strung on a string or a piece of wire will produce some of the "atmosphere" of a tambourine.

3. The thin tin lid of a frying pan, or a pie pan, suspended on a string and struck with a small mallet with a well-padded head produces a sound not unlike a cymbal.

4. Two blocks of wood, one inch thick and three inches by four inches in size, with one surface of each covered with sandpaper, produce a "swish-swish" sound when the covered surfaces are rubbed together. A nail driven in the center of the uncovered side of each block helps the child to handle this "instrument."

5. Blocks of wood struck with wooden hammers produce many different sounds.

6. The ordinary kitchen variety wooden mixing bowl, with a thin piece of parchment or rubber tightly stretched over the top and fastened securely, makes an excellent tom-tom or drum. On the outside, about a half inch from the rim, a small ridge is carved to hold the wire that keeps the cover in place. A screen-door handle screwed to the bottom makes the tom-tom easier to hold and control. For the beater, the end of a small drumstick is padded and covered.

7. Sleigh bells or any of the bells found on children's toys can also be used.

A variation in tone or sound is made by "instruments" of the same material. Try several nails or lids or materials for a drumhead, and choose the one that makes the most musical sound. With a little imagination these articles can be transformed into attractive instruments that serve an excellent purpose.

Rhythms for Older Children

The real difference between the rhythms in the primary grades and the program in upper elementary grades is based upon the difference in the children themselves. The older group has more accurate powers of observation and is interested in a wider variety of activities. The children have greater physical endurance and can play vigorously for longer periods of time. They have acquired some greater degree of muscular control and coordination. They have usually had some association with music.

Children in the upper elementary grades need experiences that will enable them to:

(a) refine movement in the basic vocabulary;

(b) direct conscious attention to music in order to respond physically to the details of this music; and

(c) acquire muscular control and coordination in activities related to the general needs of adults.

The discussion of the rhythms program for older children will be divided into two parts: rhythms for the inexperienced and rhythms for the experienced.

Rhythms for the Inexperienced. Care must be used in initiating a program of rhythms when this type of activity is "new" for a fourth, fifth, sixth or seventh grade group. The idea of moving, and moving with the teacher's approval, may induce a mild psychological shock. After all, they've been in school several years and, during this time, considerable energy—some vocal and maybe some physical—has been expended to keep them *from* moving. Lest this "new" freedom (the freedom to be natural and to do what they actually *need* to do—release physical energy and tensions) result in disorder (in the teacher's opinion) and disintegrate into chaos, their first experience in approved group movement needs careful consideration. Even though the idea is to get them on their feet and moving without self-consciousness and with enjoyment, there must be some control—control imposed either by idea, muscle, or music. Any one of these controls is sufficient in initial attempts.

One teacher used "learning the conductor's beat" as motivation for physical response to music. Television had made her class aware that conducting was an adult activity. The group learned to beat 1–2–3 while singing *America*. "Let's try to walk 1–2–3" and then, "Beat 1–2–3 while walking and singing." The class was up and moving—moving freely but within the control imposed by 1–2–3.

Clapping the hands, snapping the fingers, and patting the feet while singing a favorite song started another group on its way in movement. The percussion accompaniment was enlarged. The group "paraded" while "playing" and was soon engaged in a more creative effort in using movement as a means of expression.

The fact that two children in a class went "folk dancing" with their parents was the basis upon which another teacher built interest. She told these two she thought the class would like to learn a dance. The three of them agreed upon an easy-to-learn dance and decided which things ought to be taught first. After having learned it, the class later injected new steps and suggested other patterns—and creative rhythmic movement was a fact.

The consuming interest of a fourth grade in a nearby bridge-and-road-building project was used by their teacher to initiate rhythmic activities. The children were encouraged to watch closely the types of motion on the construction scene in order that they might be able to reproduce them in their classroom.

One sixth-grade teacher decided to use for a first experience in dramatic-play-plus-music the imminence of spring and the interest of her class in a "drama" the junior high school students in the same building were rehearsing for an assembly program.

"Why are you glad spring is coming?" "Because soon we'll go fishing and swimming, because we can play outside." "What games will you play?" "Ball, tennis, marbles, jump rope." "What other things do you do in spring?" "Make a garden and fix up the yard." As activities were mentioned, the teacher listed them on the blackboard.

Since the class was already divided into various committees, the teacher used these familiar groupings in getting started. "Charles, you and your committee plan a dramatization of sports in the spring; Alice's committee work in the garden"; and so on. After the groups had considered for a few moments, she said, "Now that you have some idea of your dramatization, we'll go to the auditorium stage where we'll have more room to move. There will be a prize for the best dramatization—the hole in the biggest doughnut you can imagine."

On the stage the children arranged themselves in their groups, and the teacher started playing *The Blue Danube* with an unartistic but commanding thump on each count 1. Movement started. The boys playing tennis found the space confining —they moved down to the aisles; those working in the yard moved down to the space in front of the seats. When the teacher observed *patterns in movement* being formed, she said, "Let's watch the swimmers." Each group did a solo performance and, then, once again, all moved at the same time. It so happened that there were plenty of prizes—one was awarded to each group with considerable ceremony.

These children were accustomed to "freedom"—they knew how to work in groups and they had had many opportunities to express themselves verbally. For them there was nothing startlingly "new" in this idea of using their bodies with controlled abandon in dramatic-play-with-music. Other children with little experience in expressing themselves verbally and with little experience in planning and carrying out plans may need more direction in their early attempts.

Rhythms for the Experienced. The program of rhythms for children in the upper elementary grades consists of extending and refining those activities developed during the earlier years in school. The children's physical growth and their previous experience affect not only the kind of responses they are able to make, but their manner of response. It is more coordinated and flowing. Their growing powers of observation, plus their greater muscular control, make it possible for them to interpret rather accurately their own ideas and the music they hear.

The situation concerning rhythms for primary and intermediate grade children is comparable to the situation in social studies. In the primary grades, there is an attempt to build up certain concepts of social relationships. Later, there is an effort to extend those concepts in some instances and to refine them in others. The same thing is true in rhythms. In the primary grades there is an attempt to build up certain responses to certain stimuli. Later, there is nothing actually *new* injected into the program, but there is an effort made to extend these responses in some instances and to refine them in others.

As their wide interests influence other phases of creative work, so will these interests contribute to the creative movement of older children. The creative rhythmic dramatizations of older children are characterized by the attention given to detail. When these children plan a rhythmic dramatization of building a house, they go to the forest, fell the trees, take the trees to the mill to get them cut into lumber, haul the lumber to the building site, and so on. Their dramatization approximates reality as far as possible.

This interest in detail extends to interest in interpreting music. Although they do not completely relinquish the idea of expressing self, there often seems to be a willingness to depend wholly on music, to be motivated, directed, and controlled completely by its dictates. When one considers the concentrated listening necessary in order to "know" what music says, it is apparent that such a group must be interested in music and find satisfaction in it. It is in this connection that the more complicated activities, bringing about an awareness of music, make their important contributions. The most difficult activities suggested in the vocabulary of rhythms challenge some groups to gain even more control in order to express the most subtle inflections in music.

Interpretation of music through physical response can take

two forms: (1) an almost exact dramatization of a story told, and (2) a translation of the fundamentals of music—relative note values, mood, dynamics, and so on.

A dramatization of a selection of program music may be an almost literal translation of the story into movement or a literal translation of the music itself into movement; for example, movement based on MacDowell's *To a Wild Rose* might be

step step hold;   step step hold;   step step step step hold

During this period when children (1) can hear and register more precisely the differences that make music—long and short, high and low, slow and fast, (2) are interested in details, and (3) are willing to make a detailed picture-with-movement of what they hear, this is the time to introduce the symbols of what they hear, and this is the time to translate feeling into symbols—important preparation for learning to interpret symbols.

Learning to recognize the symbols of musical notation and learning to interpret them is not burdensome when learning can be tied in with natural interest in detail, with a well-developed feeling for rhythm, with greater ability to hear, register, and remember, and with muscular control sufficient to react physically and consciously to what is heard. This ease in learning to read is one of the rewards (if any is needed) for the clapping and stepping, the bending and swaying, and the playing of percussion instruments in which children engaged previously. Skill in reading duration values develops by translating motion (clapping, walking, beating) into symbols and, then, translating symbols into motion (clapping) and, finally, reading words in correct time. Learning symbols for what is felt and for what has been experienced is easy. It is tied to something *within* the child.

At this time, too, rhythmic dramatizations can be arranged in music forms. One group, in summarizing its study of the community, planned dramatizations of the work of its best known citizens. Because the postman made his rounds three times a day and everyone had reason to know and appreciate him, the dramatization of the postman's activities was used as the leading "theme" of the *rondo* form, while the dramatizations of the milkman and the grocer were the other "themes." Another group had fun in working out a *theme with variations.* The "theme" was the conventional conductor's beat. The children decided that the accompaniment should beat a steady 1–2–3–4, while the "theme" and the "variations" alternated each eight measures. The "variations" included marking various note values with their feet, conducting with both hands, turning slowly in one place, and bending on every other count. Not the most scholarly working out of the form, perhaps, but those children will probably remember for a long time the exact connotation of "theme with variations."

Folk dances and singing games have a definite appeal for children of this age. Some of the dances have intricate steps and complicated patterns, but with growing techniques and control, children are able to learn difficult dances. Since folk dancing is *the* socially acceptable recreation in many communities, little motivation is required. When children make up their own singing games, there is little danger these games will be considered "childish."

Teachers must examine the activities critically and objectively to make certain that growth is taking place. For the program to contribute to the physical, intellectual, social, and emotional growth of all the children, opportunity for such development must be provided and paced throughout the whole program. It is the teacher's responsibility to make certain that *possible* results become *actual* results, that potentialities are realized.

EVALUATING DEVELOPMENT IN RHYTHMS

It is difficult, if not impossible, to say by what standards children's development in rhythms in any grade should be evaluated. It is impossible because growth and development do not automatically result from being in a *grade*. Growth and development result from a sequence of experiences, progressively more challenging through which greater skill is acquired—and experiences vary, especially in the area of music.

It is possible, however, to analyze and list *levels of development*—levels through which each individual must progress in sequence whether it be on the way from nursery school to the elementary school band or from nursery school to the concert hall. Moreover, when a concentrated effort is made to develop the dormant rhythmic sense of an adult, he too must pass along this way just as surely as a child.

Rhythmic development must be listed in terms of *physical* responses, considering that the only means by which a person's rhythmic sense can be judged is by evaluating what he does or the way he acts.

Levels of Development in Rhythms

1. Ability to recognize in music and sufficient control to show with big muscles (1) pulse, (2) pattern in pulse, and then, (3) marked contrasts in tempo, dynamics, mood, and range in pitch *at the same time* with (2).

2. Ability to recognize pulse and sufficient control to use consciously two sets of big muscles, such as walk and clap pulse, walk and clap pattern, and walk and use the conductor's beat.

3. Ability to set and maintain a simple pattern of motion and an uncomplicated pattern in sound.

4. Ability to set and maintain progressively more complicated patterns of sound, and patterns of movement involving both big and little muscles.

> Development may be judged further by evaluating the preciseness of fit between movement and regular accent, the freedom (controlled abandon) of motion, the grade or type of music (accompaniment) used, and the ability to vary motion easily in each activity on any level.

Things to Do

NOTE: This listing of specifics is offered as an aid in starting activity. Once started, the suggestions throughout the chapter will point the way. Notice that the song repertoire becomes the accompaniment for movement.

First Grade

Ask children to make the same motions you do. Start "tipping" while children learn new songs. Vary with an exaggerated motion on count 1. Make other motions *big*, lasting throughout a measure. For example, while children are sitting, they can sway or swing in carrying out an idea suggested by the words of a song or rock, pull, bow, climb and so on. After a while, as they sing the most familiar song, clap on count 1 and wave hands to side on other counts.

Other Grades

Start "tipping" while children listen to new songs and sing old songs. Ask children in second and third grades to make the same motions you do as they sing—big motions, usually lasting a measure. Notice the response. If they follow easily and accurately, follow these suggestions (the first in each group is the most simple) for children in other grades:
  1. While singing *America* (or another thoroughly familiar song written in three's), clap on count 1, wave hands on 2 and 3; clap on 1 and snap fingers on 2 and 3; walk 1–2–3, accenting 1; walk, clap and sing.
  2. Sing *America.* With one foot always on the floor and arms extended, swing or sway right and then left on each count 1. Move while singing 1–2–3 to melody.
  3. Teach conductor's beat. Use while singing *America, the Beautiful.* Beat time and walk while singing softly. Beat, walk and sing 4–1–2–3–4, giving verbal punch to the dotted quarters and three to the dotted half notes. Be certain to sing "2" on count 2 *before* the eighth note.

Prospective and In-Service Teachers

Start "tipping" while singing familiar songs and learning new ones. Use song repertoire as accompaniment for movement and learning the conductor's beat. Use the response in the activities suggested above in THINGS TO DO as a means for ascertaining the *level of development* of the group.

For Discussion

1. Discuss the muscular coordination and control of a concert pianist and a concert violinist.
2. What is the justification for including rhythms in the elementary school program?
3. Which response—walking or clapping the accent in music—requires more muscular control?
4. Notice the manner in which eight people walk, directing your attention to their freedom of motion.
5. Watch children playing games and be prepared to suggest how the use of bigger motions would add to their skill.
6. What is the role of music in rhythms?
7. When do you tell children that a "walk-walk-walk" rhythm is a quarter-note rhythm?
8. What is the proper tempo for rhythms? Illustrate: bending, swaying, marching, high-stepping, and so on in the proper tempo. Improvise the accompaniment.
9. What facts concerning accessories should teachers be aware of?
10. Discuss rhythm and hitting a tennis ball; rhythm and swimming; rhythm and the manual of arms; rhythm and ironing; rhythm and brushing the hair.
11. Which is the more valuable for a child—planning and using a percussion for ten songs or participating in a rhythm band for a PTA program?
12. Which is the more important—the singing program or the rhythms program?
13. Discuss in detail the differences in the creative effort involved in the illustrations in which music was translated into movement—the dramatization of *The Sorcerer's Apprentice,* and a summarizing series of dramatizations. Discuss the specific controls of music in each. Plan your own interpretations of each.
14. Why is the tom-tom an excellent accompaniment for movement?
15. What other signals might be used for stopping movement?
16. Plan and execute choreography for *To A Wild Rose.*
17. What abilities should a child have before he is selected as con-

ductor? Why should the conductor be changed from time to time? Why not? What is the purpose of the band as far as the leader is concerned? What is the purpose of the leader?

18. What are the limitations of a flag or wand drill as "rhythms"?

19. In what ways does the difference between primary and intermediate grade children influence rhythms for the latter?

20. The ideas of "pendulums" and "ruts" are probably two of the most important in this book. Why?

21. Demonstrate each level of development in rhythms.

Suggestions for Teachers

1. Observe the reactions of inexperienced children as they clap the beat of, first, a march and then a waltz. Notice the reactions of the same children as they stand by their seats and mark the primary accents of the same music by a sweeping exaggerated down beat. Why is it a good idea to ask them to close their eyes as they move?

2. Try allowing movement to set the tempo of the accompaniment and then allowing the accompaniment to set the tempo for movement; notice the difference.

3. Plan a pattern of movement—for example, the catching and throwing of a ball. Determine the best tempo for you. Perform the pattern *twice as fast* and then, *half as fast*. Analyze your reactions.

4. Try each of the activities listed under *Activities for Response to Music*. Clap each first, as was suggested for children. Practice those you find difficult. *You* need control and coordination, too.

5. Can you beat "four" with one hand as you beat "three" with the other? Change pattern of each hand. Try walking *one*-two, while you beat "three" and "four." If you can, you have quite a bit of control.

6. Make a tom-tom. Use it.

7. Play some recordings of popular music and decide why some are good accompaniments for rhythms and why others are not.

8. Learn the singing game *Pop! Goes the Weasel*. Plan another singing game.

9. Play on a piano, using tone clusters, the accompaniment for a dramatization of an automobile with a flat tire; a jack-in-the-box; Goldilocks and the Three Bears; a storm at sea; the color

"white"; eating breakfast; and the walk the crane and the sparrow took together.

10. The songs mentioned in this chapter are found in *Music Fundamentals Through Song*. Study your class's song book and list five songs to be used as substitutes for the songs mentioned here.

11. List the sequence in learning: the symbols for a note longer than a beat; the principles involved in a measure signature; to interpret the symbols for the relative duration values of notes. "Learning" can be said to have taken place when it (fact or skill) can be used to support the *next* in the sequence of facts or skills. The teacher must make an accurate judgment about the mastery of each step before introducing the *next*.

12. Discuss the interdependence of Evaluating Growth in Listening Ability and Evaluating Development in Movement.

13. Have your class plan and execute an additional "stanza" for its songs as suggested under item 11 of the Vocabulary.

$$\diamond\!\diamond\!\diamond\!\diamond\!\diamond\!\diamond\!\diamond\!\diamond \quad 5$$

Creating Music

Music in the school hopes to contribute to the physical, intellectual, social, and emotional growth of *all* elementary school children. The music that children create helps, both qualitatively and quantitatively, to carry out the desire for emotional growth. Moreover, creative activities can contribute to intellectual and social growth as well.

WHAT IS MEANT BY CREATIVE MUSIC ACTIVITIES

Creative music activities are those through which children themselves bring music into being. Some of the pictures that flash across the consciousness at the words "creative music" are: A child proudly and carefully practicing the new piece his piano teacher gave him to learn *by himself* for a recital three weeks hence; a group of children discussing the manner in which a song should be interpreted and *singing* it that way; children trying to decide whether the melody they are writing should go "up" or "down" at the end; and a six-year-old "making up" and beating a rhythm pattern on a tom-tom for classmates to interpret. A concise statement of this concept of creative music activities is "expression of self through music."

The child learning his recital piece and the group interpreting a song were bringing music into being (creating) by translating symbols (notes) into music. Some people think of this activity as "re-creating." The six-year-old beating rhythms on the tom-tom for classmates to interpret was not creating any "new" or startling patterns, but she was arranging her small repertoire of patterns in a new order. Using material with which she was familiar—loud and soft beats and "step" and "running" beats—she was creating just as the group writing a song was creating.

Deciding to use melody bells with a percussion accompaniment for a song is creating music. If the decision was to use melody instruments throughout, that, too, was creating. Arriving at a plan to go seven steps to the right, to stop, and then to retrace steps as a pattern of movement in a singing game is creating, too.

Creative music activities are those in which a child considers the *whole* of his awareness of music, selects parts of this whole to make his own arrangement, his own pattern.

Those who know little children well know that making up songs to convey ideas and/or emotions is a *natural* means of expression for them. Does the mere fact of going to school change them or does the fact of going to school limit the development of one of their natural means of expression?

Creating by means of movement and creating by using musical instruments have been discussed. In this chapter, creating by selecting groups of tones to enhance the words of a poem— writing a song—will be the major consideration; some melodies are to be sung and some to be played.

WHAT CREATING MUSIC MEANS TO CHILDREN

I, we, my, our are just as important to children as they are to adults. It is not selfishness or egoism, but interest in self-expression that makes them say, "Listen to the piece Harry composed," "This is our song," "May we make a song?" or, "I think this is the way this should be sung." Creative music activities mean opportunity for expressing self through music. These activities are opportunities to explore and use the language of music.

Sometimes children are not allowed to express their ideas of interpreting a song or instrumental solo. However, their idea of the music and their comprehension of the music are mirrored in their manner of performing, regardless of whether the style is one arrived at by them or their teachers. The emotional release possible through singing is valuable, and possibilities of this medium of self-expression are all too often ignored.

Children may find a means of expressing self in composing songs, too, as well as in interpreting the music of others. Composing is a natural mode of expression for little children as nursery school teachers and kindergarten teachers well know. Janie in nursery school sang:

as she swung back and forth. This little song was repeated many times—a song that was a complete expression of the activity in which she was engaged, a song that was motivated by the activity itself. More often than not, rhythmic activity and absorption in the activity will result in song on the part of nursery school children and kindergarten children.

Later, Janie, in the second grade, was a child of wider musical experience. Her description of her feelings as she swung back and forth showed her to have greater sophistication:

The impulse to create must be encouraged and directed and must be allowed to develop into musical forms. Today, child nature itself is a starting point and a guide in directing the more formal aspects of growth. There is not only children's innate love for music upon which to build a program of teaching for appreciation, and their innate love for motion upon which to build a program of rhythms to develop their rhythmic and interpretative powers, but there is also their natural tendency to express feelings through song upon which to build a program of creative music.

APPROACHES TO SONG WRITING

Songs (whether written by adults or children) are written in three different ways: (1) Words are set to a melody; (2) a melody is composed for words; or (3) words and melody are created simultaneously. Each of these methods has its unique function, each is widely used among composers today, and each has served the masters of another year. The method is determined by the motive for writing. The process of selection is simple. If a person composes a tune that is lovely, singable, or interesting, and the need for words is apparent, he tries to find words to enhance his efforts. He or another person may furnish them. If he has a poem expressing a sentiment or story that he thinks could be enhanced by a melody, he writes music for it, or finds someone to compose the tune. And, finally, if the person who is inspired to write a poem is also a musician (or vice versa), words and music may be written at the same time.

In the schoolroom each of these methods has its peculiar possibilities as well as its limitations and advantages.

Setting Words to Music

A desirable way to initiate or re-establish interest in music writing is to make up words for a familiar tune. In one instance, the teacher of a fifth grade asked for guidance in initiating song writing. Knowing her class, she felt that, once started on its composing-way, the class would find the same pleasure in this phase of creative work as it had found in writing poetry. The music specialist went to that group's room with a recording of MacDowell's *To a Wild Rose*. The record was chosen because it is melodically simple and was quite familiar. The children's discussion of the music brought forth the idea that, since the music was not gaily blatant or overwhelmingly colorful, Mac-Dowell was writing about a small rose on a secluded bush. The children felt that a breeze was roaming on the day the composer chose to write because there is gentle motion in the music. The record was played again in order that the children might reconstruct their picture to the accompaniment of the music. This hearing brought forth several new ideas and confirmed those stated previously.

The music specialist then suggested that the children make up words to fit the music while listening to the first phrase of the melody. After the first phrase had been played several times, different children were asked to sing their words. These were written on the blackboard. The group decided which set of words best fitted the music and carried out the idea of the picture. The first two lines of the poem served as the basis for the remainder of the poem; otherwise, the children would have been changing and rearranging indefinitely. As soon as the class made its decision, the first two lines of the poem were sung softly to the accompaniment of the music. During the next playing, they were asked not to sing aloud, but to wait for the next phrase and plan words for it. The second group of words came more quickly and with greater ease. This is the poem:

> Wild rose, little rose
> Swaying back and forth,
> Ah! so soft; ah! sweet,
> Red and pure, too.

Since it was a dreary fall day, the children were next asked to turn their thoughts from the rose and use the same melody as a musical setting for their thoughts and feelings about the season of the year. This poem was written to the same music:

Flowers are gone, trees are bare,
Everything is lonely.
Birds are gone with their song,
Frost is here, now.

This initial attempt at writing songs was a satisfactory experience for the children. Under the guidance of a teacher whom they did not know intimately, the motivation to write came from the music and their own discussions. It was not as unnatural a process as it would have been had this stranger bounded into the room and said, "Good afternoon, girls and boys. You are going to write a song for me today." The familiar composition and their discussion of it, and the lack of an attempt to force self-revelation upon them, combined to make their initial song-writing attempt a success.

This was not only a satisfying creative experience, but the children became aware through a different set of circumstances and through another approach that (1) they *could* write songs, (2) some words in songs are sung to two tones, and (3) the words and the melody of a song must agree in mood. This is important information for would-be composers to know and to use. Subsequent efforts of this fifth-grade group showed that the children were willing and able to use this information.

To make certain that this method of writing songs is not doomed before it starts, the melody chosen must be simple and singable. It must lie within the range of the children's voices, and if it is not familiar, it must be a tune that is easily remembered after a few hearings.

One of the advantages of this procedure in writing songs is that the only skill the teacher needs to guide such an activity is the skill to motivate. Taste and judgment are important, however, in selecting the best contributions offered; the final verses should be representative of the group's best efforts, and the words must have direct relation to the music.

Composing Music for Words

Franz Schubert is said to have created his music for *Hark!*

Hark! the Lark—a poem in Shakespeare's play *Cymbeline*—while waiting to be served refreshments in a public garden. As Schubert read this poem, a perfect melody and accompaniment took form in his mind, which he immediately notated on the menu. He was not alone in this method of writing songs. Child-composers, then, are in good company when they choose this method.

Whether the words children set to music are original or are those of a poem they enjoy is not important. The important consideration is that the poem has appeal for the children. It should be lyrical in quality so that it inspires lyrical melody.

Poems a class has enjoyed reciting in choral speech are an excellent choice in considering material to be set to music. By the time the group has worked on such poems, the words almost sing themselves. The songs written around such poems have a special charm, verve and swing that is sometimes lacking in songs composed by children. It is probable that understanding and enjoyment of the poems have contributed artistry to the compositions.

The procedure that has been used with considerable success with both children and prospective elementary teachers will be given in detail.[1] As both children and their teachers gain skill in this activity, certain steps and approaches can be eliminated. An original poem is used in illustrating this procedure.

1. Place the words on the blackboard with a wide space between lines:

> I saw a little sunbeam
> Peeking through the clouds.
> I watched it grow and grow and grow
> 'Til it wreathed the world in smiles.

2. Have the group read the poem silently.
3. Discuss the story and mood of the poem.
4. Have the group read the poem aloud with the verve and

[1] This procedure is based on the assumption that those taking part are able to read; a procedure for those who are unable to read will be found on page 149.

expression associated with good oral reading. This establishes the tempo of the song, and this tempo should *remain constant* throughout the remainder of the procedure.

5. Have the group read again in the established tempo, accenting important words.

6. Have the group read again, accenting important words and the next most important words. At this point, the reading is likely to be done in a sing-song manner; this manner of reading adds stress to important words.

7. Have the group read again while beating meter (use the forearm with elbow resting on the desk).

8. Underline important words as the children read and beat:

> I <u>saw</u> a little <u>sunbeam</u>
> <u>Peek</u>ing through the <u>clouds</u>. (etc.)

9. Place a line in front of important or accented words:

> I | <u>saw</u> a little | <u>sunbeam</u>
> | <u>Peek</u>ing through the | <u>clouds</u>.
> I | <u>watched</u> it grow and | <u>grow</u> and grow
> 'Til it | <u>wreathed</u> the world in | <u>smiles</u>.

This is one of the important steps. The bars will become measure bars in the music, thus making certain that accented words receive the musical accent. Many collections of children's original songs have been criticized because often important words and musical accent do not coincide (for example, <u>I</u> saw a <u>lit</u>-tle . . .).

10. Have children sing a melody silently at a signal from the teacher. The teacher says, "Beat, beat, sing." Her direction to beat must be in the same tempo in which the children have been beating.

11. Ask several children to sing their melody. The best of three or four responses should be repeated, and then the class should indicate its choice of the best melody. This melody should be sung by the class at least three times. The repetitions are important because they (*a*) will erase their own melodies

from the minds of the children, and (*b*) help fix the chosen melody for the children and the teacher.

12. As the class sings again, record the syllable or number names of the notes of the tune under the words on the board:

I	saw	a	lit-tle	sun-beam	peek-ing	through	the	clouds
mi	sol	sol	la la	sol	mi	do do	re	re	mi
3	5	5	6 6	5	3	1 1	2	2	3

13. Say to the class, "Sing the first line aloud and then continue singing the next line to yourselves. Beat, ready, sing."

14. Have the class choose the most interesting melody suggested and then sing it several times.

15. Write the syllable or number names of the notes of the tune on the board.

I		watched	it	grow	and		grow	and	grow
mi		sol	sol	la	sol		ti	sol	do
3		5	5	6	5		7	5	8

16. While continuing to beat, the group sings the first two lines several times, and then creates the melody of the last line in the same way as the music for the other lines was written. Notice (*a*) that the syllable names of the notes serve as a guide to the teacher, if not to the class, in remembering the tune, and (*b*) that during the singing an occasional variation will occur that makes the melody more pleasing. If the class appears to approve the changes, incorporate them in the song. The aim at this point is to make the best song possible.

17. Transfer the syllable names into notes on the staff.

(*a*) The key in which the song is to be notated must first be determined. To do this, examine the syllable names used in the melody and discover the highest and lowest tones. In this song they are *re* above high *do* and low *do*. Therefore, if the song were notated in these keys, the range would be:

The sound of *e* in "wreathed" is not an easy tone to sing on F sharp, G, or A, so the key of D or E flat would place the song in a comfortable range.

(*b*) Translate the names of notes into notes on the staff in the key of D. Place bars in front of the notes to correspond with the bars in front of accented words. (This can be done accurately if the words of the poem are placed under the staff.)

(*c*) In assigning proper values to the notes, the only question in this song is whether the signature should be $\frac{2}{4}$ or $\frac{4}{4}$ since the tones fall into groups of two's. Actually, it makes little difference. The use of $\frac{2}{4}$ will indicate a smoothness and a less sing-song style, which will add to the charm of this short tune. As the children read the poem, they probably held "clouds" longer than the "I" that follows it; therefore, "clouds" is a note of longer duration than "I." " 'Til" and "it" have to share a measure with the three preceding words, so the notes above them will be shorter. The song will look like this when notated:

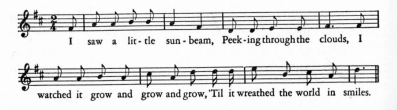

This procedure is suggested for use in initial attempts at writing music for words.

If the teacher is able to play a chording instrument, there is a second way to motivate song writing. This procedure can lead also to composing melodies with descants and two-part songs. After the poem that is to be set to music has been scanned and discussed, and important words underlined, the teacher can play a succession of simple chords. Over this accompaniment children compose a tune, singing the words silently to themselves. For example using the words of "I saw a little sunbeam . . . ," these chords would be fitting:

| 1 | 2 | 3 | 4 | 5 | 6 | 7 | 8 |

𝄞 2/4 I - - - | I - - - | I - V₇ - | I -I - | I - - - | V₇-I - | V₇ - - - | I

Each chord listed lasts throughout the measure unless another chord is indicated. A word of caution should be given to teachers who are inexperienced in improvising accompaniments: Try to have a dominant chord or a dominant seventh at the semi-cadence, and a dominant chord or a dominant seventh followed by a tonic chord for the final cadence.

Kindergarten and lower primary grade children can make tunes even though they lack skill in reading words. Since each of the preceding plans was developed on the assumption that the would-be composers could read the words of the poem, the following suggestions are made to help nonreaders compose songs:

1. The class chooses a stanza it would like to use.

2. The teacher places these words on a paper, leaving a wide space between the lines to enable her to record the notes of the tunes suggested by the children.

3. The children say the first line aloud and then sing it silently.

4. A child makes his contribution, which the teacher records and the class sings several times.

5. The children say the second line aloud; then they sing the first line aloud and the second line silently.

6. A child sings his tune for the second line, which the teacher records and the class sings several times. This procedure is carried on until the entire stanza has been set to music.

Examination of familiar songs will direct children's conscious attention to some of the generalizations that can be made about interesting tunes. They will discover the different means used to avoid both melodic and rhythmic monotony. They will be interested in learning the characteristics of good melodies. They will discover that: (a) repetition of a group of words in the poem is used occasionally with good effect; (b) monotony is avoided by varying the melody line and the rhythmic pattern

—in general, a good melody goes up and down in a variety of note values; (c) after a wide skip in the melody, there is a turn in the opposite direction—notice the pattern in *Annie Laurie* (first complete measure), *Way Down upon the Swanee River* (second measure); (d) repetition of phrase gives form and balance; and (e) repetition of a motif (small group of tones) has the effect of holding the melody together.

Consider this song:

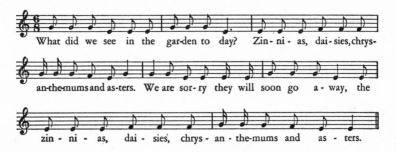

The rhythm has the variety demanded by the flow of the words, but the melody does not vary; it is monotonous to a most unsatisfying degree. The words make pictures, but the melody does not enhance them.

Notice the difference in this tune:

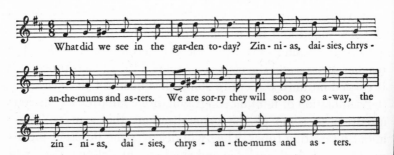

There is movement in this melody. It progresses. It dances with the "pictures."

Before attempting to create a melody, discussions as to the kind of music called for by the particular poem will bring about

an awareness of the effect of melodies a   *growth in judgment.*
In the suggestions made for initial efforts in song writing, there
was a minimum of discussion about the poetic quality of the
verse. If the poem were read intelligently, the chances are that
the melody would conform to the style of reading. However, a
preliminary discussion about the kind of music needed to enhance a verse will usually make certain that the music *does*
enhance the words. If the following questions are discussed
before composing the tune, the result will be a more truly
artistic effort, directed toward the high points of the poem:

1. What kind of music does the mood of the poem suggest?
(Gay, sad, strongly rhythmic, monotonous, and so forth.)

2. Where is the climax of the poem?

3. Where should the music be the most dramatic?

4. Where should the music ask a question?

5. Is it necessary for the question to be answered?

6. Are there any lines of the poem that seem to demand
identical melodies?

When this method of song writing is used, the words themselves form a pattern for the writing and a foundation upon
which to build. The results are more likely to be "music."

The limiting factor in this procedure is the technical skill of
the teacher. In order to carry on this activity, the teacher must
know the fundamentals of music in order to translate the tunes
into music symbols so that melodies can be notated, used, and
preserved. Fortunately, there is one device that can be used to
gain skill in the first step necessary for notating melodies.

To notate a melody, it is well to use "handles" for objectifying elusive tones. These "handles" are the syllable or number
names of tonal combinations. For the teacher who does not
have the skill to translate readily the tones of a melody into
symbols, this device for gaining such a skill is offered (see also
pages 186 and 261): Learn to sing the syllable or number names
to the notes of five or six familiar songs. After these names can
be sung as easily as the words, try to determine the names of
notes of a familiar song—*Way Down upon the Swanee River* or

Joy to the World are simple ones—as you hum the melody without looking at the book. Gaining this skill is really fun if the material used at first is simple.

It is always possible to take a course in melodic dictation or to form a class in which the skill of recording can be developed.

It is assumed that the teacher's knowledge of music fundamentals will enable her to determine the key in which the song should be notated and to assign proper values to the notes, the measure bars having been placed as the result of scanning the poem. The use of the conductor's beat simplifies the matter of assigning proper values to notes, since all notes heard on and during the *down* beat are on the first beat of the measure, all tones heard on and during the second beat are on the next beat in the measure, and so on.

Some teachers who do not have the ability to translate melody into notes have discovered another way of making a record of a tune: As it is sung, they play it on the melody bells or piano and later make a notation of the letter names of the keys used.

Even if a teacher completely lacks any skill for making a record of the tunes children make, their urge to create must not be stifled. The teacher can guide children in writing poems (or the words for an operetta), can guide them while they chant the words, and, at an appropriate time, *import* a recorder of tunes. This imported recorder might be the teacher next door, an older child, a music specialist, or a tape recorder.

Creating Words and Music

The children in the fifth grade of the Hessian Hills School were studying *Life in the Old South*. They seemed particularly impressed by the beauty of Negro songs and fascinated by the stories connected with them. When the children were saturated with this type of music, their teacher, Miss Evelyn Hunt, suggested that perhaps they would like to write some songs of that type. The next time they met in the large music room, where they could have plenty of space, she told them to pretend to do some of the kinds of work slaves had had to do, using some of the rhythms they had done before as a guide. As the children were doing their rhythms, she suggested that they make up a song about their feelings and about the way they thought slaves had felt. Their teacher said she would write the song on the board as soon as any child had his ready.

This is Joseph's song:

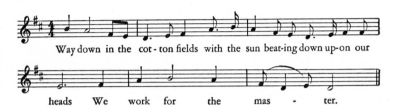

Way down in the cot-ton fields with the sun beat-ing down up-on our heads We work for the mas - ter.

Notice the use of syncopation—a rhythm characteristic of Negro music.

Naomi did not compose words to her melody. However, her use of the minor mode and her use of syncopation show that she had absorbed some of the characteristics of Negro music.

These children had been completely devoted emotionally and intellectually to their study of this phase of American life. They had evidently heard, sung, and played sufficient Negro music to have a feeling for it and to have become cognizant of some of its essential characteristics.

In creating words and music simultaneously, the "question and answer" approach to this type of creativity may give form and unity to songs. Each phrase is conceived as either a musical question or its answer. It is an extension of the procedure used with children who have aural or oral deficiencies. The teacher sings:

Where's Joan?

and Joan answers:

I'm   here!

In early attempts at creating songs in this manner, the "question and answer" idea will be carried out in the words and in the music. Finally, the "question" is musical in that it is a phrase obviously needing an answer in order to be a complete musical statement.

Some teachers have been able to guide song writing effectively by using this method, but ordinarily, teachers find it problem enough to record notes without the additional problem of recording words at the same time. In addition to the limitations imposed by the teacher's lack of skills, there is the likelihood that the songs—words *and* music—may wander pointlessly, and that the melody may lack certain essential qualities.

AN APPROACH TO WRITING INSTRUMENTAL MUSIC

The control imposed by a verse or poem is good when planning a melody for an instrument. The design, the form and the balance necessary in a *good* melody are more likely to result when a melody is conceived in terms of setting a verse to music. The pointless wandering and the omission of certain essential qualities mentioned above are almost always present in melodies written by the inexperienced. Naomi's melody has form—but she had had wide musical experience for several years under the guidance of an expert teacher.

Although conceived as a tune for a specific verse, the tune does not necessarily have to be sung—but why not? Why not have it played on melody instruments with chording instruments accompanying both singers and instrumentalists? Why not invite percussionists to make a contribution, too?

The characteristics of good melodies listed just previously apply here as well. So do the questions suggested as a preliminary discussion of the characteristics of a melody to enhance a verse.

EVALUATING GROWTH IN CREATIVITY

The consensus of experts is that "creativity" reflects a "questing quality." It is represented by the organization of processes or materials into patterns that have meaning or produce an atmosphere or actions or objects that are helpful. A true "creation," in its highest sense, will help others find beauty and meaning in their lives and surroundings, to see and understand the world about them.

If this, then, be "creativity" and if this, then, be the ultimate in "creation," what are the steps along the way in providing for growth in creativity with "music" as the material?

By what standards should a "first" song be judged? a "first" pattern in movement? a "first" four-measure melody composed on the melody bells? How much better should the "first melody" of an adult be in comparison to the "first" of a ten-year-old? Or what does a three-year-old's melody sound like? It is impossible to say. It is not impossible to judge the tenth effort, though, by comparing it with the first. The following are the levels of creativity, from the lowest to the highest, in the area of music. Within each level, however, great variation and great improvement are possible. Growth in the last three levels may take place simultaneously—in other words, one does not have to excel in singing or playing before attempting to dramatize a song, for example.

Levels of Creativity

1. Unconsciously making patterns of sound and/or patterns of movement;

2. Consciously making patterns of sound with (1) the voice and (2) instruments;

3. Consciously making patterns of movement to go with or interpret patterns of sound: Draw a tree with your arms and fingers as you move; dance "blue"; walk like a duck; do what the music says; make up a dance for this music.

4. Consciously making patterns *for* sound: music to be sung, music to be played.

For Discussion

1. What are creative music activities?
2. Describe some informal situations in which music has been created; some formal situations.
3. Should children be allowed to give their ideas concerning interpretation of a song? What difficulties may be encountered? How could these be solved? What good results could come from this experience?
4. Listen to pre-school and primary grade children make up songs as they play. Comment on what you see and hear.
5. Comment on the effect the title *To a Wild Rose* had on the words the children made for the melody.
6. Review the section in Chapter 3 on "Songs for Children."
7. What are the advantages to young composers of using a well-known and loved poem for the words of a song? How can such a poem influence the song they write?
8. Examine any ten songs in a song book to find out what devices or patterns or schemes have been used to obtain form and unity and a lack of monotony. What good can result from "young composers" engaging in this kind of activity?
9. "Monotony" may be a desired characteristic of a melody. Find a poem to illustrate this point.
10. List the possibilities and limitations of each of the three methods of writing songs.
11. Copy a simple four-line verse under a blank staff. Read it several times and finally "sing-song" it. Use conductor's beat as you "sing-song." Underline words that come on count 1. Place a bar in front of underlined words. *Sing* the tune you have almost been singing. Sing it again and again. Sing syllable or number names of tones. Write under proper words. Determine best key

for song. Change names into notes. Using conductor's beat, assign correct values to notes. You have composed and notated a song!

12. At which point in this creative effort did you have the most difficulty? What sort of practice do you need in overcoming this difficulty? Arrange to get it.

13. Your class can compose, too. Select and copy a poem on the blackboard. Scan the poem, underlining words receiving major accents. Place bars in front of major accents. As the pianist plays series of chords:

I   IV   V   I   (each chord lasts throughout one measure)

sing a tune to yourself. Individuals sing their tune. The class chooses the best tune. Notate it. You are *all* composers.

14. Write original poems. Set them to music. Have a concert. Invite your friends.

15. Discuss "creativity" in terms of *you* and the activity suggested above; in terms of a good teacher; a good parent; the skillful doctor; the true friend; the questioning or critical child.

Suggestions for Teachers

1. Sometimes the discussions about the question, "Where do you suppose all the songs in our book came from?" have been sufficient motivation for a group to become interested in writing songs.

2. Ask a child who plays a musical instrument to make up a "piece" at home and play it for the class.

3. Try No. 11 under "For Discussion."

4. Try No. 13 under "For Discussion."

$\diamond\!\!\diamond\!\!\diamond\!\!\diamond\!\!\diamond\!\!\diamond\!\!\diamond\!\!\diamond\!\!\diamond$ 6

Listening

Listening to the music composed and brought into being by others is the means by which most people gain an insight into the realm of music. Some few people will themselves bring the works of the master composers to life once again by performing them, but others, without technical and artistic skill, must depend upon the re-creators for association with music. Fortunately, recordings make it possible to hear particular compositions when they are wanted or needed. Recorded music is an indispensable aid to growth in appreciation.

Recordings can never take the place of first-hand experiences in seeing and hearing music made. "Live" music and children must be brought together. Teachers must be on the alert in seeking opportunities for children to hear music "made" in their presence. No one could list the possible opportunities because, as surely as he did so, the "real" opportunity for an individual teacher would accidentally be omitted.

A teacher in a one-room school realized that her children had never seen any musical instrument except a piano and a radio. They had seen pictures of instruments, knew the families of orchestral instruments, knew the sounds of these instruments but had never seen any of them. What did the teacher do? She called the music instructor in the Teachers' College fifteen miles from her school and told the story. As a result, the instructor and two music students paid a visit to the school and brought several kinds of orchestral instruments with them. In one afternoon, the children had an experience with music and instruments that would give them something to think and talk about for weeks. In addition, a great gap in their understanding was bridged.

The teacher has been urged, too, to direct children in making their own music. But what meager musical fare if their idea of the world of music is limited to their own inexpert abilities! They need the revelation and the inspiration of great music performed by artists.

RECORDED MUSIC'S CONTRIBUTION

Recorded music and, of course, "live" music can make a definite contribution toward getting acquainted with, understanding, and enjoying the music of this and other countries. Music in today's schools can be classified into two groups:

(1) that which contributes directly to understanding the center of interest that currently engages the attention of children, and

(2) that which expands an area in music.

To a Center of Interest

The recorded music that can contribute to a unit of work concerned with people or areas can be listed as follows:

1. Authentic music,[1] true in every detail, should receive first consideration. Native instruments are used. The vocal style and manner of singing are, of course, correct. A style of singing is

[1] See Chapter 12.

as individual as is a type of melody or accompaniment or scale. Thus, when sung by "foreigners," there is not only the possibility that the scale tones are inaccurate, but that the original style of singing has not been imitated. Recording equipment has been taken almost literally everywhere—to primitive areas of Australia and Africa, down into coal mines, to jails, to the northern part of the Near East and to the southern part of the Far East—and much of the recorded material is available to the general public.

2. *Quasi-authentic or idealized music is composed music in which the composer has used some of the characteristics of the authentic music.* This is a refined product. The arrangements are stylistically familiar. The melody, in one instance, may be authentic, but the accompaniment is arranged in a familiar manner; the accompaniment may be accurate as to style, but the true essence of the melody may be lacking; or the development may take a familiar form. The instruments used are standard symphonic instruments.

In this classification fall most of the Chinese and American Indian songs in children's song books and Cadman's *From the Land of the Sky Blue Water.* In these, the melodies are authentic, or nearly so, but the accompaniment is in "our" usual pattern.

3. *Composed idealized music in which the attempt has been made to imitate a style.* For example, Tschaikovsky in the "Dance of the Chinese Dolls," from *The Nutcracker Suite,* composed a melody in which the characteristics of Chinese music prevail and indicated the use of certain orchestral instruments to further enhance the Chinese flavor. Ravel used a classic form in his *Pavan for a Dead Princess,* but the music is modern. In his modern style he had written an old, old dance. Stravinsky used the modern idiom to enlarge his conception of a Chinese melody in the *Song of the Nightingale—A Chinese March.*

4. *Music of native composers is a valuable source of material.* In using music of this type, care must be taken because the compositions selected could well illustrate an altogether differ-

ent point. For example, Ravel, a Frenchman, wrote the popular *Bolero* which is Spanish to the last characteristic drum beat. Handel, a German, enjoyed his greatest recognition while writing in England for the English and *is* English from a musical point of view. The number of composers who are nationalistic in their style, however, is large: Tschaikovsky, Chopin, Rimsky-Korsakov, Dvorák, de Falla.

5. *Performances by outstanding music personalities of a country make an interesting study.* The fine recordings of artists of this and other days contribute to greater understanding of music and the world of music: Toscanini, Iturbi, Caruso, Traubel, Pinza, and Spaulding.

To Expanding an Area in Music

In the integrated activities program there may be an area to which recorded music can contribute little or nothing to the understanding of the whole. Rather than "draw in" materials because of a feeling that there should be some listening, abandon pretext and plan a series of "concerts" that will add to the enjoyment and understanding of music. Some titles or themes for such a series are suggested:

1. *Knowing a Composer Through His Music.* Most composers have written music children can enjoy. It is pleasant, simple, and understandable. Handel, Schubert, Mendelssohn, Haydn, Prokofiev, MacDowell, Mozart, and many others have written compositions that children with little musical background can understand. Some of their works furnish an excellent base upon which to build an appreciation of their more complicated music.

2. *Music Written about or for Children.* A series of concerts (with program notes supplied by both children and teacher), using music written for children covers the wide range from beautiful lullabies by Brahms to the opera *Hansel and Gretel* by Humperdinck. Schumann wrote *Album for the Young, Scenes from Childhood,* and *Forest Scenes,* collections of compositions that are simple musically and whose subject matter is close to

childhood. Saint-Saëns' *Carnival of the Animals* has its definite appeal. Carpenter's *Adventures in a Perambulator,* written in the modern idiom, is as delightful in its way as is *Children's Corner Suite* by Debussy. These few examples will serve to indicate the possibilities of this series of concerts.

3. *Famous Instrumental or Vocal Solos.* In order to adhere to the true meaning of this grouping of compositions, care should be taken to use music that was written for the instrument that interprets it. For example, Wagner's "Song to the Evening Star," from *Tannhaüser,* is a vocal solo; therefore, a recording in which this selection is sung should be used, even though this composition *is* beautiful when played on the cello. Chopin wrote for virtually one instrument—the piano—so orchestrations of his works have no real place in this series of concerts.

4. *Dance Music of Various People.* The *Slavonic Dances* by Dvořák, Irish jigs, the gypsy *czardas,* Brahms' *Hungarian Dances,* the Russian *hopak,* tangos, boleros, rumbas, minuets, and the Virginia Reel are included in this group of music and dances. In this musical dance spree around the world, children are given an opportunity to become acquainted with characteristic native rhythms and instruments, the melodic and harmonic traits of the music, as well as the dance forms and the dance steps themselves. Children can learn many of these dances.

5. *A Musical Trip Around the World.* Plan the trip and enjoy a song, a dance, or a composition by an outstanding composer of each country. One teacher smiles when she remembers the boy who protested because she left him in the middle of the ocean on the return voyage from such a journey "just because the bell rang."

6. *Music of America.* Young America needs to know the music of its country—the music of the past as well as the music of the present. The United States is rich in folk songs and rich in artistic interpreters of these songs.

Contemporary composers of serious music are making challenging contributions to a world once dominated by Europeans. Compositions of the following composers are available on recordings: Copland, Piston, Thompson, Moore, Cowell, Dello Joio, Gould, Harris, and William Schuman. Young Americans should know about these composers and know their music in order to be proud of their skill and artistry.

7. *A Visit from Our Neighbors.* An appreciation of the cultures of our neighbors to the north and south of us is important. Familiarity with their music will aid our boys and girls in attaining an understanding of these peoples. The folk songs portray interesting pictures of life and customs, whereas a study of instruments is fascinating.

8. *Suites.* The suites children can enjoy are numerous. Mendelssohn's *Midsummer Night's Dream,* Tschaikovsky's *Nutcracker Suite,* Rimsky-Korsakov's *Scheherazade,* Stravinsky's *Petrouchka,* and Saint-Saëns' *Carnival of the Animals* are some of the more delightful ones.

9. *Operas.* Humperdinck's opera *Hansel and Gretel* is a perennial favorite of both children and adults. Verdi's *Aïda,* Bizet's *Carmen,* Mozart's *Magic Flute,* Wagner's *Die Meistersinger,* and Thomas's *Mignon* are operas that can be enjoyed by young listeners.

10. *Modern Orchestral Instruments.* Recognition of orchestral instruments by "sight and sound" is important for full enjoyment.[2] The fact that the tone of a single instrument (for example, a violin) sounds unlike the violin section of an orchestra is one that can be observed during this series. Children should learn to recognize the tone quality of single instruments of the orchestra and the quality of those instruments playing simultaneously with other instruments.

When children can identify the instruments of the modern orchestra, some of them will enjoy becoming acquainted with the "grandfathers" of these instruments.

11. *Program Music.* Music of this type is especially fitting

[2] Whenever possible, actual instruments, rather than pictures, should be shown to the children.

for initial listening experiences with various age groups. Mac-Dowell's *Of a Tailor and a Bear* or Piston's *The Incredible Flutist* are selections of the most simple kind. They are simple because they recount rather accurately the episodes of a story. These are artless musical tales. There is no time given to philosophical wonderings and wanderings. Gounod's *Funeral March of a Marionette,* Saint-Saëns' *Danse Macabre,* Dukas' *The Sorcerer's Apprentice,* Deems Taylor's *Through the Looking Glass,* Strauss' *Till Eulenspiegel's Merry Pranks,* and Debussy's *Fêtes* are compositions listed in order of their difficulty, the first being the most simple. Prokofiev's *Peter and the Wolf* tells a story that seems to delight children of all ages. The story that the music tells attracts and holds the interest of the listeners. After interest has been caught, guided listening will bring about an awareness of the music itself.

12. Program of Marches. The contrast in mood and style discernible in a program of marches is exciting. There are notable differences in Wagner's "Wedding March" from *Lohengrin,* and Mendelssohn's "Wedding March" from *Mid-summer Night's Dream.* The first is calm and stately; the latter is gaily triumphant. The majestic *Pomp and Circumstance* by Elgar, *Marche Slave* by Tschaikovsky, *Marche Militaire* by Schubert, *Funeral March* by Chopin, *Norwegian Bridal Procession* by Grieg, *Stars and Stripes Forever* by Sousa, "March of the Toys" from *Babes in Toyland* by Victor Herbert, all carry out their composer's intent to portray marching of various kinds and are noticeably different when heard one after the other.

GAINING A BASIS FOR RECOGNITION

An important function of this program in teaching for appreciation is to supply a wide variety of experiences from which children can gain basic information necessary for recognizing, judging, comparing, or contrasting different types or styles or moods of music. For example, in order for a person to say, "That sounds like a violin, or Indian music, or a march, or a storm, or Wagner," he must have heard music of the particular kind to which reference is made. A vocabulary of essential, descriptive terms should result from the discussion of these experiences.

In providing musical experiences that will help gain basic information, there is a wealth of material from which the teacher can choose to supply a well-rounded background. Music of all types and in all moods, played by different instruments and combinations of instruments, must be included, as well as that sung by different types of voices and combinations of voices.

Just where and with what to begin in planning for growth is always a problem in this field of listening. In some schools, there was formerly a specific list of instruments and forms to be taught in various grades. The teacher in the fourth grade would know with certainty that her class had been introduced to some of these items on the list in the earlier grades. Her starting point was determined for her. If the teacher has no such list, she must find out by careful investigation and observation what the group's previous musical experience has been. The "next" experience to plan is the logical outgrowth of the last experience.

It is important that children be able to describe their feelings about and their comprehension of music; therefore, as has already been suggested, they need a vocabulary of descriptive terms. To the person who thinks that "soprano" always means a "lady singer with a high voice," considerable confusion must result from a statement that a "trumpet is the soprano of the brass choir." The adjectives "big, broad, slow, martial, loud, sweet, colorless," and their opposites, must bring to mind certain musical qualities. In addition to descriptive words, children need names of definite things in order to talk about music: march, suite, solo, violin, bass, and so forth.

GUIDED LISTENING

The teacher in charge of a class listening to music is in much the same situation as a preacher who said to his congregation in the middle of his sermon, "You look so interested in what I'm saying. You seem to await my next word with great eagerness. Actually, I can't tell whether that look of concentrated interest is a mask or whether it mirrors your true reactions to my words." Notice that the teacher is "in much the same situation as the preacher," not in an identical situation. Her particular congregation is not as well disciplined as an adult group in church; it is likely to resort to punching, pulling, prodding, and perusing if it is not engrossed in the activity of listening. It is unlikely that it will maintain an artificial pose as long as will a group of adults. The teacher can strive to gain and retain the interest of the children by skillful presentation of material and artful guidance in listening.

In planning for growth in listening, there are three things to be kept in mind:

1. Guided listening brings about greater understanding of music than does announcing the name of the selection and then playing it;

2. There must be opportunity for children to hear compositions in their entirety as well as by sections;

3. Too much talk by the teacher is as harmful as too little, if not more so.

Guided listening means "giving direction" or "directing conscious attention" to listening. Listening for specifics centers attention that might tend to roam. If the composition that immediately engages the attention is to become familiar, children must have the opportunity for hearing it as a whole—uninterrupted by any comments. However, if the point in listening is to become aware of the effect of the whole string section of an orchestra playing alone, the portion of each of several compositions thus scored can be heard. In this instance, the whole record might becloud the point. However, any composition that is to be "studied" should be heard in its entirety before sections are isolated.

Time set aside for listening to music should be used for that purpose, and not for listening to the teacher talk. Music can tell its own story with nuances and color that even the best of teachers can scarcely match. Certainly, there is need for some talk from both teacher and children, but there is no excuse for using much of the allotted listening time in this way. As soon as children have had even a limited musical experience, subsequent listening should be based upon it. Discussion in which the new vocabulary is used should follow.

Program music describes certain prescribed events, and children need to know the story to enjoy the music fully and to gain an understanding of the composer's ability in telling it.

Suggestions for Guided Listening

These suggestions are made for the purpose of giving the listeners "something to do." They are intended to bring about an awareness of music itself. They are a means of *studying* music. They will aid in stimulating an intellectual approach to music, thereby helping the listener to "know something about it."

The following are meant to serve as examples of questions and comments that will stimulate thinking about music:

1. To bring about an awareness of mood. Compare and contrast compositions as to which best carries out the mood suggested by a title. For example, ask the children to listen and decide which of two compositions is a better musical picture of "On a Quiet Summer Evening"; or place several titles on the board, including the title of the composition which is to be studied, play this composition, and ask which title fits the composition; or play a piece of music and ask the class if it remembers one that is the opposite in effect; or ask it to indicate when a definite change of mood occurs within a composition.

2. To bring about an awareness of form. Ability to recognize and remember melodies is basic to gaining an awareness of form. In a study of the rondo form, for example, the children should be allowed to re-hear the first melody several times and to hum it with the phonograph until they have it well in mind.

Simple physical responses to changes in melody are of value in showing awareness: Mark the measure accent with the right hand, with elbow resting on the desk; to indicate a knowledge of a second melody, a different part, or a change in mood, use the left hand. Such simple movements will not make noise or detract from listening. Ask children to count the number of times a melody is repeated, the times a figure is used in the accompaniment, the times the trombone says "dum, da, da," the times the violin sings *its* melody, and so on.

3. *To bring about awareness of the characteristics of different styles of music.* Discussion of these essentials is directly concerned with the music itself. Music can be discussed in terms of its fundamental elements: rhythm, melody, and harmony, together with the distinguishing quality of tone or timbre of the instrument or instruments that produce it. What makes Chinese music sound "different"? Answered in terms of its fundamental factors, Chinese music (*a*) is based on the pentatonic scale (melody), (*b*) is not harmonized, and (*c*) the accompaniment is played largely by percussion instruments (timbre). The characteristics of Arabian, Spanish, or American Indian music, or Debussy or Wagner, can be analyzed or pointed out with equal clarity in the terms of the fundamental elements of music itself. Discussion of music in these terms is like discussing bread as being either white, whole wheat, corn, raisin, or salt rising— the fundamental ingredient of the bread is used as a basis. "Good" and "tasty" are not particularly definitive in describing bread, nor are "sweet" and "pretty" definitive in describing music.

Children with little musical background can learn to tap and distinguish characteristic rhythms. They can recognize the ornamentation and unsingable quality of an Arabian melody. They can discern whether or not the accompaniment is derived from the melody and is musical or whether it is only "noisemaking." With growing musical maturity, they will be ready to discover more specifics concerning these fundamental elements of music.

Children, as well as adults, enjoy hearing again and again the music they like.

USE OF MATERIALS

Few schools have *all* the records they should like to have. It is desirable and necessary to make complete use of those owned.

The most important thing contributing to effective and extensive use of records is a file of cards on which pertinent information concerning each record is noted. Information which was found to be valuable is shown below.

NAME OF RECORD   COMPOSER   NATIONALITY   NUMBER

1. *Sources of Information About Performer:*
    (pages in reference books)
2. *Sources of Information About Music:*
    (pages in reference books)
3. *Analysis of Recording:*
    (for example, trombone solo near the beginning *or* long section by wind choir *or* bassoons prominent in accompaniment *or* great contrasts in moods *or* ethereal mood throughout *or* simple *rondo* form, etc.)
4. *Use Made of Record:*
    (for example, Maypole dance *or* dramatization of the story *or* transportation unit (rhythm) *or* good to contrast with *To A Wild Rose or* skipping *or* to enhance Corot's *Dance of the Nymph's,* etc.)

As soon as a teacher finds a new use for a record, this information should be written on the card for that record. This notation will not only serve as a reminder of the exact material used to prove or demonstrate a certain point, but it will be available for any of the other teachers. The data are added when they are discovered. They are cumulative and are the product of all teachers.

It takes some energy and time to assemble such information as this. On the other hand, assembling the information piece-meal does not require as much time and energy as does collect-ing it all at once for any two or three records to be used together. With such a card file of information about the school's phonograph records, planning a series of concerts—A *Musical Trip Around the World* or *Music Written for Children*—is not a formidable task.

In addition to facilitating planning, having such information on file will more certainly assure extensive use of the available material. All compositions have *form;* all music illustrates a *mood;* all records are made by *instruments* of one kind or an-other; and when certain types of examples are desired, difficulty in collecting information about specifics will not preclude the use of the material at hand.

RECORDS FOR CHILDREN

Time was when recordings specifically intended for children were difficult to find. The record catalogues listed a few, cer-tainly, but music for children generally had to be sought. As a result, parents and teachers were continuously asking those whom they thought might know, "What records would you suggest for our children? We want them to be interested in music and like it." Music specialists have made dozens of such lists. Finally, this thought occurred to one of them, "When they were young, Mozart, Bach, and Beethoven did not become in-terested in music through music written for children. They became interested in music through music."

Today, "records for children" can be found in department stores, drug stores, five-and-ten-cent stores, and music stores. Which ones to buy and what does one have after they are bought—those are the questions. Most of the recordings are of songs. The standards in the section of this book on "Songs for Children" *should be applied to recordings of songs.*

Several people have become interested in the great number

of "records for children" and have studied them. Parents and teachers now have several sources to which to refer.[3] Doubtless more books on this subject will continue to appear.

In addition to books on this subject, there are sources of "good" records for children—The Young Peoples Record Club is one of these. The Young Peoples Record Club issues two carefully selected recordings each month. One is for children in the three- to six-year age group, and the other for the seven- to eleven-year group. Authentic folk songs, musical games, and activity records are included in the selections for the younger group. For the older children there are, in addition, some interesting records using various orchestral instruments and even a miniature opera, Douglas Moore's *The Emperor's New Clothes.* Since the recordings are selected with the guidance of an editorial board composed of several well-known musicians and educators, the quality of the music and its suitability is without question.

Because it confirms a strong prejudice concerning music for children, a story told by Katherine Scott Taylor [4] is recounted. She was the teacher of a first-grade group of migrant children who lived in crowded labor camps and tents. These children were anything but relaxed and emotionally stable.

After trying every device about which she had read and heard to quiet children and put them at ease, the teacher finally brought a record player to school so that the professional storytellers could keep on telling stories via records. Her voice was wearing thin!

One morning during the rest period, she put one of her favorite music recordings on the player—Bach's *Air for the G String.* Four children went to sleep, the remainder quieted down. A Handel *passacaglia* was the accompaniment for lunch. Tension

[3] See bibliography for listings.
[4] "An Autochthonous Approach to Music Education," first appeared in the *Music Educators Journal,* February-March, 1949 issue. It was digested for the *NEA Journal,* then printed in pamphlet form. Later it reappeared in the September-October, 1959 *Music Educators Journal.* It would seem that one prejudice is widely shared!

and excitement left the children's voices though none remained silent during the playing. Several days later the children asked to hear the recordings again; from that time on they listened to music daily. Most discipline problems disappeared.

Beethoven's, Schubert's, and Schumann's simple chamber music; more elaborate chamber music; and then, certain symphonies! Unconscious listening, conscious listening, "doing what the music makes you want to do," becoming aware of the differences in interpretations of various conductors! Those things just aren't done in the first grade! However, this teacher had had only six college credits in music and had only an emergency certificate to teach, so she didn't know these were not the things to do! She knew only that they worked. It was as simple as this —she enjoyed music so she shared it with the children. If the evidence of learning is a modification of behavior, these children learned music. They asked for more. They were not required to learn the proper "labels," but they did learn those names for which they asked.

Read Katherine Scott Taylor's own story. Think of its implications. And remember how Mozart, Bach, and Beethoven learned to love music.

You might have been with a college teacher when she visited a second grade one day to observe a student teacher teaching music. This student teacher had previously asked about using Chaliapin's recording in Russian of the *The Volga Boatmen*. The college teacher replied that she did not think that that particular record was the best choice for a second-grade group. However, when she entered the room on that particular day, the children sang boat songs, the student teacher sang two new ones for the children, and then it was apparent that something in the way of a treat was in order. The student teacher said, "Now we'll hear the boat song I told you about this morning." The children listened attentively during the playing of *The Volga Boatmen*. Afterwards, they made such comments as these: "I saw the men come and pass along in front of me"; "Even though you said we wouldn't be able to understand the

Russian language, I knew what he was singing"; "The singer's voice was big like my father's"; "I helped pull, too, while he sang." When the student teacher said she would play the record again, expressions of interest and pleasure came over the faces of the children. Satisfied smiles greeted the conclusion of the recording. From that day to this, that college teacher has never insisted that one record was suitable for one grade, and a second fitting only for another grade, because with skillful motivation and presentation many things are possible. Incidentally, how would you have felt during that visit had you been the student teacher? The college teacher?

EVALUATING GROWTH IN LISTENING ABILITY

The only real way to judge what a person hears is by what he does. He must indicate by his behavior before an observer can tell whether he hears the repetition of a melody, the tuba playing "um-pa," or the minor tonality in a section of music. Ability to recognize instruments by their sound is as easy to ascertain as are facts about music. Behavior as a barometer of emotional reaction or appeal is easy to read. But the intellectual grasp of music itself is more difficult to judge. The levels of ability in listening to music, the levels of *conscious recognition* of elements follow:

1. Marked (then, less marked) contrasts in tempo, dynamics, mood, range, or pitch
2. Pulse
3. Pattern in pulse
4. Repetition of simple melody
5. Repetition of longer melody
6. Pattern in the development of melodic material
7. Levels 1, 2 and 3 plus 4 or 5 or 6
8. Levels 1, 2, and 3 plus 4 and 5
9. Levels 1, 2, and 3 plus 5 and 6

For Discussion

1. In what respects does the use of recorded music have advantage over radio music in gaining an insight into the realm of music? List the advantages of radio music in this respect.

2. Consult various phonograph record catalogues (there are more than two!) to get an idea of the amount of available authentic ethnic music.

3. Listen to some of the recordings listed to discover the differences between quasi-authentic and authentic music.

4. Plan the music (song material and recordings) to be used in a study of Mexico, South America, or any geographical area. Use authentic music, too, if available.

5. List some subjects or themes for "concerts" other than those given.

6. Determine a comprehensive list of terms to be used in talking about music; then plan the experiences that would provide the basis for understanding these terms.

7. Select any recording and make suggestions for guided listening for two groups: (*a*) those without much musical background, and (*b*) those with a moderate experience with music. State the specifics concerning background in each instance.

Suggestions for Teachers

1. When a child says he likes a particular composition because "It's pretty," ask him *why* he thinks so. Attempt to get him to discuss the music in the terms of music—rhythm, melody, harmony, or the instruments. Admittedly, he may not know what "harmony" is, but try to give him a concept of what it means.

2. Play a recording you think your group will find interesting. Ask what they think of it. Play it again. Ask the same question in an attempt to get them into a discussion. Note what they say. Later, play another recording and *guide* their listening. Note the difference in discussion.

3. Enlarge your class's experience by inviting musicians to perform in your classroom. Suggestions for "artists": a soloist from the local high school band or orchestra; a singer (who sings artistically!); a child or a group from another class. Ask the performer to be willing to answer questions the children might ask. To start the discussion you might question him about some

of the following: methods used in breath control, some of the difficulties to be overcome, why a particular selection is adapted to the performer's ability, or *how* the music (sound) is made by that particular instrument.

Reading Music

Music is sound. Music is sound organized in patterns. Music is sound organized in patterns that are scientifically exact. A composer works within the framework of these exact patterns called "combinations of tones." He records these patterns by means of symbols called "notes." An author works within the framework of ideas. He records these ideas by means of symbols called "words."

When an interpreter of words (a reader) comes upon the word "good," his notion of that particular word is partly guided by the remainder of the words in the sentence—". . . a good apple." Notice "partly guided." Actually, his idea of a "good" apple is conditioned by his whole previous experience with apples. "Good" is not a word that recalls an *exact* quality to each reader. A reader puts "part of himself" into his interpretation. Not so with an interpreter of "notes."

When an interpreter of notes (a singer or an instrumentalist) comes upon the "word" he has no latitude in interpretation. The "word" demands exact translation. It represents an exact combination of tones. Regardless of the interpreter's previous experience, the "word" means just what it "says"—it does not mean

It seems strange, when one stops to think, that anything can be as intangible as a tone. You cannot see it; you cannot touch it; it has little or no meaning by itself; it has life only for the instant it is made. Much the same is true of combinations of tones, but such combinations do live in the memory. Yes, it seems strange that anything so intangible as a tone demands such exactness in the translation of its symbol (reading music) to be brought to life for just another instant.

Children need power of their own in interpreting the symbols of music. The goal of music-reading activities is independent ability to translate symbols. Even though the purpose of this chapter is to show how a singer can learn to read, let us examine the ability to read music to see what is involved for the instrumentalist as well as the singer.

ANALYSIS OF MUSIC-READING SKILL

The instrumentalist who can read unfamiliar music at sight and play it accurately and artistically in the first attempt is able to do so for the following reasons:

1. He automatically comprehends the various symbols and guides to interpretation on the printed page—eye recognition.
2. He has sufficient technical ability for playing the composition, which enables his muscles to respond automatically to the impressions received by his eyes—physical response.
3. His eyes travel across the music, recognizing groups of symbols at least a measure before they must be played. By so doing, there is time for scrutiny of unusual rhythmic patterns or combinations of notes.

The singer who can read a song accurately and artistically in the first attempt is able to do so for the following reasons:

1. He automatically comprehends the various symbols and guides to interpretation on the printed page—eye recognition.

2. He has sufficient vocal control so that his voice responds automatically to the combinations of tone recalled by his musical memory from the impressions received by his eyes—vocal response (physical).

3. His eyes travel ahead of his voice in the process of symbol and word recognition. By so doing, there is time for careful scrutiny of unusual rhythmic patterns or combinations or words.

In considering what is involved in the performance of the instrumentalist and the singer, the apparent difference is in item *two:* the instrumentalist's reaction to symbols is muscular, whereas the same symbols set the singer's memory to work. For example, the instrumentalist sees the notes E, F, and G and, upon recognition, the proper muscles react in relation to strings, keys, or valves—a reaction automatic, in a rut, and without thinking. But, when the singer sees E, F, and G, he *has to remember* the sound of E, F, and G before he can produce them.

Activities to produce automatic muscular reactions differ from the activities needed to produce the automatic memory recall of the sounds of symbols. At many points along the path of learning to play an instrument and of learning to read music, the instrumentalist *needs to know* some facts not particularly pertinent to the singer who is learning to read—and the singer *needs to know* some facts not necessary for the instrumentalist. It is well to consider carefully what each group of would-be-readers and performers *needs to know* in order not to clutter up the learning process with extraneous material and activity. This is particularly true in the early stages of learning.

A young student teacher said about a lesson he gave a ten-year-old violin student: "She had difficulty making her fingers play E-F sharp-G, so I just explained to her the construction of the major scale. Was that all right?" It may have been "all right" but it is doubtful if it helped the girl. A ten-year-old beginner, attempting to hold a violin and bow while trying to manipulate wrists and arms and individual fingers in a new and peculiar fashion, did not need to know then the step and half-step pattern of the major scale. What did she need? She needed patient help in getting fingers on the proper place on the proper string and help in playing those correct tones time and time again.

The beginning instrumentalist needs experiences designed to set muscles in a rut—each combination of tone, each pattern necessitates a *new* rut. As the muscular pattern is set, the ear becomes sensitive to correct sound. Initially, no deviation of fingering is permitted in playing E-F sharp-G until that rut is partially established, at least. Later and after considerable experience, when he meets E, F sharp, and G in a different context or situation, he automatically or almost automatically chooses the handiest rut or the most logical rut in playing that combination. Many ruts must be and are established. Let others decide how long it takes for so many muscular reactions to attain the status of ruts before an instrumentalist can react without thinking to E-F sharp-G in all its possible positions on the staff in all the possible sequences of tone!

Consider for a moment that the *letter* names of notes were used in this discussion. The instrumentalist looks at a note and says to himself, "That's E" and plays E on his instrument. To do that he *needs to know* the letter names of notes. And, to arrive at the correct name, he *needs to know* the implication of the key signature, which is a shorthand way of indicating actual letter means. He learns to read actual names and he learns to make tones of the same name on his instrument. It is said he reads by *actual* position.

But letter names of notes mean nothing to a singer who does not have instrumental experience and who is starting to learn to read. Tell him a note is E or F sharp or G, and he might well answer "Isn't that interesting!" or "Yes?" His development as an interpreter of notes does not follow the path of the instrumentalist. He has, as a result, different needs. And, knowing the letter names of notes is not one of the first. Consider him, his problems, and his needs.

A singer can force himself to make about half of the 88 tones usually notated in our music, and, ordinarily, he can sing half of *those* easily. Remember that in reading he needs to recall first what an indicated tone sounds like before he can produce it, so it is good that two facts relieve him of the necessity for trying to remember the individual sounds of each of twenty-some possible sounds! The facts:

1. It is extremely unlikely that he will ever have to remember and produce a *single* tone, as such, out of context or without help, so he does not need to try remembering the sound indicated by any single given note. And,

2. *Groups of tones* are relatively easy to remember—much easier than single tones.

A melody, a song, is made up of groups of tones. The same groups occur time after time in songs. Sometimes they are identical; sometimes there are small variations. For example, each of the following songs starts with the same group of tones: *Pussy Cat, Pussy Cat, Where Have You Been? Come Thou Almighty King, The Star-Spangled Banner, Old Woman, Dixie* and *Good Morning, Good Morning*. Not only is the pattern of tone identical, but the symbols for these tones make an easily identifiable pattern: If the note for the first tone is on a line, the others are on lines; or, if the first is in a space, the other notes of the group are in spaces.

The sequence in developing a reader of music out of a singer starts by directing his conscious attention to and learning to recognize by ear certain fundamental groups of tones in the songs he sings. Then, he learns how the symbols of these groups appear on the staff. The next step in his progress is recognizing these same symbols in an unfamiliar song, remembering their sound, and producing it. His skill can be diagrammed:

Eye recognition of symbols — Memory recall of sound — Utterance.

The singer's recognition does not take the same form as the instrumentalist's—he can't remember the sound of C, for example (unless he has absolute pitch), so the letter name brings forth no response from him. He uses an entirely different aid: his knowledge of the scale names of common groups of tones and his knowledge of how these groups look on the staff. He says to himself: "*If* that note is 1 (or *do*) of the scale, that note on the next staff degree above is 2, the one on the next staff degree is 3 (or *mi*)" and so on. He reads by *relative* position, not by actual position. In so doing, he always needs some fixed point (a note) toward which to relate other notes in the group.

The singer needs certain specific guidance, certain specific experiences, and certain specific information along the path of his development as a reader, *and* at a certain specific time. The more nearly the guidance, the experience, the information and the timing are related to his need of the moment and related to his stage of development, the more likely that growth in skill will result. ("A certain specific time" is "time" along the path of his development—not "time" as indicated by his grade in school.)

Recall what the singer reading music can do and does do as he reads: (1) he can sing, (2) he can see, (3) he knows the meaning of the symbols used in music notation, (4) he can remember the sound of the notes he sees, (5) he can produce the sounds he remembers, and (6) he can understand and pronounce the words of the song in a style dictated by the words and enhanced by the melody. *That* is what is involved in reading a song accurately and artistically. Again, music-reading by a singer is a skill involving:

Eye recognition of symbols — Memory recall of their sound —
Interpretation by singing

What guidance is necessary in developing reading skill? What experiences will aid? What information will help? The answers are the substance of the remainder of this chapter.

"*When* do you introduce music-reading? *When* do you teach the dotted eighth note? *When* do you teach the letter names of lines and spaces? *When* do you teach the sharps and flats?" The answer to the first question: "When sufficient background experiences make learning easy and enjoyable." The answer to the other questions is the same: "When a child needs this information to progress further."

MUSIC-READING READINESS

Readiness to read is brought about by purposeful experience calculated to prepare the singer for music-reading. This pre-reading activity consists of acquiring and using certain information and of acquiring and using certain skills—all of which can be acquired before the actual reading process starts. Thus, the "eye recognition—memory recall—interpretation" process is prevented from becoming hopelessly fouled before it gets under way by concentrating on single aspects of the whole or complete skill.

The areas related to Music-Reading Readiness will be considered in terms of Physical Development, Important Information, and, then, Desire to Read, which is the hoped-for result.

Physical Development

Ability to sing, visual and aural maturation, and muscular coordination and development as exemplified in rhythmic control are aspects of physical development basic to ability to read.

Singing Skill. The statement that children must not try to read music before they can sing easily, accurately, and willingly is not meant to be facetious. Some teachers have attempted to teach children to read who had been in school only a few months and to whom the idea of singing with a group was still new. The desired level of singing ability can be attained in three school years *if* singing has been an important part of the music program. Private instrumental lessons, particularly skillful teachers, experience on pre-orchestral instruments all add to the sum total of readiness—and the lack of these limits readiness —but, in general, for the actual reading process to be successful it needs to be preceded by three years of rich musical experience.

Teen-agers and adults—who can sing and who want to learn to read—can learn in three or four months with expert guidance. Their years have added to their experience.

Mature Visual Power. Maturation brings about a decrease in the problems arising from immature visual perception. Young children often pay attention to the main characteristics of visual stimuli and ignore details. If, in spite of good eyesight, they do not notice differences in words or letters when asked to match them, how can they possibly be expected to notice the fine differences between notes on neighboring lines and spaces of the staff? So, we do not try to teach them to read until they can see these differences. It seems probable, too, that children who have tendencies to make reversal errors and who have not yet learned to look at a word always from left to right would have a similar difficulty in learning to read music. Unfortunately, because of the limitation of time, music-reading is generally a group project. It is fairly easy for an uncertain reader or singer to follow the tune set by the majority of the class. Thus a child who makes reversal errors may continue for days to try to read from right to left without the fact being known by his teacher. For this reason, it is best to wait for maturation of visual perception before attempting music-reading.

Mature Auditory Power. If children can sing a song correctly, it is an indication they can hear—they can hear not only sounds but tones and the often small differences between tones—else, how could they learn the tune? Of course, we don't know if they learned it after hearing it seven or twenty-seven times— but they *can* sing it, they *can* hear differences in sounds, and they *can* remember them.

It is known that very young or inexperienced children hear a melody as a *mass* of sound rather than as several groups of individual sounds. But, if a six-year-old can sing *Rudolph, the*

Red-Nosed Reindeer, it is proof he can hear the smallest intervals in our music because they are present in that melody. Such a performance indicates that his ability to differentiate between tones is keen rather than dull because, after all, he hasn't lived long enough to have heard it several hundred times! (It *could* be that the wrong song was used as an example!)

Developed Rhythmic Sense. As was discussed at length in Chapter 4, "Rhythms," the only basis we, as outsiders, have for making judgments about another's sense of rhythm is by observing what he does. "What he does" means, in this instance, walking, clapping, beating, tapping, and so on. If he carries on these activities regularly, evenly, and rhythmically, and if the sounds he makes are regular, even, and rhythmic, we judge his sense of rhythm to be "good" or say his sense of rhythm is "good." Our experience has demonstrated that if he can produce sounds *in time* by tapping, beating, and so on, he can interpret notes *in time.* Our experience has demonstrated, too, that if he can't clap or tap *in time,* he can't interpret in time.

Also, in Chapter 4, the method was given for relating rhythmic movement—walking, clapping, beating and so on—to the symbols for relative time values. These symbols are only *one* aspect of notes; the other aspect, of course, shows pitch. By relating movement to the symbols for duration, a child learns to use this one set of symbols without becoming involved with the other. Learning these relative time value symbols through developing the rhythmic sense is a most important part of Music-Reading Readiness.

Background Information

Notes have pitch and length. Music-reading for the singer involves looking at notes and identifying them, remembering their sounds and singing them. Anyone who can attain the generally accepted level of reading ability for the first grade—words, not music—can learn to *identify* notes by name in a short time. But—that is not enough. The problem is to have the name recall the sound or the note's position on the staff recall the sound. Recall, remember—recall correctly and remember accurately—that is where help is needed.

What information can help the process of remembering these elusive sounds? What information will help "harness" the intangible quality of tones? What information can help identify the notation of these tones? What information can help in interpreting the symbols for tones? What information can prevent extraneous material from cluttering up attempts at reading?

A Song Repertory. By the time children have been in school three or four years they have learned and can sing many songs. Some groups will have learned over two hundred, others about one hundred songs. These songs have been *used*—as the inspiration for dramatic play or as the accompaniment for rhythms or a percussion orchestra—and they have been sung just for the fun of singing. These melodies consist mainly of the same tones, arranged in a different order, and in different rhythm patterns and, sometimes, with different tones repeated. However, they are essentially identical groups of tones. These groups are sections of the scale, the tones of the tonic triad, the tones of the dominant chord, and the tones of the sub-dominant triad. The songs children will read consist of this same material.

Thus, in their song repertory children learn the sounds of groups of notes they will interpret in reading. The repertory becomes a dictionary of tone groups, a storehouse of groups of tones, and a collection of groups of tones. As stated above, these groups contain sections of the scale, and tones of the tonic, dominant, and sub-dominant triads.

Pertinent Facts Relating to Groups of Tones. These facts are fundamental to the discussion and to the suggestions for teaching that follow:

1. A scale is the basic pattern of tone. Each of its seven different tones has an exact relation to the other. The lowest tone of the scale is 1; the tone above is 2; and so on. In notation, neighbor-scale tones occupy adjacent staff degrees.
2. A chord is a group of notes or tones capable of being sounded simultaneously. Each tone has an exact relation to the others. When sounded one at a time, the result is a "broken chord."

3. A triad is a chord consisting of three tones occupying three consecutive or adjacent lines or spaces on the staff. In this arrangement, the lowest note of the three is the *root* (the next highest the *third,* and the next the *fifth*), and this is said to be the *root* position. When a tone other than the root is the lowest tone, the triad is said to be "inverted": 5–1–3, 3–5–1, *la-do-fa.*

Each of the three fundamental chords or triads has three names:

(1) Technical: 1–3–5 (*do-mi-sol*) is the *tonic* triad
5–7–2 (*sol-ti-re*) is the *dominant* triad
4–6–8 (*fa-la-do*) is the *subdominant* triad

(2) Number: Tonic is I (built on the first tone of the scale)
Dominant is V (built on the 5th tone of the scale)
Subdominant is IV (built under the 5th—the 4th of the scale)
Note: do is common to I and IV
sol is common to I and V

(3) Letter: The staff letter name of the root.

A few pages back there was a list of songs starting with the same three tones. Was that news to you? What information would help you recognize and sing those tones the next time you meet their symbols in print? It would help (1) to know the names of the tones and (2) to know how they appear on the staff.

The name becomes a short cut in thinking. The name eventually recalls the sound. When you know the names and see that group of notes in reading material you say to yourself: "That is the 1-3-5 group. I know what *that* sounds like"—and you sing it. Knowing its name relieves you of laborious thought: "Oh, yes, that is the group with which *Come Thou Almighty King, The Star-Spangled Banner, Pussy Cat,* and so on start." You hum silently: "Pussy Cat . . . ." "That's it" and sing.

Conscious attention can be directed more easily to identical groups of tones when their names are known.

Syllable, Number, or Letter Names of Notes. Authorities agree that the average classroom teacher does not possess enough musicianship and training to make it possible to teach music without the use of more-or-less artificial devices. They agree that the lack of musical background of the average child and the amount of experience and training he receives in music make it desirable for him to use the same devices. Experience has proved that because of the intangible quality of tone, it is expedient to objectify as nearly as possible the relationship between tones. This is done by assigning Latin syllables as names of the scale tones, or by numbering the tones of the scale and using the number as a name or by using the letter names of the notes. Each set of names has its advantages and disadvantages.

Latin syllable names—referred to as the *"sol-fa"* syllables—are artificial but have been in use since the Middle Ages. *"Do-re-mi"* are part of our culture (even though their sound seems *not* to be, at times!). These names have the advantage of being easily pronounced: one syllable and no difficult final consonant.

Number names have advantage because 1-2-3-4-5-6-7 is a familiar concept—but as names, they are cumbersome to sing. They become even more so in singing chromatics—"3-high 4-5."

Letter names, too, are familiar. The instrumentalist uses letter names but they, too, are cumbersome to sing—"E flat-G-B flat."

The advantage of number names and syllable names is that combinations of tones—1-3-5, 5-7-2, 4-6-8, *do-mi-sol, sol-ti-re* and scale sections—make a pattern in sound that is the same for every key and a pattern in notation that is consistent. While there *is* a pattern in the notation of E flat-G-B flat, this pattern of relationship is not so easily observable. Considerable experience in music is necessary before it can become a tool in learning.

Syllable and/or number names have definite advantages as the means of harnessing tone and as the means of identification.

How are these names learned? They are introduced by rote as an additional stanza of a song—and learned by repetition.

Older children and adults can learn them the same way—but the process can be speeded for them by writing the names under the notes of well-known songs and singing them repeatedly.

Names must be tied to the proper tones through singing. There is no point in *saying* names.

Syllable or number names of notes are learned by rote. The best songs to use are favorites—folk songs are excellent. Children are likely to have learned these melodies correctly. Folk songs are replete with tonic, dominant, and sub-dominant chord tones. Thirty or forty songs sung with note names will cement the relation between sounds and names. A list of songs in which basic groups of tones are found follows:

Scale and scale sections: *Joy to the World; The First Noel; Sweetheart Out A-Hunting; Pussy Cat, Pussy Cat, Where Have You Been?; Chumbara.*

Tonic chord (four tones): *On a Bicycle Built for Two; The Star-Spangled Banner; Goin' to Leave Ol' Texas; The King of France; On Top of Old Smoky.*

Tonic triad: *Oh, My Darling Clementine; Blow the Man Down; Red River Valley; Rice Pudding; Taps; I've Been Workin' on de Railroad.*

Dominant triad: *Careless Love; Where Has My Little Dog Gone?; Bridal Chorus; Oh, My Darling Clementine; Pussy Cat, Pussy Cat, Where Have You Been?; God of All Nations; Down in the Valley.*

Sub-dominant triad: *Jacob's Ladder; She'll Be Comin' Round the Mountain; Careless Love; Oh! Dem Golden Slippers.*[1]

In this activity, names of groups of tones are learned. Sometimes it will be evident that the relationships between name and tone are becoming established and that the sound recalls the name. The sign: when children can "feel their way" along a tune and assign correct names to melody tones. *Joy to the*

---

[1] Most of these songs may be found in Louise K. Myers, *Music Fundamentals Through Song.* Englewood Cliffs, N. J.: Prentice-Hall, Inc., 1954.

World or *Long, Long Ago* or *America* are good choices for initial "feeling" if the note names have not been learned by rote. They are good choices because their melodies consist mainly of adjacent scale tones. The teacher may have to supply the name of the second tone in an interval or skip—the first *sol* in *America,* for example.

In this activity the tune recalls names. The goal is to have the names recall the tune.

After children can "feel their way" along several tunes with little help from the teacher, they are ready for this activity— one that is more directly related to the goal:

1. Place the names on the blackboard in a vertical column.

2. Ask the children to sing 1 or *do* as the teacher points to it; and then, the ascending and descending scale, as the teacher points.

3. Ask the children to sing as the teacher points. (The teacher points the melody of *America* without telling the children beforehand.)

4. Ask the children to identify the song. They probably will not know—even though they can sing the note names of this song!

5. Tell the children to *listen* as they sing again. Repeat the process, when the song has been identified.

6. "Point" the melody of another favorite song.

mi	3	
re	2	
do	1	
ti	7	
la	6	
sol	5	
fa	4	
mi	3	
re	2	
do	1	8
ti	7	
la	6	
sol	5	

(The teacher needs to point to the "next" tone an instant before it is to be sung, and the pointing should be fast enough so what the children sing bears some resemblance to the tune as they would sing it.)

In this activity, the names recall the tune. It approximates the ultimate aim—but recognition of symbols is not involved.

Thus, those convenient handles for tone help identify groups of tones and can help in remembering and recalling tones.

A knowledge of their appearance on the staff is helpful, too.

Relative Position of Scale Tones on the Staff. A singer reads music by interpreting the relative position of notes on the staff. Certain patterns in placement can be observed. They never vary. They are the same whether notes are on the bass, tenor, or treble clefs. Even the instrumentalist, who reads by *actual* position rather than by *relative* position, uses knowledge of these patterns. Again, they are:

1. adjacent scale tones occupy adjacent staff degrees; and,
2. when the root of a triad is on a line (or in a space), the 3rd of the triad is on the next higher line (or in space) and the 5th of the triad is on the next higher line (or in space).

How are these patterns in placement learned? By being so informed, and by placing patterns on the staff and by directing conscious attention to them in the notation of music.

Some activities that aid learning follow:

1. (*a*) The teacher places a note on the first line of the black-board staff. Then, while placing the notes [2] of an ascending scale (no key sign), she sings on scale tones. "This is 1 of the scale, this is 2; this is 3" and so on. Then, the children sing while the teacher points to the notes: "Line-space, line-space."

   (*b*) The teacher places a note on the first space and sings and writes another ascending scale. A descending scale. The children sing "Line-space," then the number and/or syllable names while the teacher points to the notes.

   (*c*) The teacher places notes 1-2-3-4-5 in the key (but without key signature) of a song in the children's book they know how to sing but for which they do not know note names. "This is 1-2-3-4-5 (or *do-re-mi-fa-sol*) in this tune. Find those notes in your book and read the words under them." (Reading words under notes is an excellent means of identification.)

---

[2] Use dots for notes. They are more easily altered to make different kinds of notes than whole notes.

2. (*a*) Place the following notes on the blackboard staff:

(*b*) "*Do* can be on any line or space. When *do* is on the second line, where are *re-mi-fa-sol?*" Write notes. "When *do* is on the second space, where are *re-mi-fa-sol?*" Write notes. And, so on. The teacher, then the children, write.

(*c*) At another time, consider each of the above notes to be 3 of the scale. Write 3-4-5-6-7. The teacher and the children write.

(*d*) Consider each to be *sol*. Place *sol-fa-mi-re-do*.

(*e*) Consider each to be 1. Place 1-3-5. Get the pitch from a pitch pipe and sing each group in pitch before writing the next group. Place 5-3-1 and repeat as above.

(*f*) Consider each to be *sol*. Write *sol-ti-re;* and *re-ti-sol*.

(*g*) Consider each to be *fa*. Write *fa-la-do;* and *re-la-do*. (This is one of the few activities suggested in which names are sometimes *said* instead of sung.)

3. (*a*) The class sings the first six measures of *America* (or a melody which contains groups of adjacent scale tones).

(*b*) The teacher, placing 1 on 3rd line, says, "Repeat it a little slower while I write those notes." (Use dots—no symbols for relative note values—and insert measure bars as they occur.)

(*c*) The class sings again while the teacher points to the notes.

(*d*) Repeat the process, using the last four measures. (For a song other than *America*, choose a section containing fundamental chord tones.)

The purpose of this activity is to establish the fact of relative position of notes on the staff—an "if" and "when" position—and to establish recognition of the relative staff position of familiar groups of tones. Recognition has been established when children, having been told the name of the first note in a tune they know—but not note names—can look at the notes, register their position, and then, supply and sing the correct names. This is the test of skill in recognition.

Knowledge of Symbols for Relative Time Values. A tone has pitch and it has length. Groups of tones have pitch and groups of tones make a pattern in time, a pattern in rhythm. Information about the pitch aspect of groups of tones—their sound and their representation on the staff—was derived from songs children know. Similarly, information about the duration aspect of tones—the pattern they make in time, their rhythm pattern—is derived from songs children know.

Procedures for acquiring this information were the substance of Chapter 4, "Rhythms." They will not be repeated here.

Children have absorbed that information—both muscularly and mentally—when they can look at an unfamiliar song, study it momentarily, and, after the teacher says "One, two, three, one, two, begin," can start counting aloud and tapping the values of the notes in the melody or when they can read the words in time while using the conductor's beat.

Acquaintance with a Keyboard. Melody bells, resonator bells, the xylophone, and the piano keyboard objectify the tonal relationships inherent in scales and triads. They make it almost possible to *see* tones. There are many reasons for making these instruments generally available for children to use—but one of the most important is that they remove tone from the realm of the intangible and place it in the realm of things; and they remove tone from the realm of memory and place it in the world of objects to be manipulated.

Think about a child who can start on any of the keys of any of those instruments and play by ear the first four measures of *Row, Row, Row Your Boat,* or *Three Blind Mice* while singing the number names of tones—just think what he *could* learn! And, after thinking, teach him!

1. Each tone is a separate thing;
2. 1-3-5, 4-6-8, and 5-7-2 sound alike; therefore, their interval construction is the same;

3. The notation of white keys occupies all the places on the staff, so black keys *have* to be notated in terms of white keys because there is no place left on the staff for them;

4. 3 and 4 of the scale are closer to each other than are 4 and 5; 3 and 4 are the same distance apart as are 7 and 8, and so on.

Some of that information might not interest him right now— but when a child wants to know or has to know, he can *see* it on a keyboard instrument.

The Facts on the Printed Page. Children must be familiar with the facts on the printed page of songs before the actual reading process can start. Some in the list below are almost too obvious to mention—but, lest they be overlooked, they are included. They have to be learned *some* time and the time to teach them is before actual reading starts.

1. The word arrangement of a poem under a staff is different from the poem printed as such.

2. The name of the composer (or the source of the melody) is the name at the right above the first staff; the name on the left is the name of the poet.

3. The clef sign and the key signature indicate *actual* pitch and the *correct* pitch for singing, so the song will be neither too high nor too low for comfort. The actual pitch comes from the pitch pipe or the piano or the tone block.

4. The implication of the measure signature (learned while translating movement into symbols).

5. Notes that look alike, sound alike; measures that look alike, sound alike; and lines that look alike, sound alike.

6. Words or their abbreviations or symbols indicate tempi and volume.

Desire to Learn to Read. Certainly, the *desire to learn to read* is a most important phase of music-reading readiness. If the child has had the varied experiences and has acquired the skills suggested previously, it is reasonable to expect that the culmination of these activities will be a felt need for learning to read music. In the field of language, pre-school and kindergarten experiences cause children to anticipate keenly the day when they will learn to read. As a matter of fact, many children want to go to school solely for that purpose, and are disappointed in their first day because they did not learn to read.

It is need for a skill that impels learning—and this is as true in music-reading as it is in the mastery of any other skill. Three or four years of well-rounded musical experience—interesting, pleasurable, and varied enough to challenge the child's abilities—will bring about a keen desire to investigate further the world of song.

Perhaps the most important contribution this section on pre-reading experiences has to make is the idea that a complicated skill becomes easy when single aspects of that skill are developed one at a time. Skill in reading *can be* (and *was!*) broken down into parts. When each part is acquired, ability to read is a fact.

The experiences that bring about a singer's readiness to read music can be summarized as follows.

This Experience	*Results In*
Three or four years of singing in school	Easy use of singing voice; a vocabulary of tonal combinations; time for maturation of visual and auditory perceptive powers.
Rhythms	Feeling for time values; automatic use of the conductor's beat; knowledge of symbols for relative time values.
Rote learning of note names	Familiarity with *sol-fa* syllables, number, or letter names.
Ear training	Recognition of sounds by syllable, letter, or number names.
Handling song book	Familiarity with the material on the printed page.
All these	Desire to learn to read.

Learning to read is the culmination of many learnings and many experiences *paced* throughout three or four years of

school life. Careful examination of the listing above will disclose that the only essential lacking in actually "reading" is
recognition of the symbols for the level aspect of tones. Such
background and experience preclude the possibility of a feeling
of utter loss and amazement when the child is confronted with
a book of songs, opens it to the designated page, sees a mass
of dots on lines, and is told that the first note (what is a note?)
is *do* (what is *do?*). Then he is told to continue reading. Continue? Why, he hasn't even started!

TEACHING MUSIC READING

Two fundamentals of music notation must be basic in teaching recognition of symbols. They *never* change. They apply to
the viola player in a symphony orchestra and to the nine-year-
old in the third grade. When the nine-year-old becomes that
viola player he does not have to do any "transfer of learning"
—when he learns these principles, they are in effect *always*. They
are the common core of essential understandings of notation
and of essential skill in interpretation. They are:

1. The sameness in pattern of the relative position of scale
tones on a staff, and

2. The sameness in pattern of relative time values.

Teacher time-and-energy and learner time-and-energy are
both conserved when the fact of relative position of scale tones
on a staff is learned: when *1* of the scale is on a line, *2* of the
scale is always on the adjacent space above; when *1* is on a
space, *3-5* are always on the next above spaces; and so on,
Always indicates a pattern. *Always* includes the *F* and *C* clefs
as well as the *G* clef. Learning a pattern takes less time than
going through countless experiences necessary to *discover* a
pattern. Recognition of patterns in the notation of the level
aspect of notes is a short cut in reading. There are patterns in
the duration aspect of notes, too.

The measure signature designates the basic pattern of the
notation of duration values of notes in a piece of music. Within

that pattern are other patterns: one tone to a beat, tones longer
or shorter than a beat, two or three even or uneven tones to a
beat. Actually, patterns in notation are few. They occur over
and over and over again. Thousands can recite: "The upper
number means there are three beats in a measure and the lower,
the quarter note is the beat note." So they do—but can those
thousands automatically interpret a measure filled with quarter
notes or two eighths on each of three beats? The viola player
does—and the nine-year-old can, too, especially when duration
values are tied to muscular reactions and learned independently
from level values and learned in patterns. Learning a pattern
takes less time than assembling facts to discover a pattern.

Good methods of teaching music-reading and teaching language-reading have much in common. Four practices that are
fundamental to successful teaching of language-reading will
now be adapted to the teaching of music-reading.

1. Treat a group of notes as a sentence. In music, *re* (2)
acquires character only when it is found in groups of tones.
It is *do-re-mi-fa-sol* (1–2–3–4–5) or *sol-fa-me-re-do-ti-do* (5–
4–3–2–1–7–1) that recalls a definite musical sound, not *re* by

itself.  means just that. It does not mean

The vocal result of the musical phrase notated above is likely
to be ‖ if this combination is
conceived as four separate and distinct tones, each requiring
much time for deciphering. Key feeling and relationships are
lost. Fundamental tone connections are taught exactly as word
combinations are taught: by singing them from cards, by singing them from the blackboard, by singing them from charts,
by singing them from books. The tune of the combinations and
the syllable or number names are familiar because they have

been encountered many times in songs. *Eye recognition is the only new element.*

Phrase repetition and measure repetition—so common in children's songs—present an opportunity to emphasize *likeness* and sameness in both rhythm and tone patterns.

2. An adequate supply of reading material on each level of difficulty is needed. The teacher may have to copy songs on the blackboard, but it is with constant repetition that skill comes. She may have to purchase or borrow books that have additional easy material, for if the children have not mastered the reading of simple songs—simple as to tonal combinations and rhythmic pattern—they are not ready to attempt complicated materials. Consider the great amount of material of equal difficulty necessary for teaching reading. A comparable amount of music material is necessary. The importance of gaining skill in reading common simple tonal combinations cannot be overstressed. This is the basis upon which all music-reading depends.

3. The correction of inaccurately sung tonal groups should be made in the same way as mispronounced words are corrected. Repeating these inaccuracies only fixes them, and no opportunity should be permitted for gaining wrong tonal impressions. A famous piano teacher once said that for every incorrect finger used, or incorrect key struck, in a given passage of piano music, twenty-five correct repetitions are necessary to eradicate the errors! Classroom teachers should remember this. When the class sings the syllables *do–mi–sol* (1–3–5), *re–fa–la* (2–4–6), and the tune sung is *do–re–mi* (1–2–3), *re–mi–fa* (2–3–4), the teacher should sing immediately the correct tune for the syllables. When the teacher says, "Think, Jane, think," Jane may "think," but if she thinks too long the wrong connection may be cemented.

In reading (*a*) if the children sing the *tune* correctly yet are consistently wrong in naming the notes, they are having difficulty manipulating a crutch they obviously do not need; (*b*) if the names of the syllables are right and the tune consistently wrong, the children are not ready for music-reading because recognition of the symbols does not result in the immediate recall of the *tune* of the combination (*eye recognition of symbols* is supposed to be the only new element in sight-reading but, in this instance, the children lack one of the most important skills of music-reading readiness—they need the experience of singing with the syllable names many more melodies learned by rote); (c) if the names of the notes *and* the tune are consistently wrong, the class is not ready to attempt to read music. The results of investigating their general readiness for reading will point the way for subsequent practice.

Should the class *say,* not *sing,* the names of notes of a new reading song? This operation is similar to saying the individual letters of words in reading a language. Syllables or number names of notes have less relation to a tune than individual letters have to a word. If the teacher believes that saying the names of notes has value, her reasoning process is, "If the class gets the names of the notes right, then they will be able to sing the tune correctly." As a matter of fact, the *tune will be correct only if the names recall the correct tones.*

While teaching, *remember:*

1. *Recognition of symbols* must be the only new element. Once children recognize notes, their names must recall their sound.

2. This activity is learning to read in order *to sing;* therefore, vocal effort should approximate singing.

3. When children know the relative staff position of groups of tones and when they can show they recognize the symbols of tone duration, they can read any song in their book as long as you are there to tell them where *1* or *do* is. So, you tell them. . . . When they are in fifth or sixth grade, they can learn the implication of a key signature and learn to find *1* of the scale in two sessions of about five minutes each. It is much more important that their time and energy be spent first in recognizing

groups of symbols, remembering their names and singing them. Singers do not *need to know* the letter names of lines and spaces and how to find *do* until they go off someplace by themselves and try to read a song. They are not likely to do this while in the third or fourth grade. Instrumentalists need these facts—but not singers.

4. When children are recalling the sound of the symbols they recognize, Teacher, *you keep still.* They have followed your singing for years. They are expert. So, if you sing with them, you might be judging and evaluating your own effort exclusively!

5. When one of their hands is not engaged, it should be automatically marking the conductor's beat. That pattern frames a measure as do the measure bars. It is an excellent aid in learning.

6. A song to be read can either be considered as one the teacher thinks or knows children will want to learn and add to their repertory or as just a means for gaining reading skill. In either case, the teacher must be aware of, or better still, can mark her book for quick reference to show (1) repetitions in material—groups, measures, lines; (2) familiar combinations; and, (3) unfamiliar combinations—particularly, the interval resulting from the last note in one phrase and the first of the next. A glance at a page so marked enables the teacher, then, to direct conscious attention quickly to important places.

After using it for reading purposes, the repertory song can be discussed: the poet and his poem, the composer, the mood, and so on. Reading only parts of a repertory song and learning the remainder by rote can give children great satisfaction in early stages of learning to read.

GUIDING MUSIC-READING EXPERIENCES

Music reading was "introduced" when children saw their first song book and realized that those dots on the lines were the source of a tune. It was "introduced" when they tapped the

relative values of notes and played a percussion accompaniment
from a score. It was "introduced" when they noticed that like
notes sound alike. All these activities, hopefully, prepared children for the time they would look at a new song—and read it.
It is sometimes difficult to determine just *when* they can read
(and so easy always to tell when they can't) because there
needs to be preparation for each song for some time. "Preparation" here means "directing conscious attention to specifics" in
order to capitalize on previous experience as well as to make
certain no mistakes will be made.

Suggestions

The following suggestions related to guiding music-reading
experiences are intended for use with those who are *ready* to
read—*ready* in terms of *music-reading readiness:*

1. Clap or tap the note values of a tune while counting aloud.

2. Read the words in time while beating.

3. Direct attention to the level aspect of notes: "Are there
repeated measures or sections? Read words under them (in
rhythm)."

4. Discuss general characteristics of the melody line—scale-
like or broken chords.

5. "The key signature indicates *1* is in the second space.
Where is the tonic triad? What is the first tone? the second
tone?"

6. Give the correct pitch of *do.* "Sing *do* and the first tone
of song. Hold it." Then, "Beat, beat, beat, one, two, sing"—and
the class sings the names in time.

7. Repeat this process at least twice. Then, sing with "loo"
and follow with words.

Rather than trying to perfect the song at this time, follow
the activity by directing attention immediately to another song
in the same key and, if possible, with the same general melody
characteristics and proceed in the same way.

If two songs are used as is suggested, remember: *they have not been learned.* The next day, "prepare" children again—and repeat. Children (and others) learn to read by reading.

The process can be varied: (1) After directing attention to repeated measures or sections, read and sing these; (2) direct attention to easy parts (scalewise) and read those; (3) place more difficult or less familiar groups on the blackboard, study them, identify them as part of the song and, then, sing the whole song.

These next suggestions relate to helping those who lack the thorough preparation or readiness for reading as outlined herein. Getting aural, visual, and kinesthetic feeling has to be telescoped into less time and experience—children have to acquire information and have to acquire feeling almost simultaneously with using it. Prerequisites, however, are: (1) some awareness of and some ability to respond to duration symbols (through familiar songs); (2) knowledge of either syllable or number note names; and, (3) a concept of the line-space-line and space-space-space and line-line-line position of scale and triad tones on a staff. With these as a basis, proceed in the following manner.

1. The teacher places on the blackboard staff a six- or eight-note pattern selected from a song for which children know note names.

2. While the teacher points to these notes, she sings the pattern several times; then, the children sing while watching the board.

3. The children find the pattern in melody in their books, "box" it with their index fingers, and sing it while looking at the notes. Children identify a repetition of notes by reading words under it and then singing note names and words.

4. The teacher suggests that the children (*a*) turn to page so-and-so, (*b*) find the identical pattern, (*c*) identify by reading words, (*d*) sing names and (*e*) words.

> *Note:* This procedure resembles closely that of learning to identify and use a new word. And, beating time with the con-

ductor's beat is even more important for this group of children than for the "ready" group because it helps establish a muscular *rut*.

Teaching Letter Names of Notes

The easiest and most efficient way of teaching the letter names of notes is: (1) to teach the letter names of white keys on a keyboard instrument and then (2) to show where these keys or sounds are written on the staff. Since the sequence of the alphabet is familiar, point out and play an A on the keyboard and say: "The next key above is B, the next is C—what do you suppose the next is?" and so on. Ask individuals to find A's on the keyboard. When the pattern in names is recognized, place a note (dot) on the second space of the blackboard staff. "This is A; this is B; this is C; what is this? (D) and this?" Place A again, and then a dot on the second line: "This is G; this is F; what is this? and this?" When all the space on the staff is "used": "We need more lines and spaces on which to put the remaining notes—so we'll add some." "Turn to page 3 in your books. A is on the second space—how many A's in the first line? the second? How many B's in the third? C's in the third?"

At another time, teach that the black key below A is A flat, below E is E flat, and so on. These are *new* names. Then, the black key above A is A sharp, and so on.

No real keyboard available? Hang a cardboard picture of one where all can see it. Or, place a dot on the second space of the staff: "Notes have letter names, too—A, B, C, D, E, F, G. The name of this note is A, this is B, this is . . ." Place a note on the second space: "This is A, this is G, this is F . . ." and so on.

To test knowledge of names: Read letter names of the notes in a song, disregarding implication of key signature.

Teaching Key Signatures

The singer *needs to know* only some of the implications of the key signature. He needs to know how to find *1* or *do* in order to find the correct pitch for starting a song. Not until late in his experience does he need to know that five sharps is the key signature for the key of B, for example—and some children will never need to know.

The efficient procedure is to establish the principles involved in finding the key tone. The principle regarding keys with sharps in the signature: the sharp farthest to the right (the last sharp) is on the same staff degree as 7 or *ti* of the scale; therefore, *do* or *1* is on the next staff degree. To demonstrate the principle: the teacher places the key signature of four sharps on the blackboard staff and directs thinking by the statements and questions below; she erases the last sharp (fourth line) and the signature of three sharps remains; she directs thinking along the same line again; she erases the last sharp, and so on.

Statements and questions about a key signature with sharps: "You have observed that *do* has no permanent place on the staff—it has many places. The group of sharps and flats at the beginning of a song tells where *1* or *do* is in that song. On the board are the four sharps often found at the beginning of a song. Is the sharp on the fifth line or the fourth farthest to the right? The sharp farthest to the right—the last sharp placed there—is on the same staff degree as 7 of the scale. If that is 7, where is *1?* What is *do*'s letter name? *Do*'s letter name is E and the song is in the key of E. Therefore, to give the correct pitch for a song, I play E on the piano or my pitch pipe and that is the sound of *do* for this song." Erase the last sharp—and start thinking again, and show how the principle works. Later, children turn pages of their books, examine signatures containing sharps and tell where *do* or *1* is and give its letter name.

The principle for finding *do* in songs having flats in the key signature: the last flat occupies the same staff degree as *fa* or *4*. To establish: place flat on the third line of blackboard staff. "When there are flats in the key signature of a song, the flat to the right is on *4* of the scale. Where is the flat? Count up or down to *do*. Where is *do?* What is its letter name? Therefore, one flat is the key of—?" Place the next flat in key signature—

and repeat. A "short cut" principle: the next to the last flat is
on *do*.

Next, have the children examine songs in their books to identify signatures made up of flats, locate *do*, and give *do*'s letter
name and the name of the key.

Teaching Chromatics

The name "chromatics" suggests the power and purpose of
these notes—they add color (*chromo-*) to music. Since they are
tones foreign to the key indicated by the key signature, they
can effect harmonic, as well as melodic, variations in the music.
The names of these new tones have to be learned. However,
there is an inconsistency (perhaps "inaccuracy" is a better
word) that arises concerning the naming of chromatics.

In our system of notation, in which consecutive lines and
spaces of a staff are used to record the tones of the scale indicated by the key signature, there are obviously no available
places left on the staff for recording chromatics—those tones
foreign to the scale. Therefore, chromatics have to be indicated
in terms of the notes of the existing scale. For example, although there are several places on the various staffs to indicate
G, there is no place to indicate the half step above or below G
(the next line or space above is A; the next line or space below
is F). Therefore, the only way to show the tone a half step
above G is to place the symbol ♯ in front of it. The only way to
show the tone a half step below G is to place the symbol ♭ in
front of G. G and G sharp or G flat have no key or tonal relation
to each other—each is separate and distinct.

Chromatics indicated as being higher than a given note seem
to have a closer relationship to the next higher tone than to the
altered note. Chromatics indicated as being lower than a given
note have a closer relationship to the next lower tone rather
than the next higher. For example, *fi* seems to be closer to *sol*
than it is to *fa*; *te* seems to have a closer relation to *la* than to *ti*.

Hint for teachers: The distance between *sol* and *fi*, *te* and *la*, *mi*
and *ri* is the same as between *do* and *ti*—a half step. To sing

sol-fi correctly, think of a *do* on the same pitch as *sol;* sing *do-ti-do,* then *sol-fi-sol* on the same pitch—and it (*sol-fi*) will be correct.

Children have sung chromatics in many songs. *Eye recognition* of their symbols is the only new element. Each chromatic is a new symbol so each must be taught separately.

In teaching, follow the suggestions on page 202, in which combinations of notes from familiar songs are placed on the blackboard, sung and discussed, identified in the melody, and so on.

Teaching Minor Mode

Just as *do–mi–sol–mi–do* establishes the *feeling* of the major mode or scale, *la–do–mi–do–la* establishes the feeling for the minor. *Fi* is a common chromatic.

The tones of the minor scale are:

la	ti	do	re	mi	fa	sol	(si)	la
6	7	8	2	3	4	5	(high 5)	6

Reading in a minor key proceeds the same as reading in a major key. It is well, however, to emphasize the combinations of tones that establish minor tonality—*la–ti–do–re–mi* and *la–do–mi.* The way to emphasize is, of course, by singing songs containing these combinations. If children do not know the following songs, they should learn them (or others containing the same groups of tones) before technical facts about minor keys are introduced:

> *The Battle of Jericho* (The first eight measures of this song
>   and the next one are excellent for establishing the *feeling*
>   for minor tonality.)
> *Charlie Is My Darling*
> *Where Do You Go?* (*la–do–mi*)
> *Zum, Gali Gali* (*la–ti–do–ti–la–mi–la*)

The Pre-Orchestral Instrumentalist

The discussion of instrumentalists early in this chapter—the way they read and the way they learn—includes performers on pre-orchestral instruments as well. The advantage pre-orchestral instrumentalists have is that they can enjoy satisfying music-making experiences without spending months in acquiring technique. The instruments are easy to play—and they are easy to teach and they are wonderful "lures for further learning." It is true they have limitations as instruments of music—limitations of range and limitations of tone—but only those most musically sophisticated who are, at the same time, uninformed as to the needs of children, would deny their value.

There are two general types of such instruments: melody-making and accompaniment-making. Psalteries, xylophones, melody flutes, flutophones, melody bells, and the like are the makers of melody. Recorders can be so grouped—but fine recorders are real instruments. Autoharps and harmolins make accompaniments. Of course, guitars and ukeleles do, too, but the selection of the proper place on the proper string so as to produce the proper chord requires long fingers and more practice than does the manipulation of a bar that automatically selects the proper strings.

At what age are they introduced? Some say not before the third grade—and then one sees a kindergarten teacher accompanying children on an Autoharp while one child plays correct tones on the tone blocks and another plays the last three tones of a repeated section on the melody bells. One hears a group of children in the third grade playing melodies and descants on flutophones. On the other hand, the third grade across the hall is still trying to play the first piece in the flutophone instruction book after two months of effort—but those children are allowed to "play" only fifteen minutes a week. One visits a college class and finds the harmolin being used not only as a source of material for harmonic dictation but also as an accompaniment for original songs. One visits a sixth-grade group and hears beautiful three-part flutophone playing, with an original descant on the melody bells accompanied by three Autoharps. Other visitors in that room are four boys from the second grade waiting to carry the Autoharps and bells to their room so they can play.

And a teacher said to her summer school music instructor, "This has been quite a summer for me. I've learned to play three musical instruments: the flutophone, the Autoharp, and the piano!" On the piano she had learned to play a major triad (1-3-5) on every key—by ear, with both hands—and could go up and down the keyboard with ease and assurance, to say nothing of satisfaction and enjoyment. She could use those triads as accompaniments for songs. She forgot, however, to mention the drum, bells, and rattles she had played for the first time in a percussion accompaniment. So, it *was* "quite a summer"!

At what age are pre-orchestral instruments introduced? Any age. How? "This is a flutophone (or Autoharp or recorder)." If it is a wind instrument: "You take it and play it—find out how the high tones are made, and the low tones. See if you can "find" a tune you know. Try *America*." If it is a chording instrument: "Play the G chord, then D, and back to G. Hum *America* and play those chords as you hum." Later: "Neither of those fits *that* place? Hunt around and find the correct one."

Back to that "third grade across the hall" for a moment. It is difficult to forget those children—their eyes eager as the flutophones were distributed. Their behavior, exemplary: they waited for a signal from the teacher before picking up the instruments; at another signal, they assumed a "correct playing position"; and at still another signal, they played G. Several children had difficulty, they received individual attention, and the group played G. One child was unsuccessful. He was helped. This time: a G in concert. Then, attempts to play A— and finally, an A in concert. Time was up. The instruments were collected, disinfected and taken out of the room.

There were so many questions a visitor dared not ask: Had the children ever had the chance to "play around" with an instrument? Why not spend time on G, A, B, and C instead of just G? Did the teacher think the children would *always* make

a perfect G when they would meet G later? Why only a maximum of eight minutes playing time? What did she think muscles could learn in that short time at infrequent intervals? Did
she think that experience was a "lure to learning"? Or, did she
think?

Players of melody instruments read letter names of notes, but
kindergarten and first-grade children are likely to play number
names because of familiarity with numbers. Players of chording instruments read letter names of chords or technical names
—I, IV, V. Each group knows how to interpret relative time
values since they were learned in relation to movement.

Instruction books for beginners are readily available and are
excellent. But before children use books they need opportunity
to investigate and experiment with their instrument. It is desirable that they learn to play tunes by ear before learning to
play by note, just as they learn to sing by ear before learning to
read notes. In playing by note, attention is divided between
handling the instrument and recognizing the symbols.

Now that the value of playing pre-orchestral instruments
(and the piano) is widely recognized, more and more song
books for children include chord markings for songs. If chords
are not marked, the teacher can mark them. If the teacher does
not know the letter name of the root of a chord in order to mark
it in the book, she can ask someone who does know.

It is possible that in no other area of music can people have
so much fun—with so little background, with so little effort—
as they can in making music with these instruments. Combined
with percussion (rhythm) instruments, delightful effects can
result. Even the musical sophisticate is often forced to applaud
them.

Reading Part-Music

Skill in reading part-music is acquired in the same way as
skill in reading a melody: learn to sing by ear; learn symbols
of what is sung; learn to identify those symbols in new material.

"By ear and then by eye"—that's the way.

The "by ear" preparation includes: singing descants and obbligatos; singing with chordal accompaniment; singing the root of the triad to which the melody-tone-on-the-accent belongs; playing descants, playing chordal accompaniments; and playing the root of the triad to which the melody-tone-on-the-accent belongs as an accompaniment. It would seem that all the music-making activities discussed in this book conjoin in preparing children for singing and reading and playing music in parts. They do.

When this pre-reading activity is neglected or is not planned carefully, nor participated in thoroughly, two-part singing or two-part harmony is likely to sound like one-and-a-half-part harmony.

Children are "introduced" to part music when they engage in any of the activities mentioned just previously.

Examination of songs used to introduce the notation of a second or third part reveals that melodic and rhythmic patterns are simple. The pattern of notation must be discussed; first, in a song children have learned by ear, and then, related to the song they are about to read.

It is suggested (1) that the second and third parts not be considered as competition to melody, but as a factor that enhances the melody; (2) that the opportunity to sing the harmony part be alternated between sections of the class to help eliminate the development of a forced, hard, chest tone while singing "alto"; and (3) that phrases be harmonized before the complete song is harmonized.

When pre-reading experiences have been rich and when these suggestions are followed, skill in reading *and* singing three- and four-part music is readily acquired.

EVALUATING MUSIC-READING SKILL

The singer's ability to read music is the composite of several skills, including knowing certain facts and how to use them.

He must have all these various skills—*the lack of any one precludes his ability to read.*

Each skill contributing to music-reading has been isolated and discussed, and a test for each indicated. Certain facts and their implications have been isolated and discussed. Means of teaching these facts have been presented. (A knowledge of facts is easy to test—children show that they know them or that they don't.) In the section "Desire to Learn to Read," a summary of pre-reading experience is given.

The author is unwilling to isolate again each contributing skill and a test for judging whether or not it has been acquired; and, she is unwilling to list again the facts needed by a singer in reading music. This unwillingness results from the conviction that this material is so important that each student should make his own listing of necessary skills and tests for each. Such is the suggestion in item 2, below. It is further suggested that after each student has made his own listing, the class arrive at a consensus, and the consensus report be written in the back of this book for a quick reference when the *need to evaluate* arises.

For Discussion

1. If you are skilled in playing an orchestral instrument, in doing art work of any kind, or in playing golf or football, summarize the skills that culminate at the high point of the activity. What is the first skill you must acquire in that particular activity? The second? What is the next skill without which you can progress no further?

2. List the contributing skills that prepare a child to read music. What activity develops each? What is the "test" for each?

3. What purpose is served by the devices (tonic *sol-fa* syllables, number names, and letter names) in learning to read music? State the advantage of number names over syllable names, syllable names over number names, and letter names over syllable names. Which of these media is the best? How do you teach chromatics in your choice of media? Are letter and number names "devices"?

4. What remedial measures are needed if a group consistently

sings the names of notes correctly when reading new music but does not sing the correct tune?

5. Some of the section *Background Information* is intended for teachers and some for children. From this material select specifics to insert in the statement "Before they are ready to start reading vocal music, children must be able to .... and must know ...."

6. List the facts singers need to know before they "need to know" the implications of the key signature.

7. Assuming an excellent teacher each year, list only the activities directed toward gaining music-reading skill that would prepare a group of children to be willing, accurate readers of music in four years.

8. Look through twenty consecutive pages of songs and circle each tonal group that includes tonic chord tones, dominant chord tones, and sub-dominant chord tones. The order of the tones in the group is not important—that is, *sol–do–mi* is *still* tonic, and *do–la–fa* is *still* sub-dominant.

9. Look through the next twenty pages of songs and circle each group of four consecutive scale tones and five consecutive scale tones—ascending or descending.

10. List six songs that provide the "feeling" for minor tonality. What tonal groups are found? Are all songs written in the minor mode "sad"? Prove your point.

11. What do you think of the writer's "unwillingness," as stated in the section on "Evaluation Music-Reading Skill"?

12. List the activities mentioned which are designed to develop skill in "aural recognition of tonal combinations." Why is it impossible for singers to learn to read without this skill?

13. Learn to sing three popular songs with note names by "feeling" your way along the melodies.

14. Give the sequence of experiences by which learning to use the tonic triad is paced in the singing approach to learning music fundamentals; the relative position of scale tones on the staff; a major triad. "Use" is the key word in this assignment.
Give the sequence for pacing those same learnings for children who have ready access to or who can play the piano. It is quite probable that knowing these sequences and *acting* as if they were known is the identifying mark of a good music teacher. "Knowing" gives direction to planning the "next" experience.

15. *From Movement into Symbol* in Chapter IV actually belongs in this chapter. Why, then, was it not placed here?

16. Write a two hundred word essay, starting "Music-reading readiness is characterized by ...."

17. Write a one hundred word paragraph explaining how reading vocal music is the result of three automatic responses.

Suggestions for Teachers

1. Evaluate your class's readiness to read in terms of "contributing skills." What is the *next* experience it needs?

2. Which types of mistakes does it make in reading music?

3. Make some notes on the pages of your music book that will save time while the children gain skill in music-reading. For example, look at the first reading song in your book written in the key of F; circle tonic, dominant, and sub-dominant chord groups, and underline scale-wise passages; and at the bottom of the page, write the page number of the next song in the book written in the key of F. Mark it the same way. Do the same for several songs. This will save time during music-reading sessions.

   If your group is concentrating on time values, make similar notes concerning pages as you did for tonal groups.

4. It is *truly* as easy to play the flutophone and the Autoharp as this chapter suggests it is. Try—and you'll be amazed and delighted.

5. You, too, have a "musical" ear. Use it in learning to play 1–3–5 up and down the piano keyboard. When you can, remember that you can now play I and IV and V in every major key and V in every minor key. With this skill you can now play nice chord accompaniments for singing—and you are now given permission to "break" the chords if you so desire.

6. Explain the difference between the needs of a singer in learning to read and the needs of an instrumentalist in learning to read.

7. Explain the differences between the procedures suggested for guiding singers who are "ready" to read and those who are not.

8. Explain why there is relatively little discussion of reading two- and three-part music in this chapter.

9. Explain the way the song series (music books) used in your school "handles" part-singing. Point out how it differs from the way described in this book.

━━━━━━ II

Implementing

the Program

8

The Classroom Teacher

In the final section of Chapter 1, it was stated that in the elementary school music program children should gain:

1. The ability to use music as a means of self-expression and communication (which includes being able to manipulate the one musical instrument all elementary school children possess —the voice).

2. An understanding of the musical expression of others, which implies a consciousness of music as an art.

3. An awareness of as much of the science of music as is necessary to give meaning to music as an art.

What attitudes concerning music should the elementary classroom teacher have to direct such a music program? What experience does she need to fit her for guiding the music program? What abilities must she have? What training is necessary to fit her for teaching music?

ATTITUDES

The most important assets the elementary classroom teacher can have for carrying on the music program for her class are: (1) a consciousness of joy in musical activity, and (2) an awareness of the joy music may bring to others. Without these feelings about music, the teacher's guidance will be insincere, without purpose, and without effect. With these feelings, her teaching will be sincere because she will enjoy the activities along with the children. Her verve and vivacity will result in enthusiastic teaching. Her teaching will be effective because she will be guiding an aspect of personal enjoyment and development that she believes to be really important. Since music has brought joy into her life, she will want to share it with others. Enthusiasm begets enthusiasm.

Attitudes, feelings, and sympathies are the result of experiences. We all know that sometimes the attitudes, feelings, and sympathies we have about things, ideas, and people seem to be without logic. However illogical ideas may seem, they are, nevertheless, the results of experience. Since certain feelings toward music are the most important assets an elementary teacher can have when it comes to teaching music, it seems pertinent to ask what experiences will result in such attitudes. Even though we plan conscientiously and carefully what appears to be a logical program of experience, the results cannot be guaranteed. We are dealing with emotions, intangibles. However, certain experiences seem most likely to turn the emotional tide in the direction of these desirable attitudes.

Desirable Pre-Service Experiences

The discussion of desirable pre-service experiences of classroom teachers is based upon these assumptions:

1. Prospective teachers are musical—they have innate capacity for musical reception and talent for making music.

2. There is an area of music that will "fit" and satisfy the emotional being, the creative being, the physical being, the

intellectual being, the social being, and the spiritual being that is a prospective teacher.

3. They are susceptible to the "lures" for catching interest and enjoyment, for catching a desire to learn; and the "lure" implicit in "teaching *for* appreciation."

4. They will teach as they were taught.

5. Music is *something to do* as well as something to learn about.

Analysis of these assumptions discloses that teachers-in-training are considered as "children-a-few-years-later," that they are inherently those same individuals. The unknown factor, of course, is how their in-the-meantime experiences have conditioned their natural aptitudes and their natural talent for making music and their natural interest in music and music-making. The "known" is (1) what they were like as children and (2) what they will be expected to do as teachers of children through music. Therefore, it seems wise to base suggested experiences and activities for developing them into teachers on those two known facts, capitalizing on or erasing and substituting for the "unknown" as the case may be. Thus, the following experiences are desirable in teacher-training, guidance in each being influenced by the philosophy and the procedure inherent in Teaching *for* Appreciation:

1. Experiences designed to develop innate equipment for making music through the activity of making music. The musical memory, the musical ear, the sense of rhythm, and the voice are the innate equipment. The first three are developed in singing and in making music "by ear" and "by feeling." The wide range of "by ear" and "by feeling" music-making activities is the same for adults as for children and includes all those discussed under Music-Reading Readiness and Rhythms; namely: singing by ear (rote), "harmonizing," playing melody and chording instruments by ear, and making percussion accompaniments—all this without becoming involved in interpreting notes.

2. Experiences designed to permit the expression of self through music. The activities in which self can be expressed are singing, movement and dramatic play interpreting musical compositions, planning accompaniments for movement, dramatic play and singing and planning melodies for poems—all this without becoming involved in interpreting notes.

3. Experiences designed to bring about awareness of and an acquaintance with the various areas in music. Activities directing conscious attention to and resulting in an acquaintance with music are: singing, interpreting musical compositions by movement and dramatic play, planning percussion accompaniments, and listening, directed and/or free.

These activities that develop the innate equipment for making music, that permit the creative being to use music as a means of expression, and that bring about an acquaintance with music, serve two purposes; (1) they are the best possible for inculcating positive attitudes and feelings regarding music, and (2) they provide a foundation, laid deep in muscles and memory, upon which to build certain skills, a foundation within them and within their experience to which the technical facts of music can be tied and related. All this leads to the following—

4. Experience designed to develop skill in reading music. In these experiences, skills contributing to independent music-reading skill are acquired: aural recognition of fundamental triad and scale tones, the symbols for the duration values of tones, and familiarity with the "handles" of tone, for example, the keys on keyboard instruments, the holes on flute-like instruments, and the syllable and number names of scale tones.

5. Experience designed to learn methods of teaching. Activities directing attention to the sequence of learning and to the method used in guiding and pacing learning are related to the sequence of *their* learning and to the method by which *they* were taught. Analyses of these personal experiences will then reveal the "why" of method.

SKILLS

The person guiding the program should have certain abilities in order to carry on musical activities. Some skills are purely technical skills in music, whereas others are those that contribute to all effective teaching. The order in which these requisites are discussed is not intended to indicate their relative importance.

The elementary classroom teacher should have the ability to sing artistically, to read music, to record music, to teach, to select materials, and to play some musical instruments.

Sing Artistically

This ability is of prime importance for two reasons. First, children will tend to sing no better than their teacher, since her singing sets the standard. Second, artistic singing is more pleasurable and satisfying than the plodding, stodgy, unimaginative kind. "Artistically" means accurately as to notes and rhythm—in time and in tune—in a style that enhances the mood of the song. It means pronouncing the final consonants of words, sliding from one tone to another only when the composer indicates a slur. "Artistically" means with a lilt and swing that belong to the particular song that is being sung, to bring out the important musical phrase. Finally, it means singing with expression.

Read Music

Ability to interpret the symbols of music is necessary in order to learn new songs. There are not enough music courses in all the colleges today to make it possible for every prospective teacher to learn every song she might have occasion to use in her teaching life. Without the ability to read, her repertory contains only the few songs she can learn by rote—and opportunities for teachers-in-service to learn songs in this way are limited. She will have little comprehension of what a page of music says or means. Without this ability, she is definitely handicapped after she has taught her class all the songs she knows. Imagine not being able to read a four-line poem about a chickadee to a group of first-grade children unless one had learned this poem in college!

Record Melodies

Few of the songs children write are worth saving for posterity, but many are interesting enough to be added to a class's repertory. When a creative effort is recorded, the creative being is greatly encouraged and satisfied. Recording or notating is a job for the teacher.

Teach

The principles that result in effective teaching of arithmetic, reading, social studies, or spelling also apply to teaching music. There is no sacred or mysterious ritual that teachers have to master in order to teach children music. The principle of arousing interest is efficacious in trying to teach reading *or* in trying to teach music. The principle of readiness applies to learning certain skills in arithmetic *and* in music. True, the teacher has to be able to chart progressive steps in arriving at a goal—and the way is much easier if the horse is before the cart; it is much easier to teach a child to skip to music if he knows how to walk or march to music. There is another striking similarity between teaching arithmetic or social studies and teaching music. The teacher must *know* the music she is expected to teach, just as she must *know* the arithmetic or social studies she is expected to teach.

Preventing errors in music-learning is done the same way as in other subject matter areas. Correcting errors depends on an ability to hear them; then, analyzing them, and, applying remedial activities.

Select Materials

The word "select" is used advisedly. Consider the implications of this word in connection with a piece of clothing. "Selecting" a coat implies consideration of some or all of these points: Does it fit the exact requirements of a certain occasion? Is it what is needed? Will it be useful for any other purpose? Is it similar to or is it in marked contrast to other clothes? Is it worth the price? Even though you like it or you do not like it, even though it fits or it does not fit, the process of "selection" involves all these (and perhaps other) considerations. Before arriving at the point where the answers to these questions had to be considered, you had to know where to go in order to find a supply from which to choose.

"Selection," as applied to materials to be used in promoting musical growth, involves the same considerations—exactly the same. The teacher must know where to go to get needed material, whether it be records, songs, information about compositions, or instruments. To make the business of selection less arduous, first-hand acquaintance with books of songs, music encyclopedias, and other sources of information is desirable. Each composition should be selected with an eye to its subsequent use, selected as carefully as the new garment is selected. These questions must be answered: Does this song or composition contribute to growth in interpretation? Does it crystallize a certain desired mood? a necessary technical point? If it does answer a certain need, what other purpose can it serve? If a record is being considered, what instruments are prominent, or what is the form of the composition, or what is the mood? Does its intrinsic value merit the time and energy required to learn it? "Selection" means judging, and it means using discrimination. It does not mean teaching the song on page 25 just because the children have finished learning the song on page 24. Certainly, it is possible that those songs belong together, but the logical *next* one might be on page 98.

A college girl who was doing student teaching made an appointment for a conference with her college music teacher. She wanted to discuss what to do in music. She had previously observed the children in her class when they had been engaged in musical activities; she was ready to answer intelligently the questions her teacher asked: How well do they sing? What abilities do they have in rhythms? What do they know about musical instruments? And so on. After this appraisal of the musical background of the children, the student, with the assistance of her teacher, was then able to plan activities that would bring about growth in the various phases of music. All this information was necessary in order to *select* materials for the *next* step.

The selection of material can be guided by relating it to the sequence of learning outlined in this book and by relating it to the level of development.

Play Musical Instruments

Ability to play musical instruments is important for two reasons: (1) It is evidence of a certain amount of comprehension of "music," and (2) it makes possible a richer program in the classroom. The contribution of instruments to the music program was discussed throughout Part I of this book. Ability to play "by ear" and "by feeling" has been discussed, too, as the desirable way of becoming acquainted with instruments and with playing. Hopefully, the outcome is the desire to play "by note." Ability to play "by note" is the aspect of playing that denotes some comprehension of "music"—and "by note" is the qualifying distinction of playing in this next discussion (with one exception).

Ability to play the piano, any of the standard orchestral instruments, the flute-like pre-orchestral instruments, the Autoharp, and the harmolin is an indication of ability to read music. The teacher who can read music has the means of learning new material.

Too much importance should not be placed on "ability to play the piano" because of the generally optimistic interpretation usually made of such stated ability. Too often it is interpreted as "being able to play well" or "playing so that others enjoy it." Mere "ability" is worth little if the playing is neither artistic nor rhythmic. Rather than playing done in a style too closely approximating stammering and stuttering, hemming and hawing, hunting and pecking, let's have no piano playing in schools, let's not subject children to *that!*

"Ability to chord on the piano" or "ability to play tone clusters"—ah! those are two other things! A well-developed sense of rhythm is necessary for playing both, little technical facility is required for the first, and none in the second. Chords, played on the piano, make delightful accompaniments for singing. They can easily be taught to children, too. A person with no "ability to play the piano" can fit a precise and exactly right accompaniment to children's dramatic play and movement by playing tone clusters.

The information necessary for chording can be acquired easily and almost casually.[1] When an individual is equipped intellectually for finding the proper chords to play on the piano, he is also equipped to discover the proper chords to make on other chording instruments.

Chords on any of the so-called "social" instruments can make interesting accompaniments for singing—and techniques for playing the Autoharp, harmolin, ukulele, guitar, and banjo can be acquired in a relatively short time. The very name "social" implies that such instruments are close allies of teaching *for* appreciation. And it is *in* hearing and *from* hearing tones in chords that people get the aural experience basic to harmonizing.

Teachers need the ability to play a melody instrument and a chording instrument. Under the hands of some few, the piano serves the purpose of both.

Improvisation. "Improvisation" or "improvising" has different connotations among various groups although its meaning—"to compose extemporaneously"—does not vary. To one group, it suggests a highly musical and technical skill in extemporaneous composition that follows formal designs. In the other sense and to another group, "to compose extemporaneously" is a more

[1] The method is the basis of *Music Fundamentals Through Song*, by Louise K. Myers. Englewood Cliffs, N. J.: Prentice-Hall, Inc., 1954.

informal, less technical utilitarian sort of activity, judged primarily as to whether or not it accomplishes what it set out to do. Used in this way, "improvisation" does not preclude the possibility of a fine musical effort, but it can be done by persons who are not highly skilled musicians.

"Making up" or improvising accompaniments has been referred to often in this book. They can be simple or complex—depending on pianistic skill. Often, the more simple, the better. So little music is available for children's movement in dramatic play, it is fortunate that simple accompaniments will suffice and that little skill is necessary for playing them. Willingness to try on the part of the teacher *is* necessary, though.

A group of second-grade children was dramatizing the winter sports it enjoyed. Coasting, one of their favorite sports, was to be included. Several children worked out the actions. First, the long hard climb up the hill with an occasional pause for breath, then, the thrilling swift descent. Music for this? They searched. Finally, the teacher sat down at the piano and played something comparable to this:

Did this seem to be what they needed? A climb was suggested. The heavy chords implied pulling and tugging sleds. At the top of the hill, there was time to get turned around. The brilliant glissando complemented their idea of exciting descent. Yes, it would do.

Notice the exclusive use of the tonic chord. The whole thing is simplicity itself. But, it served its purpose to provide music for a bit of rhythmic play. It satisfied the need of the children at that moment. Had the teacher been more proficient, she might have used a more interesting chord progression. However, the teacher's willingness and ability to contribute to the procedure more than made up for her lack of superlative pianistic power. If she had not been able to furnish this music, just what *could* they have used?

Sometimes the need for a more complex accompaniment is apparent. A group of fourth-grade children, studying the importance of transportation to the life of their city, was greatly interested in the newspaper reports of the difficulties a ferry boat encountered on one of its trips across the lake. The group went to the docks and talked to some men who knew the story. They found out that, after the boat had started on its trip, a sudden freak storm had been responsible for considerable damage and for difficult going for part of the trip. As suddenly as the storm had descended, it had moved on, leaving comparative calm.

The children were motivated to dramatize the event after their visit. In their discussion they decided that the voyage had three distinct parts: a calm beginning, a terrifying struggle with the elements, and a refreshing cessation of turmoil. They said that music for such a dramatization would fall into three-part form. After listening to several phonograph records that portrayed calmness, turmoil, and then calmness on water, the group rejected the available music as not conforming to its ideas and asked the teacher to "make up" some. Under a simple tune a barcarolle accompaniment was improvised. That, she was told, would be fine for the beginning, and if she could make it less calm, it would be suitable for the last part, too. The middle part satisfied them when the music dashed and slashed.

Was the result "music"? Probably it was more like "music" than the accompaniment in the first example. The second teacher had more pianistic ability than the first. The second group of children had had more musical experience than the first group. But, what a fine experience they all had had as the teacher made the music to their specifications—"selecting" and rejecting parts of the proposed accompaniment.

What training is necessary to prepare the elementary teacher for guiding the music program in her classroom? What experiences would best prepare her for this part of her teaching? There is concern not only about the amount (number of courses) but about the *kind* of training. In the preceding discussion of attitudes and skills that are desirable for the teacher, some suggestions concerning such training were given. Some of the following recommendations are specific, and means by which they can be accomplished have been suggested; others are general, with reasons given for their inclusion. These recommendations are not necessarily ranked in order of their importance, with the exception of the first one, which should receive unusually careful consideration.

Recommendations

1. All prospective elementary teachers should know, from first-hand observation and participation, the part music plays in the elementary school program. In this way they will understand what skills and background are needed in successfully carrying on the music activities of the classroom. In many institutions it is possible for a prospective elementary teacher to complete her teacher-training courses and *never see a music lesson taught to children.* This is not only possible, but, in too many colleges, it is unhappily the fact.

Institutions that train music specialists are most likely to delimit the observation and participation experiences of the prospective elementary teacher. Student teaching facilities are at a premium. Since it is desirable for those students who are specializing in music to have experience in teaching music, the limited facilities available for observation and student teaching are assigned to them. This practice unfortunately works hardships on the prospective elementary teacher as well as the prospective specialist who will have to work with these teachers later in their various classrooms.

Observation of, and participation in, guiding experiences in music are necessary for prospective elementary teachers, then, because they: (a) give them an awareness of the function of their courses in college, (b) give them an awareness of the place music plays in the elementary school program, (c) make it possible for them to accept the help of a specialist in their actual teaching toward their common purpose—to enrich the lives of *all* the children through music.

In institutions training music specialists, the music majors too often are the preferred members of campus choral and instrumental groups. Prospective elementary teachers are again denied experiences that are vital. Singing and playing in choral and instrumental organizations are important to their growth, too.

2. An extensive singing, rhythmic, and creative experience should precede any formal attempt to learn how to read music. Too often, music—a language of feelings and ideas—is taught in a manner faintly resembling a drill on a multiplication table. Too often, the college student's introduction to music is through the science of music rather than through the aesthetics of music.

3. Prerequisites for technical courses in music should be imposed. Imposing prerequisites for technical courses (for example, the beginning courses in reading music [2]) would insure that the time would be used in learning to read and not in learning to sing.

4. Since the musical backgrounds of students vary greatly at college entrance, arrangements should be made to assure the actual growth of each student. This necessitates more than imposing prerequisites for technical courses and making remedial courses available. Students should be divided into sections composed of those of equal ability. This will preclude the possibility of the winner in a piano contest and the violinist in the local symphony attending class with students who have had no

[2] Learning to play pre-orchestral instruments is just as effective for adults in learning to read music as it is for children. A combination instrumental-vocal approach is best for both.

musical experiences since the fourth grade. If the group cannot be divided into *four* sections, perhaps it can be divided into *three*. If not three, *two* sections are better than *one*. It is a matter of scheduling these classes when the master schedule is made. This is the way to make certain that the best students as well as the weakest make progress.

5. Regulations should prevent the possibility of a student's taking Music II before he has had Music I. Imagine taking French II before having had French I just because of program-making difficulties!

6. Learning to teach music should be the result of (a) personal experience in learning music, (b) the observation of music teaching, and (c) a responsible effort to discover the implications, for teaching music, of principles learned in Child Psychology, the Psychology of Learning, and the methods courses in other fields. Music is taught in conformity with the same principles. The time and effort of prospective elementary teachers should not be wasted in a so-called "methods course" for which they are not ready. The time and energy could be spent more profitably in adding to their musical equipment.

7. Conscious effort must be made to broaden the musical background of these students. The following will serve as examples of possible means: (a) Offer class and individual lessons in voice, piano, and orchestral and pre-orchestral instruments; (b) make glee club, choir, band, and orchestra participation possible; (c) offer extra music courses to be chosen as electives. The only contact with music many prospective elementary teachers have is in their two or three required courses.

8. The philosophy of teaching advocated by the elementary education department of the college should be exemplified in all the courses students are required to take. For example, if the philosophy of teaching is "areas of experience," then this philosophy should pervade teaching in the college. Otherwise, the students will have *heard* about it, *read* about it, perhaps *seen* the workings of it in the demonstration schools, but will not have *experienced* it. Unless students are aware of the work-

ings of that philosophy, unless their lives have been affected by it, it remains in the realm of speculation for them.

If philosophy-as-it-is-taught and the workings of philosophy-experienced-by-students do not harmonize, considerable confusion will result in the minds of students. There must be considerable self-education on the part of students. If broad implications and interrelationships are not made evident to the college student in courses, he will be forced to juggle the minutiae of a dozen different subject-matter courses, selecting this and discarding that in an attempt to arrive finally at formulae of causes and their results. This is a tremendous task to impose upon young people.

This extremely important matter of articulation and integration of meanings should not be left to the students. It should be directed by the mature and experienced. The students have a right to expect guidance in discovering the broad implications and interrelationships of learnings. They are some of the important outcomes of a college education that will function in all subsequent teaching. Such guidance is one of the major responsibilities of any faculty group.

Nor should the important matter of articulation and integration of meanings in the area of music and learning music be left for students to discover independently. They must know how their learning was paced over the entire program and how their skills and understandings were built sequentially. This will answer as many times for them as for teachers the question what to do "next." Making students aware of this sequence of learning is one of the major responsibilities of any faculty group.

MEN AS ELEMENTARY MUSIC TEACHERS

Men students have often asked whether or not they can successfully teach little children to sing. The men were thinking, of course, about the obvious difference in range between the adult male and the child voice.

If you have been concerned about this, remember (1) while

learning to *speak,* children hear men's voices and still learn to speak in their normal child range, and (2) it is almost impossible for a child to force his voice into the male range.

It is possible that one or two children in a first-grade group may try to match the male voice in a session of individual work. There is not much point in telling the child to sing "higher"— a concept of "higher" is probably what he lacks. Ask the class to model "higher."

Some men have used their falsetto voice in singing with and for inexperienced children for a little while.

For Discussion

1. What effect does "liking music" have on a teacher's teaching of music?

2. Examine your feelings about music. Recount the experiences that resulted in these attitudes. Are they logical? If they are negative, what experiences caused them? What might help change them? Have discussions resulting from the material in this book changed your attitude? How?

3. What four activities are necessary in a teacher-training program in music? Would you arrange them differently? Justify your arrangement.

4. Of those skills listed as important for the teacher which is the least important? What substitute can be made for a total lack of this skill? Which is the next least important?

5. Re-read the story in Chapter 6 about Katherine Scott Taylor and the story of the second grade and the recording in Russian of *The Volga Boatmen.* Discuss the implications of those stories in answering the question: "What is a good record for my third grade?"

6. If you think this is too much to expect of the elementary teacher, what do *you* think she should be able to do? What kind of a program in the schools will result from *your* ideas?

7. Be prepared to talk for five minutes on *The Teaching of Music,* transferring to music-teaching what you have learned about the teaching of reading (language).

8. Give an illustration of artistic singing. Sing the same song in-artistically.

9. Why is it desirable that the classroom teacher be able to play

the piano? Which of these reasons applies equally well to being able to play the 'cello? The flute? The guitar? The harmolin?

10. Upon what basis is the *next* experience in music planned?

11. Discuss "improvisation" in relation to rhythmic dramatization. Improvise music for the story of the ferry boat, using chords or tone clusters.

12. Which is the better accompaniment for rhythmic dramatic play: a good composition that *almost* fits the children's ideas of the proper accompaniment, but for which they must make certain alterations in their plans, or a poor improvised accompaniment that exactly meets their requirements?

13. Play chords on the piano so that they will suggest (1) heavy pulling; (2) quick, gay marching; and (3) "fairies dancing." Play tone clusters to suggest the same.

9

The Music Specialist

A teacher whose major training has been in the field of music is called a "supervisor," a "director," a "specialist," or a "consultant." This expert and the classroom teacher work together in making it possible for music to make its greatest contribution to child development. There is a close relationship between the two—the efforts of one complement those of the other.

The specialist whose responsibilities lie in the area of elementary school music has an interesting, challenging, and difficult job. To the community, he is the expert in charge of the music program. To the administrator, he is an authority on music, an organizer, an executive. To the classroom teacher, he is a source of help in things relating to music. To the children, he is the "music teacher"—and their connotation of "music teacher" is entirely dependent upon past and present association!

What kind of a person should this expert be? What qualities

of leadership are desirable? What preparation best fits him for the ramifications of his important work in the community? How can his particular skills be used to the best advantage?

HISTORICAL BACKGROUND OF THE "MUSIC SUPERVISOR"

When our forefathers realized the importance of free, universal public education, there were not enough well-educated, responsible teachers available. To compensate for this lack of education, the plan of using experts in certain subject-matter areas became established. Commonly, these areas were physical education, drawing (art), handwriting, and music. These experts supervised the teaching of these subjects. It was necessary to tell teachers what to do, how to do it, and when to do it. It is well recognized in all fields of activity that the amount of supervision needed depends upon the competence of the workers.

A pattern of behavior was established by these experts in addition to a pattern for the *use* of their time. Dealing with incompetent personnel, these supervisors too often became small dictators, who inspected and reported to higher officials.

When classroom teachers became better trained and more competent, they resented that pattern of behavior that had become fairly well established. They resented the dictatorship imposed by supervisors. Supervision such as this was held in ill-repute. But at present the label, "supervisor," is disappearing —it had too many bad connotations for too many people. "Specialist," "consultant," or "director" are currently the more preferred terms.

THE MUSIC SPECIALIST

In a child-centered school there is no place for dictatorship and inspection. In some instances it *may* be necessary to tell the teacher "what, how, and when to do." The manner of "telling," however, is different. The authoritarian air has been supplanted by one of cooperation and willing assistance. And, the teacher has received in pre-service training the basis for understanding the "why."

Today, the school is the result of a cooperative effort on the part of the community, administration, teachers, children, and experts. What sort of persons should these specialists be in order that their talents and skills make rich experiences in music possible?

Personality

The music specialist must be pleasant, gracious, and emotionally mature. He must be efficient and, most important of all, he must like people, including children. Each quality is indispensable. Notice the use of the word "must." If *any* teacher lacks any one of those qualities, *permanent damage is likely to be done to the personalities of children*. Damage to a child's inner self should be avoided more conscientiously than should giving the incorrect name to a musical composition. Notice, too, that those are the same qualities you like in people as well as in teachers!

It may be that the general concept of "artistic temperament," as applied to musicians and those who work in the arts, has helped some people forgive and fondly remember evidences of bad manners and irrational child-like behavior on the part of teachers. However, most people have condemned the behavior. The ill-mannered, emotionally immature, and insecure do inestimable damage to children and have no place in the classroom.

Efficient. "Efficient" means delivering the book that was promised, arriving at a designated place at the agreed-upon time, bringing the phonograph *and* the records *and* the needles (if all that equipment is needed for a demonstration lesson), or planning a meeting so that, having started promptly, it can end at the designated hour. "Efficient" means the ability to appraise honestly the worth of activities in relation to time and energy. It means being ready to discard the "old" as well as to adopt the "new." It means using time to the best advantage.

There must be time for reading professional literature in addition to fiction and nonfiction, for listening to radio and watching television, for professional and social engagements, for scheduled and unscheduled school activities, for in-service improvement of teachers (including the specialist), for community and school extra-curricular events, and so on. The music specialist must be efficient in order to be even moderately successful.

Likes People, Including Children. More important than being pleasant, gracious, emotionally mature and secure or being efficient, the teacher must like people, including children. Some of us prefer to work with things rather than with people. "Liking" implies being interested, trying to understand, sympathizing, making an effort to help, and seeking opportunities for association. There could be no worse fate for an individual who prefers working alone or with things than to have to live and work continuously with children. It would not be fair to the children for them to do so, either. Adults who cannot tolerate children or who are irritated or bored by them have no contribution to make as teachers. Even though they have absolute pitch, can sing a hundred beautiful songs, can correctly identify all the subordinate themes in each movement of thirty symphonies, they lack the essential quality of teachers if they do not like people.

Democratic Leader

The ability to work with others and to give direction to their activities while inspiring them toward their best effort is the essence of democratic leadership.

The person who has this gift does not appear to "boss" when answering a request for help or when asked to assist in making plans. Nor does he "talk" cooperation while completely disregarding the suggestion of others.

Probably the finest quality in such leadership is its power to inspire enthusiasm and the desire to improve. This power has in it, too, the ability to recognize even the most minute indication of initiative or interest and, having recognized it, to choose the proper way of nurturing it.

The qualities of democratic leadership presented here are the ideal toward which the best practice is being directed. Honest self-appraisal will show the thinking person how he can more nearly approach it.

Skills

The specialist whose responsibilities lie in the field of elementary music must have the same skills as those listed for the classroom teacher. He must be able to (1) sing artistically, (2) read music, (3) record music, (4) play musical instruments, (5) select materials, and, (6) teach.

There is some difference of degree, however. The specialist's efforts in each endeavor must result in perfection, an unthinking, unconscious perfection. These skills are the fundamental "tools of the trade." Proficiency in their use, the distinguishing mark of the specialist, is necessary so that energies may be directed toward the bigger job at hand. That job is to promote child growth and development through music, to appraise situations and to plan for growth and improvement. There is no time or energy for learning to manipulate "tools."

Someone may ask, "Don't you think that knowing music and knowing about music and musicians should be included in the list of skills for the specialist?" The answer is "Yes, that is included in the skill 'ability to select material.' In this the specialist must excel. Re-read what was said about it in relation to the classroom teacher."

"Select materials" implies, too, an awareness of the sequence in learning and the skills that support this learning. Having appraised the skill of a class to transfer movement into symbols, for example, or to apply the principle inherent in the relative position of scale tones on a staff, the specialist must be able to "select" from all possible materials and activity that which will extend or reinforce this skill—and "select" almost without thinking.

Later in this chapter—in the section *The Unwilling Teacher*—is a brief summary of what "teaching music" is. That summary is intended as reassurance for a particular kind of teacher. In relation to the "specialist," however, that level of teaching is considered to be below the *barest minimum*.

The teaching skill of the specialist is based on a grasp of general principles rather than on less important specific learning. Specific learning applies only to situations that are identical —but principles transfer to other problems. Not only is the skill of the specialist based on a knowledge of principles but his use of these principles is a measure of his skill!

The specialist must have to a great degree skill to assess learning. Having assessed, there is need to know what to do: reinforce by a different approach or go on to the *next* in the sequence. The decision, of course, is based upon whether or not previous learning will function in subsequent learning, whether it will support subsequent learning.

Training

This will be no discussion of how many college hours of study it takes to make a "music specialist." Music faculties and competent committees of the Music Educators Conference have given of their time and energy, talent, and skill in suggesting courses of study that will insure the student's gaining the "tools." Such courses of study have been revised as the people they will work with (classroom teachers) have become more competent and able in guiding the various phases of the music program in the elementary school.

It is the area of nonmusic training that is often neglected—the area of relationships between the whole school program and music, children and music. And too often, the study of children is only superficial.

Limitations. The training that results in the specialists' mastery of "tools" and the pattern of background experience that develops some of the desirable leadership qualities are, at the same time, responsible for producing the greatest weaknesses of the music specialist. These are:

(1) a lack of awareness of the nonmusical background and experience of many people,

(2) a lack of knowledge about and association with children, and

(3) a lack of acquaintance with the philosophy of the school program and with the program itself.

At the moment when specialization is crystallized in the choice of curriculum, it is all too likely that association with nonmusic students and activities cease. This delimitation of experience with "outsiders" is almost a natural result of training to become a specialist. The business of gaining "tools" is time- and energy-consuming. During the period of concentrated study (college years), the "rest of the world goes by" without the attention or concern of the student who is specializing. Law students, engineering students, medical students, music students—all these, preparing to become highly trained specialists, associate only with their own kind during their years of training. They live in their own small worlds.

That small world in which particular skills and background are obtained is, unfortunately, only a fraction of the whole. The about-to-be specialist will have to learn of the whole by indirection if not by direction. Some of them are not successful at self-direction. They make bad mistakes. They waste valuable time—theirs and that of others.

Because of his isolated position in pre-service training, the music specialist is often unaware of the lack of knowledge about, and interest in, music on the part of many people. To the specialist, music is *the* thing. To the nonspecialist, music is *a* thing.

In the elementary school where the specialist will work, the place of music is quite different than it is in a music school (or department).

In the Elementary School	*In the Music School*
Music is fun	Music is a subject for serious study
One of the many paths of learning	*The* path
A means of enjoyment	A means of livelihood
A means of self-expression	Material governed by the strictest of rules
One of many possible choices	*The* choice

These points of view concerning music are diametrically opposed. The product of the music school needs some *leavening* experiences that will transform his respect, his regard, and his reverence for his subject-matter into the more normal attitude of the nonspecialist. Perhaps, what is needed is a series of planned experiences that will enable him to see music's real place in the lives of other people. Few but professional musicians—a small segment of the whole—would say that it is most important, and none of them will be found in the classrooms of the child-centered school.

Suggested Remedial Procedures

1. If a student who is preparing to become a music specialist in the field of elementary education could spend one half-day each week throughout his pre-service training years with children in a classroom in charge of an expert classroom teacher, he would

    (*a*) become aware that there is more than music in the program of the elementary school,

    (*b*) become aware that there is a wide range of musical aptitude and talent and interest,

    (*c*) have the opportunity to study children in relation to what he has learned about them,

    (*d*) have the opportunity to study the *art of teaching,*

    (*e*) watch how music and other areas of subject-matter promote child growth and development,

(f) see the integrated activities program in action and, thereby (it is hoped!) absorb its philosophy, and

(g) gain a background of practice and procedure against which to evaluate the effectiveness of his own teaching and activity.

All of this can be learned in one half-day a week—one tenth of a student's time. When these things are not learned the teaching effort of music specialists is unsuccessful and ineffective. A half-day a week cannot be spared? In what other half-day period could the student learn so much? Nine tenths of the time is spent in gaining mastery of "tools"; surely one tenth could be devoted to gaining an understanding of how they are to be used. Such time cannot be used more advantageously—and it counteracts the effects of isolation resulting from specialization.

It was stated that this discussion of training would not include a discussion of hours and courses, and now, here is a plea for three hours per week of the student's time! This might appear to be inconsistent. It is—but it is such a simple, satisfactory way for a student to learn so much that is of paramount importance.

2. Students need some "fun" or "creative" or "social" experiences with music. Such would be completely in accord with the specialists' future activities, and they can well serve as a bridge between two diametrically opposed philosophies. In their pre-service training, music specialists need experience in

(a) interpreting music by means of rhythmic or dramatic play,

(b) improvising piano accompaniments for their classmates' original rhythm patterns,

(c) writing songs, as individuals and as members of a group,

(d) assembling *all* the curriculum materials to be used in a study of, say, transportation—not just the music materials,

(e) helping people in learning to sing—not so much experience in helping them learn to sing *better,* but in learning to *sing,*

(*f*) notating original songs,

(*g*) appraising skills and the results of skill, and

(*h*) suggesting a "next" area to be developed.

Such experiences will help prepare the specialist for the specific things he will have to do. Not only are some of these experiences "fun" but many of them include group activity. This is good for a person who will most surely spend most of his teaching time with groups. The specialist-in-training must of necessity be interested mostly in one person—himself. He needs some experiences that will direct his interest and concern to others.

3. Children study the cultural patterns of groups other than our own. A glance at some of the subjects in which they are interested will show a type of study that is common. Here is a list:

> Our Neighbors to the North of Us
> Our Neighbors to the South of Us
> People Who Live in the Arctic
> The American Indian, and so forth.

In order to guide the children in learning about people of other cultures, the specialist must know their music. He must know the essential characteristics of the music itself, the instruments that produce it, and the ways in which it is used, and where to find out about it. He must know how to organize and present his knowledge so that it will enhance the children's understanding and not confirm their prejudices. And, he must know that the manner of introducing American Indian music to children in the third grade is different from the method used for those in the sixth. For younger children the emphasis is on the *visual* and the *feeling* aspects.

POSSIBLE ROLES IN THE SCHOOL PROGRAM

The talents and skills of the music specialist are used in as many different ways as there are specialists and elementary programs. It would be an unusual coincidence for any two to have exactly the same duties and responsibilities. It is the specialist's relation to the music for *all* the children in the elementary school that will receive major attention here.

As was mentioned previously, music specialists are known by any of several names—music supervisor, music consultant, music director. Rarely, if ever, is he known as an "itinerant teacher of music" which is what he quite often is! "Director of music" is usually reserved for those who coordinate and give direction to city-wide programs, the details of which are the direct responsibility of other specialists.

In the area of elementary music there are two general types of positions—the music consultant and the "special" music teacher. Because the use of a specialist's ability and energy as a consultant is the ideal use as well as the most economical, that role will receive first consideration.

Music Consultant

The ideal music consultant is a master musician who is a skillful teacher. He is an excellent leader who can work co-operatively with others in providing opportunities for children to develop emotionally, physically, and intellectually through music. The economical use of his time, energy, and skill demands that each be used to the greatest advantage of the greatest number of children. Ideally, he is used as an expert in any other field is used—to make a diagnosis, to aid in making plans, to analyze data and show their implications, and to demonstrate media or methods. Ideally, he is a *service* available to classroom teachers in providing a rich experience in music. Actually, the way in which he is used depends upon the concept of his job in the minds of administrators and classroom teachers.

The following illustration shows how expert time, energy, and skill may be used economically and uneconomically. In one situation, the expert goes to Miss Allen's classroom at Miss Allen's request on *a* Tuesday morning at 10:30 to direct activities likely to arouse children's interest in creating rhythms. In the other situation, the consultant goes to Miss Allen's classroom *every* Tuesday morning at 10:30 to direct activities in music. In the first instance, Miss Allen presumably felt that once a line of thinking had been started in her class, she could plan and guide subsequent activities. In the second, unless Miss Allen and the consultant have thoroughly discussed the methods and materials to be used, it is uneconomical to have the consultant go into Miss Allen's room, "take care of the children" for a designated period, say "Goodbye!" and leave.

Activities for the Consultant. Activities such as the following should be the major concern of the consultant:

1. Meet with curriculum committees to show music's contributions to various areas of interest.

2. Arrange demonstrations to determine, for example, the status of a group of children's reading readiness skills.

3. Plan and carry out in-service training experiences for teachers.

4. Help individual teachers start certain phases of the program or suggest procedures *after* a phase has been started.

5. Work with other specialists toward making the program better and over-all teaching more effective.

6. Plan for more use of available teaching aids and music materials and plan for expanding such aids.

7. Suggest means of expanding the music program in order to take better care of children's needs.

Note that in those activities the *whole* of the consultant's skills is used. Note, too, that the best use, the economical use, demands that classroom teachers have a certain degree of competency in the area of teaching children through music.

Most consultants will find it necessary to engage somewhat in the activities of the "special" music teacher.

The "Special" Music Teacher

The "special" teacher of music must have the same talents and skills as the so-called "consultant." However, there is one important difference. *It is the duty of every "special" teacher to be so successful that he will work himself out of his job!*

What are the implications of such a statement?

A "special" teacher is an "itinerant" teacher. He goes from building to building, from room to room, day by day, at specified times. He darts in; he teaches a lesson (presumably the *next* one on *his* outline or plan); he darts out.

Today, his plan called for him to teach, among other things, the song

> Little snail upon the wall,
> When, I wonder, will you fall. . . .

He did—and left.

What he had no opportunity to learn was that, just before he arrived, the class had discovered that the people in the Belgian Congo eat cassava and that they, too, eat cassava but call it "tapioca." That discovery was of considerable interest to the class. There was little concern about the snail and its probable future—a lack of concern mirrored in a lack of enthusiasm. The children were excited about the people and life in the Belgian Congo. They would have pursued that interest into the realm of music had there been the opportunity to do so—but Mr. Itinerant knew nothing of their interest. He was teaching music from his outline.

On the other hand, had Mr. Itinerant had a previous conference with the teacher or had he been present during the time when the children were discussing the Belgian Congo, Mr. Itinerant would have (1) been *aware* of the children's interest, at least. If he were an alert person, seeking an opportunity to share with children his knowledge of the music of Africa, he would have (2) taken the responsibility for listing and providing the music materials that would add to the children's information about that region. If he were a conscientious person, he would have (3) assembled it, delivered it, and discussed it with the teacher and suggested ways for using it.

It is supposed that Mr. Itinerant was employed as a "special" teacher because classroom teachers could not or would not teach music. (Much more will be said about this later.) When he embarked on this peculiar pattern of flitting in and out of classrooms, doing all the teaching himself, and having no conferences with the teachers, he was not helping the teachers, and he was not helping the children. Did the children ever sing or create rhythms or listen to recorded music or write songs from one Tuesday at 10:30 until the next Tuesday at 10:30? Mr. Itinerant does not know. If the children sang a song with more ease today than they did yesterday, he may suspect but he does not know.

On the day that Mr. Itinerant (1) becomes aware of the special interest of a group, (2) provides music materials to enlarge that interest, and (3) confers with the teacher about the ways and means of using those materials, he will begin the process of working himself out of his job. He has started teaching children instead of music; he is traveling the correct path. (There is considerable difference between teaching a dotted quarter note and teaching a ten-year-old.) He will be well on his way if, at the end of a semester, he can have this sort of conversation with himself:

"Miss Adams taught all those songs suggested for the Transportation unit herself after I sang them to the class a few times. For the previous unit I had to teach them all.

"Miss Chalmers 'guides the listening' in her class so constantly I guess I'd better suggest that the class needs the opportunity to listen occasionally without guidance.

"Jack and Herbie have improved in their singing more in Miss Jameson's room than they did in either the first or second grade. She certainly accepted the challenge of its being every teacher's duty to help each child gain the use of his singing voice.

"Perhaps I should suggest that Miss Young use some of the

songs her children wrote as the motivation for beginning reading. Little did I think they'd spent almost all their time writing
songs the day I helped them write their first."

When Mr. Itinerant can have such a conversation with himself, it indicates (1) he is an analytical person who knows the
processes of development; (2) he can plan, give direction, and
inspire; (3) the classroom teachers are becoming more competent; and (4) Mr. Itinerant is working himself out of his job
as "special" teacher.

As soon as Mr. Itinerant and others of his kind become more
interested in *child* growth and development than they are in
music program growth and development, and as soon as they
realize that intellectual growth in music is a natural, easy
process when child interest is great, their unusual talents and
skills will be used more advantageously.

ADMINISTRATORS AND THE SPECIALIST

It would be an unusual coincidence for two specialists to
have identical relationships with the administration for the
same reason that it would be an unusual coincidence for any
two music specialists to have identical duties and responsibilities in their school programs. One specialist may work directly
with the superintendent, another with the principal of a school
or the principals of several schools. The specific pattern of
activity is a result of the relation to the administration pattern.

Reason for Employing a Specialist

There are several reasons why an administrator may employ a
music specialist. He may (1) accede to the demands of the
community; (2) continue to carry out the long-standing community policy regarding music; (3) wish to start a music program because of a personal conviction as to its value to
children; (4) realize that the pre-service training of his teachers
will enable them to use the services of a consultant, or that the

lack of pre-service training demands the use of a "special" teacher; or (5) start to carry on a music program because it appears to be "the thing to do."

Criticisms of Administrators

When an administrator employs a music specialist, he hopes he has found an excellent teacher, a good musician, and a pleasant, happy individual who loves and understands children. He knows exuberant, energetic, efficient specialists who work well with young and old, inspiring and helping them to learn through music. *That* is the kind of a specialist he wants. But, sometimes, he is disappointed!

There are two types of criticism he makes of specialists in which he voices his disappointment: (1) that concerning behavior revealing undesirable personality traits or a lack of understanding of children, and (2) that related to singing.

The *true* incidents and bits of *actual conversation* that follow illustrate undesirable personality traits or a lack of understanding of children.

1. Miss William shrieked at Harry, "This is the last time I'm going to tell you to stand right there. Now, do it and don't let me see you move out of turn!" The other children stopped in shocked silence. Then Arnold said to his neighbor, "Gosh, that's nothing. Remember last year when she threw a book at Tommy?"

2. In a meeting of teachers of the fourth grade Mr. Stillwell, the music specialist, said, "Well, it seems to me that if the other teachers here can follow directions, you, Miss Jepson, ought to be able to do so."

3. The chairman of the classroom teacher curriculum committee said to the consultant: "We thought you would be interested in hearing some of our ideas about using music in this unit that. . . ." "No, I don't think so—I believe you'll find mine better."

4. Miss Evans, the music director, did not attend the meeting

of principals at which a proposed expansion of the music staff was to be discussed. She went for a ride in the country.

5. "I just can't do a thing with those teachers in Barnard School—they won't cooperate with me."

6. "You're the first music teacher we've had who didn't get mad at us when we didn't do well."

7. "Of course they're sick and can't eat their lunch. It's 12 o'clock and they usually eat at 11:30. They have been out in that hot sun practicing for two hours!" said a classroom teacher, explaining children's behavior in the lunch room.

Were the administrators being too critical in relating those incidents and reporting those conversations? What does each reveal about the specialist involved?

The second criticism—related to singing—is all the more interesting because many other adults in our society voice it, too! It is that, all too often (1) those children who do not sing well are not allowed to sing; and/or (2) those children who do sing well lose their desire to sing when they have to "drill" continually to perfect a few songs.

If you believe that it is the first and major responsibility of a music teacher to give children the use of their singing voices, then you teach them to sing. It is easier, of course, to call them names—"Blue Birds, Yellow Birds, or Green Birds"—and to tell them to listen and learn how! But it does not make sense for a music teacher not to teach children to sing.

One superintendent said, "Our Mr. Underhill can't understand why music in the Junior High gets such a small amount of 'support' from the youngsters. What he does not realize is that those children think of music as singing the same songs over and over to make them perfect—that's all they did in the elementary grades. Now, at their first opportunity to *choose* music, they will have none of it."

People like to sing; rather, they like to sing until they have unfortunate experiences that change that like to dislike.

Adults who launch vehemently into tales of woe about their

dislike of singing as children (as adults they have more control over their activities and refuse to allow themselves to get into situations where they might be supposed to sing), have been heard to say: "All we ever did in music was to sing syllables"; "I was interested in cowboys, not cowslips—all those songs about flowers!"; "We practiced and practiced the same old songs—nothing could please him"; and "When I went from the country to the city school, I didn't know what they were talking about—all those fa-la-la's. I just stopped singing."

PROFESSIONAL RELATIONS

The music specialist has certain obligations, certain duties, and certain responsibilities as a member of the staff of public school employees. Some of these are defined or dictated by the administration, some by tradition, and some by common sense. Those defined by the administration relate to the specifics of the particular position of a particular specialist; those defined by tradition are the result of the impact of former personalities on the school program; and those defined by common sense are often only the dictates of generally accepted concepts of politeness and courtesy.

There is a pattern of behavior the music specialist must be guided by in relation to other members of the staff and in relation to the profession.

Administrators

The work to be done by a particular specialist is inherent in the type of position for which he has been employed. As was suggested previously, with the position—consultant or "special" teacher—goes a certain pattern of activities. This pattern is the result of administrative thinking concerning the use of a music expert in carrying out plans for child growth and development. In some schools, the desired activities are based on the concepts of the superintendent of schools; in others, they are based on the ideas of a principal or a group of principals; and in still others, the activities defined for the specialist result from the ideas of many. In any case, the expert works within the pattern suggested by the administrative officers. Because of his varied responsibilities, a superintendent often delegates to school principals his authority to use the expert's time and energy to the best advantage of children and classroom teachers. The principal of the school in which a specialist works is the key figure in making plans and carrying them out.

A principal is responsible for what goes on in his school. He is equally responsible for what does not happen. As the responsible person, he knows about his teachers—their skills and their weaknesses—and he knows about the children. He knows about the school program, and he knows about the music program. Because of the responsibility resting on him, because of his knowledge of the individuals in his school, the music specialist is expected to plan and work cooperatively with the principal.

Since he is responsible for his school, the principal wants to plan the music program with the specialist. Because part of the music expert's time has been made available for a particular school, the principal there wants to know when the specialist must change his plans, if only to notify the teachers. He is interested in the equipment in his building, so he wants to be consulted and to plan cooperatively for improvements. When a city-wide program of music is being considered or a school festival is being planned, he wants to be kept informed of developments.

It is important to note and to remember that a principal's interest in his school is not just a personal sort of whim or fancy. Nor does he take upon himself the responsibility that has been described. State laws and the rulings of local boards of education charge the principal with the responsibility for the personnel and program of his school.

Other Music Specialists

In most communities those people who are interested in music often join forces to make a definite civic contribution. Such a group may often work and play together in a semi-social-professional way. These people, the music personnel of the school staff, the private instrumental teachers, the church organists, and the choir directors—all have music and music-making as an interest. The more closely this group can work together toward common goals, the more the community and the children and the individuals themselves will benefit.

School Personnel. Should there be only one music specialist employed in a school system, he will get his direction from, and plan his program with, the superintendent or the principals. His program, his area of interest and responsibility will be clearly defined. However, when there are several experts on the staff, there are some suggestions which, if followed, will make for a more harmonious situation in which to work. They are made in the hope that energy and time will be used to the children's advantage and not dissipated in unproductive, useless worry and controversy. These suggestions are simple:

1. Make certain that specific duties and responsibilities are clearly defined and understood by each individual. Each person must be made to feel free to seek clarification of details he does not understand.

2. The over-all plan for the whole school music program should be the result of the cooperative effort of the staff.

3. Each person on the music staff should be informed as to the major activities of the others. This does not mean that Mrs. Johnson should know where Mr. Samuels is each hour of each day. It means that if Mr. Samuels' three elementary schools are planning a joint music festival, Mrs. Johnson should be so informed. A staff meeting once every two months is suggested so that general and individual plans and activities can be discussed.

4. One must give credit and a "thank you" to those to whom credit is due for their part in an activity. One teacher who attained more than local fame by dramatizing the folk music and literature of the community later isolated herself from many in that same community because she had not given credit to those

who had helped her produce the first programs. One of her school-teacher friends had directed the dances for the pageant, one had planned and supervised the making of costumes, and another had recorded the songs. Even so, only one name appeared on the program—that of the "producer." As the program became more elaborate, the "producer" found that her once willing assistants had vanished. She had never thanked them publicly or privately.

Private Teachers. The private instrumental or vocal teacher and the public school specialist have a great deal in common that can be utilized—teaching, children, and music. The specialist should take the initiative in cooperating with the private teacher for the benefit of all the children.

One of the great advantages (and it takes so little time) that can come from school personnel and private teachers working together is in establishing a common vocabulary and a common method. "Measure signature, meter signature"—they mean the same thing; "quarter note, beat note"—in the early study of music, they mean the same thing; "key signature, key sign"—both mean the same thing. Agreement as to what terms will be used may prevent a child from becoming confused.

Consider the manner of counting time; in rhythms, the child learns to *feel* two pulses to a beat, but in his piano work he counts "one–and–two–and." Soon he may be required to count "one–a–and–da two–a–and–da." When his private teacher is aware of some of the devices and experiences enjoyed in the classroom to gain the *feeling* for four tones to a beat, he can use that knowledge in his own teaching. Beethoven who wrote the song in the school book is the same composer who wrote the piece in the book of piano selections and who wrote the *Fifth Symphony* heard on the radio. There is only one Joseph Haydn and one Franz Schubert. Cooperation between the school expert and the private teacher can result in enlarging the child's awareness of the realm of music; it can lead him, too, to realize that music in school and his out-of-school experiences have much in common.

Sometimes children who can read and play piano music easily and readily have no idea that those same notes can be sung. This is sometimes true of other instrumentalists. A few pointed suggestions and a modicum of help by the private teacher would clear up the relationship of notes and tune.

Much of what the private teacher needs to teach can be taught just as effectively by using the material in the school song books. For example, many piano teachers teach the fundamental chords (tonic, dominant, and sub-dominant) early in a child's period of study. What better way to have children use this knowledge immediately than by applying these chords to the melodies of the songs in the school song book? Then, too, these children will have the added satisfaction of accompanying their classmates' singing.

Just as piano manufacturers once feared that radios would lessen the demand for their products, so private teachers once feared that an organized program of music in the schools would lessen the demand for private lessons. But both have found that a greater demand for their services resulted. There is evidence, too, that orchestral instrument class lessons offered in the schools have created an even greater demand for private instruction.

If the two groups who teach children through music and teach music to children can exploit the commonness of purpose, children will benefit greatly.

Classroom Teachers. The music specialist is sometimes regarded by classroom teachers as being in a semi-administrative capacity. Perhaps it is because the over-all planning of the music program necessitates close relations with administrators. Perhaps it is because administrators rely on specialists for carrying on vital parts of the school program; or because of the leadership demonstrated by the specialist in all-school or all-community affairs; or because respect for musical ability alone places him in a somewhat preferred group. It is a fact, though, that music people are often regarded as being "special."

This real or implied semi-administrative rating in the minds of classroom teachers imposes added responsibility on the specialist. His professional behavior must be above reproach. Specifically, he does not indulge in small, inconsequential chatter about teachers or school personnel. Should a principal ask his opinion about the teaching skill of a teacher, only the principal and the specialist know of the question and the answer.

This regard for the expert's position and talents makes the role of the successful specialist a difficult one. He needs to use all possible means to gain the teachers' confidence. He must prove his worth and integrity. What concrete suggestions can be made to help him?

Since classroom teachers have said many times that an arrogant dictatorial manner is the characteristic that antagonizes them more than any other, the specialist should be consciously zealous in striving toward the ideal of democratic leadership. And, since there is more than a hint of a feeling of superiority in arrogance, he should attempt to appraise honestly his talents and weaknesses. If the appraisal has been honest, his list of weaknesses will no doubt surprise him. If he concentrates on eliminating them, he will certainly leave little time for conscious or unconscious admiration of his ability. An interesting contradiction, this: Although the specialist must *be* a superior musician, he must never give any indication that he thinks he is a superior person!

Community. There is community interest in those who are a part of the schools since the schools belong to the community and are one of its important assets. More and more, music specialists are expected to take an active part in community musical life and to exert leadership in this area. The life of the specialist in the community, therefore, has two phases: (1) that of an individual and (2) that of a professional musician associated with the schools.

As an individual, the music specialist's personal pattern of living and behavior will not differ from the accepted norm for the community. His manner of dress will not be conspicuous. His actions will be those of a well-bred person.

As an individual he has certain rights. He has the right to vote according to his political views, to choose the church in which he will worship, to speak for those things in which he believes—these are the fundamentals guaranteed by the Bill of Rights. When a person becomes a teacher, he should not lose the rights that the Constitution of the United States guarantees to its citizens. Should he find himself in a community where it is not possible for him to exercise these rights, he still has one important remaining right—the right to leave. If he has any self-respect, he will exercise it.

As an expert in music education, the specialist should assume leadership in coordinating the musical life of the community. In some instances, such coordination is a fact, so the public school expert's role is that of another cooperative agent. His role should be a more active one than that of "furnishing" music for various occasions. He should use his ability (1) to perform and take part personally in musical groups, (2) to organize and direct groups of adults, and (3) to suggest areas of activity to be developed or explored.

Two organized professional groups—the National Education Association and the Music Educators National Conference—have prepared codes of ethics for the teacher. The code prepared and distributed by the National Education Association lists and discusses ethical behavior for all teachers. The codes prepared by the Music Educators National Conference [1] relate to those aspects peculiar to music education: relations with the press, information about copyright laws, relations with dealers in supplies, regulations governing merchandising procedures, and relations with the American Federation of Musicians. It is important that *every* teacher and *every* music specialist procure and study each of these codes. In each is described the ethical patterns for behavior to be followed in various situations—situations that arise daily in the professional life of the teacher and the professional musician.

[1] Music Educators National Conference, *Music Education Source Book*. Washington: The Conference, 1951.

In relation to using copyrighted music in Audio-Visual Education, Mr. Leonard Feist, president of the Music Publisher's Association of the United States, Inc., says:

> It is not hard to learn what he (music educator) may or may not do. If he wishes to make use of a copyrighted musical composition from regularly printed copies other than for non-profit performance, he must communicate with the copyright owner asking permission and explaining just what use he plans. The name of the copyright owner appears on the bottom of the first page of each composition, placed there by law and with this very purpose in mind. There will be varying policies among different publishing houses, dictated by their own ideas of what is best for their own purposes. But permission *must* be obtained.

Incidentally, this parenthetical remark is at the end of the article: "This article is *not* subject to copyright. It may be used for any purpose whatever without permission. . . ."[2]

IN-SERVICE TRAINING PROGRAM

The development and expansion of the music program to its greatest potential is the responsibility of the music consultant. An effective in-service training program for the specialist and the classroom teachers is the best means of assuring this. There will always be new areas to investigate and new avenues of learning to try and to choose even though the specialist and all the teachers have had the finest available pre-service and in-service training. And it is through a timely, well-planned program of this kind that the "special" music teacher becomes a consultant.

There are always those teachers who are working for undergraduate and graduate degrees. Their choice of in-service courses and experiences is often circumscribed by the requirements of the particular institution in which they are matriculated. Those who plan in-service courses for teachers—this dis-

[2] Feist, "*In re*: The Use of Copyright Music for Audio-Visual Education," *Music Educators Journal*, April, 1954, pp. 22-23.

cussion is pertinent to the music expert as well as the classroom teacher—must remember (1) there are many demands on teachers' time and energy; (2) teachers *will* take credit or non-credit courses when they meet a need the teachers themselves feel; and (3) courses can be planned with the cooperation of a college faculty, thereby satisfying both individual needs and institutional requirements.

For the Specialist

The education of a music specialist never ceases. Some of it results from planned experiences, some from incidental, un-planned experiences. The person who can honestly appraise his own weaknesses and skills will be most likely to plan intelligently for his own growth and development.

Objectivity in appraisal is essential. The teacher who has specialized in voice should ask himself if he really knows chamber music literature; the pianist should ask if he knows choral literature; and the violinist, if he knows opera. Each should question his familiarity with the best contemporary music. By "familiarity" is meant knowing the music itself, not "acquiring a package of facts" about it or its history. An objective analysis such as this will point the way for further study.

It is essential that the specialist keep those skills he has, even as he plans for his growth and development. Thousands of dollars and years of practicing are required to develop even mediocrity in the performance of music. It is a shocking waste for skills to be dissipated or allowed to disappear.

Singing or playing in fine musical organizations is an obvious activity for the specialist. However, for many, such groups are inaccessible. In these instances, the specialist may have to *find* a pianist with whom to play two-piano music, the string players with whom to form a trio, quartet, or small ensemble, the organ-ist with whom to play piano-, violin-, flute-, or trumpet-organ music, or other members for a vocal ensemble. Should the spe-cialist be an outstanding performer who gets little satisfaction from playing with those of lesser ability, he can learn to play a new instrument. Thus, he can take pride in, and gain satisfaction from, developing his new skill.

Attending professional meetings is another means of learning. At many conferences of music educators it is possible to observe rehearsals and conductors. There is the opportunity to hear, meet, and talk with the outstanding members of the profession. Earlier, it was suggested that music teachers should attend the meetings of teachers of reading. For years experts in this field have been studying the problem of teaching reading, and they have discovered much that can be transferred to the teaching of music reading.

Specialists say informal meetings with other music specialists in the surrounding area have been one of the most rewarding activities in which they have engaged. The teachers in neighboring communities have many of the same problems. Time spent in this way is highly profitable even if it does nothing more than make one more satisfied with his own school situation! But it is likely that a great deal more than that will result from such gatherings.

In pursuing graduate study, the specialist who is keenly aware of a serious lack in his background training that limits the effectiveness of his work can often persuade a faculty committee to give him permission to take the course that will fulfill his special need.

Probably the finest in-service training a specialist can receive will come from his own effort—his own analysis of each activity in which he engages. What would have made the demonstration more effective? Why did none of the specially invited guests come to the school concert? Why did the children in the fourth grade not sing in assembly this morning? Why was the account of the rhythms program not printed in the local paper? Each one of those activities required energy and effort. Analysis may bring to light the reasons for the minor failures. If analysis does not, discussion with competent observers surely will.

For Classroom Teachers

In planning an in-service training program for teachers, ask them what they need or would like to have made available and let them help with the planning. After they have taken part in a suggested activity, have them answer the following questions: Did you get out of the course what you had hoped to get? What changes would you suggest if that opportunity for study were again made available? What opportunity for study would you like next?

If the teachers have confidence in you, you can ask them to sign their names to their evaluations. Then you can seek out those who were not completely satisfied and discuss the reasons for their reactions. If, however, they dare not tell an unfavorable truth to a semi-administrative person, there is little point in asking for an opinion. The answer too surely will be "Oh, it was just wonderful," whether they thought so or not.

Demonstrations of Teaching. It is the consensus that a demonstration of teaching is a most valuable means of teaching teachers *how*. Demonstrations are even more effective when teachers themselves demonstrate. This is true whether it be showing how to guide listening, how to sing for fun, how to make physical responses to music, or how to write songs. Many teachers can carry on an activity once they have an idea of how to begin and how to proceed. The best way to show them is to guide them personally in the activity.

In planning a demonstration *of* teaching, the following items are important.

1. Information sheet. When teachers *observe* teaching, it is important they know *what is being demonstrated*. Each person present should be given a mimeographed sheet on which pertinent information is set forth. For example:

Demonstrator: Miss Hargrave, Second Grade, Wilcox School
Purpose: To show the variety of means by which this group's vocabulary of rhythms can be extended.
Minor Points:

1. Watch Harold, the second boy on the left of the third table; until last week he had not engaged in any rhythmic activity. We do not know why he was unwilling.
2. Alice and Margaret, seated across from Harold, have not learned to skip.

This information is important for everyone and will enable a visitor who is late to become acclimated in a few moments. Time will not be consumed in talking about irrelevant matters in the discussion period—for example, why didn't the children sing more? This was supposed to be a concentrated effort toward extending existing skill by means of a variety of activities.

In some instances it is possible for observers to meet in a room away from the children and to receive a brief summary of the plans.

2. *Time.* The *when* of a demonstration using children is always a question. If the children are kept after school, they are tired; their parents have to be consulted. If the demonstration is scheduled during school time, arrangements have to be made for the classes of those teachers who are going to observe. School time is the ideal, of course, because it is the *natural* time for children. In some schools, there are assistant teachers who can function while the regular teacher is away. Should only one teacher from each building be away at the demonstration hour, the principal will often teach in her place. Those concerned with the demonstration should be asked to make suggestions about the best time.

3. *Demonstrator.* It is better to have a classroom teacher, rather than the specialist, demonstrate for teachers. Teachers, then, cannot say to themselves, "Of course, *he* can guide children like that—he's a musician, he knows music!" The specialist has an important advisory role in the planning, and he can lead the discussion, but teachers will have more confidence in their own ability to "do that" if they see a nonspecialist demonstrate.

4. *Children.* The more normal the demonstration setting, the more normal the children. Ten, fifteen, or thirty visitors is

enough of the "unusual," so, in so far as is possible, children should be in their own room, in their own places, and in their school clothes. A demonstration should not be quite a party. Say to the children, "I have invited some guests to share with us our Pan-American Program" or "Mr. Eldridge would like some other teachers to watch our rhythms this afternoon." If the teacher does not get excited, the children are not likely to do so.

5. *Types of demonstration.* In general there are two kinds of demonstrations: those that show creativity and those that do not. In the culminating activities of an area of study, there may be original poems or songs or dances, but the creative effort was expended before demonstration time. In a demonstration to show children "creating" their next unit of work by discussing and planning the music activities, there must be no hint that the discussion had been held previously. In a demonstration announced as "Children Creating Rhythm Patterns," it should be evident that the children are making up these patterns now, not practicing patterns they know.

Classes. Aside from courses teachers take in their work for degrees, there are classes related to music and music teaching that they enjoy. These do not necessarily have to be taught by the specialist, but he can assume the responsibility for finding out which are possible and, in some cases, make arrangements for them. Many such classes do not need to run for a semester—a series of six or eight sessions is sufficient.

A series of recorded music concerts in which recently acquired material is played is not only pleasant but worthwhile, especially if well-prepared program notes are distributed with the suggestion that they be filed and used as background material information for children, too.

An experienced square-dance enthusiast may organize a series of sessions for teachers.

Piano class lessons for adults are popular. There is now available a considerable amount of material for the adult beginner, which takes into consideration the size of the adult's hands and the fact adults can easily reach the piano pedals. Classes for persons who "used to play the piano" are important, too.

Classes in the "Fundamentals of Music" may be of interest to some. Since chord-producing instruments are so valuable in the classroom, a class designed to teach chords is an asset. Actually, this would not be a course in fundamentals nor in harmony, as such, but would combine materials from each.

In only a few weeks an adult can learn to play some of the pre-orchestral instruments: melody flutes, tonettes, flutophones, and so forth. The Autoharp is a simple instrument to learn. There is quite an interest in some places in playing recorders,[3] which are not quite so easily learned.

A series of demonstrations in the use of equipment is of great value since audio-visual aids contribute to learning only if they are used. The value of equipment is increased threefold if teachers themselves have the opportunity to experiment with it and learn to use it.

THE "NEW" TEACHER

The *new* teacher may be a beginning teacher or one of experience who is new to the school system. In either case, each appreciates it *even if she does not need* attention early in the school year. It has been said that many potentially good teachers have been lost in the first month's floundering—floundering in a maze of newness. Since it is possible to get facts about the pre-service training of these new people, the specialist is in a position to offer aid and to guide intelligently.

In many schools it is the custom for an "old" teacher to be assigned as a special assistant or guide for the "new" teacher— an excellent custom. Someone—guide, principal, or specialist —needs to give the "new" teacher an idea of the music background experiences of her class, and, if she seems to require them, suggestions for possible immediate activities in music.

[3] Popular sixteenth- and seventeenth-century flute.

One ninth or one tenth of the school year is gone if the first month is spent just floundering.

THE "UNWILLING" TEACHER

The fact that some classroom teachers are unwilling to teach music is one with which the specialist must concern himself. The reasons for this unwillingness are important. Whether they be real or psychological, the reasons must be found in order to change the attitude. A discussion of possible reasons follows, the psychological first because they are more important and more prevalent.

If a person's voice does not measure up to his concept of a "nice" voice, he or she is reluctant for anyone to hear it. If it did not measure up to some other person's concept—a person in authority (for example, a former teacher)—and that individual made a public pronouncement about its quality, more than likely the person resolved then and there that no one else would ever be able to criticize his voice again. Circumstances such as these may have been the cause of the tremendous self-consciousness of some adults who will not sing. The singing voice is a personal, intimate thing—much more intimate than those who sing easily realize. Singing, then, becomes one of those activities in which he will not engage in the presence of others. Too often, all activities that can be a part of music are shunned in the same way.

There may be a real, as well as a psychological, basis for unwillingness to teach music. It may be that a teacher does not have any idea of how to teach it.

Show and tell these teachers what "teaching music" is: singing or playing recordings of songs often enough for children to learn them; talking about the "pictures" in songs and/or dramatizing the story; beating time while singing or listening—conductor's beat or indicating the down beat, clapping, tipping, and snapping fingers or singing 1—2—3 (or beats) to melody, allowing children to experiment with and learn to play pre-orchestral instruments; teaching syllable or number names of melody tones; making percussion and/or chording accompaniments for songs; and allowing children to learn folk dances and singing games from records.

Help them by furnishing needed technical information: list in the teacher's book the chords to be made on the Autoharp, the letter names of tones to be made on melody bells; the syllable names of melody notes of a song; and most important, furnish necessary materials.

Some teachers have refused to try music-teaching because the pattern to which they were accustomed relegated those activities to an itinerant music teacher. Solicit aid in changing the pattern, if need be.

THE "NEW" MUSIC SPECIALIST

The music specialist who accepts a new position owes it to himself and to his position to become fully informed about his job and the community in which he will live and work before the opening day of school. When the opening day comes, he should be established in his living quarters; he should know about his specific responsibilities; he should have become acquainted with the school principals with whom he will work; he should know where the various schools are located and how to reach them. He must be familiar with any reports made by his predecessor, and he must be aware of the fact that many, many times he will hear "Mr. Predecessor did it this way!"

People are afraid or suspicious of some kinds of change. If Mr. Predecessor were a popular and respected person, the *new* specialist would be wise to inaugurate changes slowly, to keep his opinion of Mr. Predecessor to himself, and to set about making his own place in the school community. It is not a waste of time to prove one's worth before changing a well-established concept of desirable behavior. It is not a waste of time to talk over proposed plans with those who are concerned with them.

WAYS TO INITIATE A MUSIC PROGRAM

The first music expert employed by one community scheduled a music assembly in each school every two weeks. The program of one of the assemblies at the end of the first two months is described below.

The children in the third grade played their melody flutes, and the expert played the piano accompaniment. Brahms' *Lullaby* was their selection. The class played it through once; next, the best flutist stepped forward and played the melody while the class hummed it; then, all repeated the tune.

The orchestra performed next. Its contribution was simple, but the audience of second-, third-, and fourth-grade children enjoyed it. The orchestra, too, repeated its piece several times with variations.

Then, came the "treat." The specialist's wife, a superb violinist, played fast, gay, colorful music and told the children its story—gypsies dancing around their camp fire. As an encore she played the selection a second time.

The other "visiting artists," the sixth-grade class, sang two songs for the group.

That was all. It was simple and pleasant. The child who played the flute solo had never been chosen to do anything before. The little boy in the back row who had forgotten to bring his flute was allowed to stand with his group. The child who went up to the stage during the violin solo was allowed to remain near the violinist. The specialist was "selling" participation and enjoyment.

The specialist said that the program two weeks before had included a performance by a man who had gained local fame as a clarinetist—his "clarinet" being made of a piece of rubber hose, a five-and-ten-cent store funnel, and a clarinet mouthpiece.

Band and orchestra directors have been envied because of the rapidity with which they can prepare groups for public performances. The advent to the classroom of pre-orchestral instruments, however, has made it possible for the vocalists, too, to "show" their work in a comparatively short period of time.

Another specialist—the first the community had had and in her first position—examined the material in the superintendent's files and discovered that most of the elementary teachers in her schools should be able to teach their own music. In the first weeks of school she visited and planned with those about whose capabilities she was in doubt. She arranged for one class in each building to start work immediately on melody flutes. In another she found the "makings" of a small orchestra, which she organized and directed herself. In another school, group singing was promoted—and in seven weeks the assembled group sang almost as a good chorus. A teacher who was a folk-dance enthusiast aroused interest in that activity in her school. In each school a separate activity was emphasized.

When questioned about this plan, the specialist said, "I thought it would be a good idea this year for each building to specialize. Toward the end of the year I plan to have a 'festival' in which all these activities will be a part. During the festival, all the people of the community—children, teachers, parents, administrators—can get more than a hint of the diversified activities of a good music program. Next year, then, they will know of a wide range of activities from which to make choices."

"But you've started almost everything about which you know this first year!"

"Well, we'll expand this program next year, and I'll go to summer school and get some more ideas for us."

The specialist, in conjunction with the administrators, can decide which activities will receive first consideration. There is danger that individual effort be divided among so many activities that none is particularly successful. For this reason, opinions of others as to the relative importance of activities should receive careful consideration.

Singing is one of the important aspects to be stressed immediately in an organized program—everyone singing for fun.

Community songs, patriotic songs, fun songs—the same books or song sheets made easily available for everyone everywhere in town. Moving to music—clapping, stepping, bending, swaying—is the first cousin of singing, so rhythms can become a part of the program early. The idea is to get as much participation on the part of as many people as is possible. Key signatures, the form of the symphony, and the range of the piccolo are important but not necessarily the best selling points for a music program. The introduction to music is making music and the activities should result in satisfaction for the community.

PUBLICITY

Good relations between the school and the community are important. In smaller towns, individuals know of the activities by hearsay; in larger towns, they learn about the school program mainly through the press. It is important that citizens be informed and informed truthfully and accurately.

One community became aroused because three thousand dollars had been appropriated for band instruments. "Too much money for frills" was often heard. Had the news release given to the paper contained the price of each specific instrument, instead of mentioning the total amount, the community reaction would have been different. "Band instruments certainly cost a lot. Sixty dollars for that horn the Johnson boy plays! But we need it, though."

Books have been written on educational publicity from which a specialist can gain worth-while information.[4] He is told how to write stories for papers, and how to write them so editors will print them.

School news is important local news. For really important programs, a reporter and often a photographer will be assigned to cover the story. But, editors need to know of the program before they can assign personnel to cover it.

Some school systems designate a certain individual as the

[4] See Bibliography.

person responsible for supplying material to the press. In such a case, the specialist channels information about music activities through that person.

There is a real difference between attempting to get publicity for a music program and to gain publicity for one's self as an individual. The specialist should be overly careful in not crossing the line that marks that difference. Individuals have ruined themselves in the eyes of the community by seeming to seek fame for themselves rather than trying to inform the public of events or programs. Acclaim should come from others—acclaim must not be instigated by the specialist.

PUBLIC PERFORMANCES

Whether children are "sharing with their neighbors" the songs they enjoy about farm animals, or whether they are taking part in a pageant with hundreds of others, there are two principles that must be followed: (1) The children must not be exploited, and (2) The program must result from their normal interest and study.

When adults decide to include children in a program of any kind and preface their ideas of using them with "Wouldn't it be sweet if . . . ," or "Wouldn't it be cute if . . . ," children are likely to be exploited. Any time children do not gain as much from participating in a program as do those who observe, children are being exploited. "Exploit" in this instance means "to draw an illegitimate profit from." What *good* would a child get out of waiting two or three hours after his bedtime to appear on a program? If that child won a scholarship for college as the result of so doing, it would be eminently proper for him to appear—once!

Nor is it right for adults to impose on a child a plan that has no real interest for him nor one that does not satisfy any felt need. He has an interest in the programs he helps devise, in the dances he helps create, in the songs he helps write, in the music he helps make—those are his, they contain an important part of him. What conceivable interest could he have in taking part in a Triptomaniac Dance so that a person in a town twenty miles away could satisfy his desire to become famous as a folk pageant director? The child loves folk dancing in his classroom, and he fancies himself one of the "folk" as he dances. Because he has studied them and knows about them, he finally identifies himself with them. But he has no interest in a Triptomaniac Dance or in the would-be folk pageant director—he hasn't even heard of Triptomania! And, who has?

There is considerable difference of opinion about the use of masses of children in a program. Can it be justified on the basis of promoting child growth and development? Adults probably enjoy watching seven hundred children dance around so many Maypoles (if they can see all the children from where they sit). The individual child, however, gains all there is to be gained from dancing the Maypole dance by dancing it in his own schoolroom or auditorium.

Some people think the largest program in which elementary school children should take part is the all-school program of their own schools. In an elementary school there are ample opportunities to gain the desirable experience that comes from appearing on programs and performing for others. Should the state or the town declare that next year is to be devoted to its Tricentennial or its Golden Anniversary celebration, the whole school is a unit large enough to make an impressive showing *for adults*. It is a unit small enough for children to have an active part in the planning. They can study the whole story, become interested, and know *what* they are doing when they take part in this celebration. After a period of study, a committee of teachers and children can propose that this class develop one phase of the program and that class develop another. The good comes from planning together, performing together—not from furnishing an evening's entertainment for some person who would rather be some place else.

In the all-school program (and in the room program) the children interested and talented in art make the scenery and design the costumes. The hospitality committee writes invitations to special guests, greets those guests, and introduces them to other guests. The children taking part in the program sit watching the performance until it is their turn to appear. It is a friendly, informal affair that everyone feels is his.

Costumes for elementary school children should be simple. If any considerable time, energy, or money is required for making them, they should be used again or be converted into ordinary wearing apparel. Improvising is the best practice.

For example, the Christmas choir can be costumed in sheets. Fold the sheet the short way and drape it around the shoulders, pinning it securely at the neck. Place a large, round, black cambric collar around the neck, pinning it in the back. If each child holds a flashlight with both hands, the light of which is covered with red crepe paper, the effect will be impressive. The cost of the material for collars is much less than that of one choir robe. Crepe paper collars are even less expensive—but the cambric collars can be used again the following year.

Speaking of exploiting children, Miss Wagner had an interesting experience. After having heard a famous boy's choir, she organized a choir of boys from the fourth, fifth, and sixth grades of her school. It made its first appearance at a PTA meeting. Those who heard the choir were thrilled, and one of them invited the children to sing at the Rotary Club. The Rotarians enjoyed the performance. In the month following the first concert, the choir received invitations to sing morning, noon, and night. Every organization in town wanted to hear it. What was to be done about accepting this overwhelming number of invitations to sing? Miss Wagner conferred with her principal and superintendent. You may not agree with the way they solved the problem, but it did make it possible for the youngsters and their director to be in school for the major portion of school hours, and it did allow them to receive almost their normal amount of sleep. It was decided that the choir would not appear before groups of less than three hundred people on the basis that *the children would gain the same benefits from singing for*

three hundred as it would from singing for thirty or fifty people.
How would *you* have solved the problem?

For Discussion

1. What are the academic requirements for an elementary teacher's certificate in your state? How many teachers are there teaching on emergency certificates?

2. What personal qualities do *you* think a teacher should have? Do you know any really good teacher who does not possess those qualities?

3. Why did you decide to become a teacher? Be honest in your answer. Can your reasons be justified in relation to children's needs? What would you really like to do instead of teach? Why don't you?

4. Give some examples of child-like behavior on the part of adults. Why do you think they act that way? Give some examples of your own child-like behavior.

5. Explain how a course in the History of Music is a "tool."

6. Re-read the material on skills for the classroom teacher, page 217-223. Indicate specifically just how the specialist must excel in each skill.

7. How can a music specialist find out about the philosophy of the school in which he is about to start teaching?

8. List the ways in which the purpose and the program of the Music School (or Department) make the student more interested in himself than in others. In what activity is he dependent on others?

9. Suggest other activities in which a consultant might engage "to the greatest advantage of the greatest number of children?"

10. Which do you think the better practice: to adjust the teaching to the children or to hope the children will adjust to the teaching?

11. What *are* the differences between teaching a dotted quarter note and teaching a ten-year-old child?

12. Which of the administrative reasons for employing a music specialist are likely to result in the most favorable atmosphere in which to work?

13. State some infringements of the copyright law you have observed.

14. Think of the best "leader" you know. What are the characteristics of his leadership?

15. You have "heard" that the director of music in the neighboring town is going elsewhere next year. You would like that position. What line of procedure is suggested in the National Education Association Code of Ethics?

16. Give some instances of unethical behavior.

17. What in-service training can you suggest for the specialist who is two hundred and fifty miles from any organized music group or other specialists?

18. Give some examples of the exploitation of children. Can it ever be justified?

19. What are some current radio and television programs of particular interest?

20. Ten classroom teachers have indicated they want to learn to play accompaniments on the Autoharp. They can sing and enjoy singing but they have no background in theory or fundamentals. You have agreed to teach them in eight two-hour sessions. You will use the community-type songbook each has because many of the songs are familiar. The problem: Outline your plan to teach them the necessary fundamentals. At the end of the sessions they must have learned enough theory to figure out the proper chords to accompany all the reading songs in Book IV of a song series. Remember: number and syllable names of notes are "theory," relative time values are "theory," I, IV, and V are "theory." Pace experiences so that in the eighth session the sequence of learning will result in the group being able to translate I, IV, and V to letter names of chords. Because of the limitations of the Autoharp, the students will need to know how to transpose, too! Is this quite an assignment? It is—if you don't know the sequence of learning— but it may be small in terms of what you, the music teacher, may be asked to do with a group that can't or won't sing!

10

Guiding Experiences

in Music

Music is one of the important means by which children can grow and develop physically, intellectually, socially, and emotionally. It is a means rather than an end. This concept of its place in the whole school program is the basic factor underlying the fundamental philosophy and the principles guiding all activities.

PHILOSOPHY AND PRINCIPLES OF TEACHING

Activities in music are directed toward two objectives:

1. Teaching children *through* music, and
2. Teaching for appreciation.

These objectives, at variance with the old aim, "teaching music to children," result in principles of teaching that differ from the old—they differ in approach, they differ in method, and they differ in hoped-for results.

The principles guiding music teaching are:

1. Plans for growth and development are made upon the basis of existent attitudes and skills;

2. Attitude and interest are more important than skill;

3. All experiences with music affect attitude and interest; and

4. Child interest and need are basic in selecting teaching materials.

Analysis and Evaluation

Emphasis on teaching children through music rather than attempting to fit them into a pattern of standards or a pattern of "grade level" achievement is the fundamental precept. Background experiences and skill in the various areas of the music program are analyzed and evaluated. The analysis and the evaluation point the way toward experiences needed to provide growth—they point the way to the "next" procedure. An analysis of the abilities of a group of children in the fifth grade might show, for example, that it lacked certain reading-readiness skills or a feeling for note values or command of the medium to be used in reading. Under these circumstances, it would be futile to try to teach these children according to a previously determined pattern of Fifth Grade Music—as futile as trying to teach them William Cullen Bryant's *Thanatopsis*.

A list of grade-level standards in music is valuable though, because it points to logical steps in musical growth. The standards are the ideal. Too often it is not emphasized that the ideal of achievement is possible *only* if each preceding step has been mastered. So few groups in our schools have had consistently expert guidance in their music experiences that for most the ideal is impossible to attain. Too often, there is the futile attempt to fit the children into the pattern of the suggested ideal rather than to make a program to fit the children. As an aid in making a program that fits, steps in growth or levels of attainment in each separate activity have been listed in this book so that a teacher of a fourth grade, for example, can analyze and evaluate correctly her group's status in each phase and then guide them *on* from that point.

Importance of Attitude and Interest

Developing a skill for which there appears to be no possible use appeals to adults as little as it does to children. Today, thousands of adults are enrolled in public speaking courses. Many of them have had such a course in high school or in college. At that time the course either was required, or it was selected because of the convenience of the class hour or because two more credits were necessary; but it was not chosen because of a real interest or a felt need. Why are they repeating the course, then, and spending extra money and energy? Because they are interested and feel a need for this skill. Acquiring skill has so much more point when a feeling of need is present. It is as true in music as it is in any other field. A favorable attitude toward, and an interest in music are more likely to result in the desire to learn than in gaining skills *per se*.

It is hoped that some or all of the wide range of activities in music suggested—making music, listening, rhythms, or creating—will interest him and will touch a responsive chord in the inner self of a child, will catch his interest and add to his pleasure as a child and, later, as an adult. The effect on him of a single activity is likely to color his tolerance of, or his interest in, all the others. Thus, teaching *for* appreciation becomes an important principle as does the realization that method must be adapted toward this end.

As the man said, when describing the school music experience that resulted in an unfavorable, disinterested attitude toward singing: "I was interested in cowboys, not cowslips." The truth inherent in that statement is acknowledged implicitly by basing the selection of teaching materials on child interest. Not only will interesting material more readily be accepted by children, but it can be used to teach the facts of music just as effectively as uninteresting material. Had a search been made, a cowboy song could have been found to illustrate the same musical point as did the cowslip song. Interesting material is essential for effective teaching.

EXPERIENCES IN MUSIC

Children can become acquainted with music and activities connected with music by (1) using it in the integrated activities program, and (2) studying an area in music unrelated to the major curriculum center of interest. In the first instance, music is used to provide a broader understanding of an area; in the second, its own intrinsic worth is the reason for its use.

Music in the Integrated Activities Program

Today, all the possible avenues of approach are pointed toward learning in an area of interest. The question about music is not "What music can be used in this unit or project?" but "What can music add to further understanding?" Music is used as one of the avenues of learning—music is a means of widening understanding. The reason *The Volga Boatmen* is used in a study of Transportation is that the music is a picture in sound of a type of transportation—a picture more than photographic in delineating feeling. In a study of communication, the "talking drum," as found in the Belgian Congo, enlarges the concept of the wireless. The mechanism is simple. Children can make up codes. In the study of a primitive people, the utter simplicity of their music further substantiates the idea of a simple pattern of living. The question of using music is always "What can it add to understanding?"

In an activities program children learn through doing and experiencing rather than through just talking or reading. Children's natural play habit of "let's pretend" is capitalized upon, adding many vicarious experiences to the real. It is the doing,

whether actual or pretended, that is important. It is the thinking, the planning, the carrying out of plans that is important.
And, as music enhances a concept and controls movement in
demonstrating an idea, music makes its contribution to learning.

Study of an Area or Phase of Music

In Chapter 6 recorded music's contribution to expanding an
area in music was discussed. Attention is again directed to that
discussion. Twelve areas are suggested for an organized study
of music. Those programs, as well as many others, enhanced
not only by recordings but by all the media suggested in this
book, offer possible means through which to study music not
related to a major curriculum area.

PLANNING FOR GROWTH AND DEVELOPMENT

Teaching music in the elementary school is easy. All one has
to do is to guide children through successively more advanced
experiences. That is all "teaching music" is.

How does a teacher know where to start? First, she analyzes
the actual status of the children's attitudes, and interests, and
determines the level of development of their skills. The following is an analysis of the status of one group:

Singing: Tone quality needs improving; more precision in
attacks and releases necessary; enthusiasm great; half the class
can repeat accurately a four-measure melody after hearing
it once; six poor singers, and so forth.

Rhythms: All except three children can clap, step, and skip
rhythmically; eager to make up simple rhythm patterns; most
have imagination and use big muscles freely.

Creating: They have had considerable experience in creating
rhythms and writing songs; dramatic interpretations of three
musical compositions were varied, freely and willingly executed;
little copying of neighbor's ideas.

Listening: Guided listening experiences appear to bring satisfaction; attention seems to wander a little during long periods of "finding out"; seem to enjoy listening to music once "studied" or through which they were guided several times.

Thus, the analysis shows where to start. What does a teacher do "next"? She provides opportunity for the children to experience the next more advanced step in each phase of activity.

In this book, two means of evaluating skills are available and, therefore, two sources for reference in planning the "next" step or activity:

1. The material related to a major area of the music program is presented in a sequence representing a developmental pattern. The "first things first" idea in the sequence of development implies that when children can do *this* in the sequence, they are ready for *this* which is "next" in the sequence.
2. The material related to Evaluating Growth in each area contains the same ideas but is stated in a different set of specifics related to accomplishment.

The teacher is referred to the following chapters in this book for guidance in planning and evaluating experience in

Singing, Chapter 3;
Rhythms, Chapter 4;
Creating, Chapter 5;
Listening, Chapter 6;
Music-Reading Readiness, Chapter 7; and
Music-Reading, Chapter 7.

Examples of Analysis, Evaluation, and Planning

To illustrate further the points that (1) guiding music experiences is easy, (2) what must be done first, and (3) what is to be done "next," some examples of analysis, evaluation, and planning concerning specific groups are here given.

Group 1. Third Grade

ANALYSIS AND EVALUATION: Previous area of interest—the American Indian.

Singing: Good tone quality but lacks enthusiasm; Helen, Irene, Tommy, and Joe still need individual attention.

Listening: Emphasis was on the ways in which Indians *used* music.

Rhythms: Bending and swaying predominate free interpretations.

Creating: No "making up" experiences.

PLAN: Area of interest—Eskimos.

Singing: Dramatize all songs in an effort to arouse more enthusiasm; give individual attention to "poor singers," using class as model and as an aid.

Listening and Rhythms: Direct attention to drum beat in recorded music; use drum beat to motivate: walking to quarter notes, running to eighth notes, slow walk to half notes (feeling *for* note values—reading readiness).

Creating: In songs or stories, point to activities possible of dramatization and give opportunity to dramatize; have class make up Eskimo Dance or dramatize activities to music.

Possibilities: Eskimo stalk game—slow walk; sled dogs—running step. Write a poem about Eskimos that will fit Eskimo tune, and, if a considerable amount of Eskimo music is available, play it often so children will get the "feel." Is such music available?

Group 2. First Grade

ANALYSIS AND EVALUATION: First day of school. Children have had no kindergarten experience. Need orienting to group singing and movement.

PLAN: Sing three or four songs known to appeal to children; sing them several times during the day. After the group has heard them several times, ask questions about the story in the songs: "What was the little boy's name?" "Listen again and find out what the leaves did." Second day: Repeat songs, ask more questions about meanings, ask children to clap softly (or "tip") with singing; ask children to sing a phrase that is repeated often. Third day: Repeat second day's activities.

Group 3. Fourth Grade

ANALYSIS AND EVALUATION: Group has had three and a half years extensive and good experience in music. Music-reading readiness is investigated. It is found that group lacks competency in supplying syllable or number names for combinations of tones.

PLAN: Concentrate for two weeks on singing all the melodies for which children have learned the syllable or number names of notes. Sing a phrase of a song with "loo." Have children answer with syllable or number names, especially scale and chord passages. Before starting third week of concentrated study, tell the children *why* they need this skill and *how* it will help them when they start to read music next week!

Group 4. First Grade

ANALYSIS AND EVALUATION: First day of school. Children have had kindergarten experience. Level of development of singing and movement needs to be determined.

PLAN: Sing three or four songs known to appeal to children. Sing several that the children learned in kindergarten. Invite them to sing these with you. Repeat songs the second day. As children sing, attempt to discover those who need individual help.

Group 5. Fifth Grade

ANALYSIS AND EVALUATION: New teacher of the group can discover in the children no spark of interest in any phase of music. She knows nothing of their previous experience except that "they were supposed to have had music" in the other grades.

PLAN: Make arrangements for an unusual, dramatic experience —for example (1) take the front off a piano and investigate how tones are made; (2) arrange to have class "go through" a pipe organ; (3) invite a vocal or instrumental soloist to give a concert for the class, and discuss the construction of the musical instrument after the concert; (4) bring ukulele, banjo, or any such instrument to class and sing to the group with instrumental accompaniment; (5) procure some tonettes or melody flutes and learn to play them with those members of the class who want to learn; (6) invite the sixth-grade group to repeat its Folk Dance program for the class; or (7) listen to and discuss a particularly attractive composition of program music. If one of these experiences does not arouse a spark of interest, try another; for example, teach them to beat 3's and then walk while beating. When interest (or at least, tolerance) is aroused, use it as a basis for further study or investigation.

Group 6. Sixth Grade

ANALYSIS AND EVALUATION: Second month of school. Previous experience in music consisted entirely of a little singing of community songs. Available materials: sixth-grade music text in hands of each child. Available equipment: teacher's pitch pipe and a music book she owns. General area of study: Mexico, which will be continued next month. Activities during first month of school: Sang songs learned previously; teacher twice sang song about Mexico from her book; class aware of fact that there are two songs in their book labeled "Mexico"; one boy said he had heard "Mexican music over the radio at home once."

PLAN: Continue singing songs learned previously, using them as basis for (1) learning conductor's beat and (2) accompanying any rhythmic activity; learn "teacher's song" by rote; learn Mexican songs in text. If any of these is a folk dance, teach some folk dance steps even if they are not *the* ones suggested for the music and even if only six children are interested in learning them. Plan accompaniment for these songs on (1) claves (two sticks tapped lightly), or (2) castanets (blocks of wood) or clapping and snapping fingers. Try to interest some child in making a drum and use this drum in accompaniment of songs. Introduce "marimba" in as many ways as possible—pictures and stories—hoping someone will be interested in making one (eight glasses or bottles, containing graduated amounts of water and producing the tones of scale when the glass is tapped, is a *marimba;* also, eight pieces of hard wood of graduated lengths producing scale tones when tapped make a marimba or a xylophone). Aim at using rhythmic dramatizations in culminating activity *even if the music used as accompaniment is not Mexican.*

Group 7. Fifth Grade

ANALYSIS AND EVALUATION: Group leaders are "sophisticated," interested only in popular songs; refuse to sing material in their books; ape a popular teen-age group in as many ways as possible.

PLAN: *Teach* no popular songs, but teach syllable names of the notes of some. Teach them to "conduct" a favorite song. Use recurring rhythm patterns as material for gaining a feeling for note values. Analyze form. Should it happen that one melody has been "lifted" from the classics, obtain the original and use it for listening. If a song pertains to any specific group or place, use it as motivation for studying that group or place. Capitalize on the *good* that is in the material and hope to guide toward wider interests. (One teacher who had such a group broadened its interest by using music recorded in Africa and included the folk songs sung by Josef Marais.

She also showed the group how knowing syllable names of notes can make it easier to play a tune by "ear" on the piano.)

Group 8. Sixth Grade

ANALYSIS AND EVALUATION: Eight overgrown boys have been transferred to the group. They have had no previous experience in music and constitute a disrupting influence in the class composed of musically interested, experienced, and capable children.

PLAN: To find out if boys can sing, teach a simple, new "fun" song to the entire class and listen carefully to the boys' efforts. If they do not do well, re-read the section on "The Poor Singer" and apply some of the suggestions to the situation. Be wary about asking boys to sing alone. If they can sing, make up a simple series of tones that harmonize with some favorite songs. Teach them to the whole class and then help the boys to sing those tones while the class sings the melody. Plan and use percussion accompaniments. Show them how to make xylophones. Make it possible for them to make a contribution to the group and its endeavors. It is not their fault that (1) they were transferred; (2) they have had no experience in music; (3) they are overgrown; and (4) their voices are changing. After a week or so, it is possible *they* could make helpful suggestions about what they could and would do. Perhaps one of them could make some scenery for a play or some cases for the recordings. They must be brought into the group and made to feel comfortable.

> *Note:* Quite often groups of children from an outlying area are transferred to the fifth or sixth grade of the elementary schools in town. Too often, these children are considered an "out" group. Their *new* teacher has the same responsibility for them as she has for the "in" group.

Group 9. Fourth Grade

ANALYSIS AND EVALUATION: Area of interest—China's contribution to our country. No music materials—recordings, or songs available.

PLAN: Introduce the pentatonic scale: sing *do–re–mi–sol–la* (1–2–3–5–6). Make a tune by singing *la* between each tone of the scale. Sing *mi–sol–la;* hold *la.* (If a piano is available, *play* these combinations, too.) Select simple Chinese verse; place it on the board and scan; sing pentatonic scale tone combinations again to re-establish tonality. Using these tones, make up a melody for the verse. For "authentic" accompaniment (use sparingly) refer to the section on the "Music of China" in Chapter 12. After several experiences such as this, the group will have the "feeling" of Chinese music.

Group 10. Sixth Grade

ANALYSIS AND EVALUATION: Singing is the only background experience. Most of the songs the group knows—including *all* the community type songs—have been learned incorrectly. Phonograph records and piano not available. Only material is a community song book for each child.

PLAN: Since it is more difficult to correct a song learned incorrectly than it is to teach a new song, ignore all the old songs except a few community songs. Teach new songs correctly and concentrate on developing physical response to music. Teach conductor's beat while you sing one of the incorrectly learned songs. *Do not allow the class to sing wrong tone or time again.* If, for example, there are wrong tones and time in *The Star-Spangled Banner,* sing it while the class beats. Next, have the class whisper the words (not singing), exaggerating those that fall on Beat 1 throughout the song. After hearing the correct tune several times, invite the class with your hand to sing the sections they sing correctly; signal them to stop singing before the incorrect sections are sung; and invite them to start again, and so forth. After learning the conductor's beat, class can learn to walk or step to tunes. Teach them to "harmonize" melodies; provide experiences that will make them enjoy learning every song in their book. Use the words to inspire individual research and group activity and as suggestions for art work. Even such meager resources can be used to great advantage and for great enjoyment.

Group 11. Fifth and Sixth Grades

ANALYSIS AND EVALUATION: Organized music program is being introduced this year. A little group singing comprises the total background experience of the children. The sixth grade will enter Junior High School next year. Which phases and activities of the music program shall be included in plans for these children this year?

PLAN: (1) Give each child the use of his singing voice and the opportunity to develop and enjoy his sense of rhythm. (2) Concentrate on the "feeling" aspects of music: favorable attitude toward it, interest in it, willingness to participate in it. (3) Give each child a concept of *how* tones are made: experiment with instruments to discover the relation of size and length of vibrating material to pitch. (4) Realizing that the concept of the relation between a tone produced vocally and its symbol is more difficult to gain than is the idea of the relation between pitch produced by manipulation of strings, keys, or holes and its symbol, teach children to play a simple instrument such as a tonette, melody flute, or xylophone-like instrument. (5) Make it possible for children to hear some of the world's fine music. If most of the group have radios, direct attention to scheduled programs. "Guide" out-of-school listening by giving specifics for which to listen —musical instruments, composers, and so forth. Try to guide those listening experiences in such a way that school time can be devoted to those phases that require personal direction. (6) In assemblies teach "fun" and "camp" songs.

> *Note:* Continue to expand the program for next year's sixth grade. (Those children are now in the fifth grade.)

Group 12. The "New" Music Teacher

ANALYSIS AND EVALUATION: The "new" music teacher—new to the school or new to the children or new in experience—is about to meet groups of children for the first time.

PLAN: Before the meeting, the "new" teacher should: (1) find out the children's general musical background experience and their teachers' background and attitude toward music-teaching; (2) meet their teachers, if possible; and (3) if the new teacher is supposed to "teach" at this meeting, get specific information as to some songs the children know and their experience in rhythms—"specific" means a *list* of favorite songs.

A gracious social atmosphere should permeate this meeting: the teacher introduced to the children and the children introduced to the teacher, and "You sang for me, so I shall sing for you." For the music teacher, it is a "bait-throwing" occasion—"bait" of the finest, most attractive kind; music most likely to appeal, made by the new music teacher. For example, a group of folk songs children in the whole school might learn to sing in assembly, sung by the teacher and accompanied, perhaps, by the Autoharp, piano (if it can be played while looking at the children) or violin; or songs children know, sung by the teacher, then by children and teacher (a favorite song is excellent "bait") and repeated with a simple rhythmic response added; or songs sung by the teacher and then played on a recording with children responding rhythmically—the recording to be left with the children, the songs to be learned before the next visit. The same program can be repeated for several groups.

> *Caution:* Be armed with specifics: a list of songs children know and a list *you* know. Have a plan—it's easier to change a plan than to have to devise one on the spur of the moment. You can discuss your plan with the classroom teacher before meeting the class. Your plan will make you act as if you *knew* what you were trying to do, as if you were certain, not floun-

dering, because you *do* know. Don't say "Do you want to. . . .?
(What would you do if they said "No"? That question can
become an irritating and bad habit.) Say, instead, "Let's. . . ."
Don't say "Do you know . . . ?" and expect children to be able
to sing what they say they "know": they might mean they have
heard it or they recognize it. Find out ahead of time what they
know. Don't talk much about what you're going to do—*do* it.
You make music and let them make music. Music is the area of
common interest and music is the point of contact and music
is the medium for attaining the desired goal of aiding children's
growth and development.

For Discussion

1. List specifics of music's possible contributions to the physical,
   social, intellectual, and emotional growth of children who are
   studying the "Natural Resources of Our State."
2. Examine two series of music texts. Select books of each song
   series (music texts) that should be in the hands of children in
   each grade during the first year of an organized music program.
   Justify your selections on the basis of child interest and need.
3. Justify your selection of books for each grade during the second
   year of this program.
4. Plan a program of activities for the children of the fourth grade
   in the same school as Group 11, discussed on page 283.
5. In some communities when books are adopted, the sixth book
   of the series is placed in the sixth grade regardless of whether
   it fits the needs of the children. *Problem:* Analyze the ability
   and background of a sixth-grade group (or "make-up" an analysis). Using the sixth-grade book of any series as a basis, plan a
   program that will result in the growth and development of *your*
   sixth-grade group. (*That* is an example of fitting material to
   children, rather than of trying to fit children to material.)
6. Plan an outline of the "sequence of growth" in each area of
   the music program. Save it and use it as a checklist for planning the "next" activity.

Suggestions for Music Students

1. Music's contribution to social studies is important. Examine
   the Courses of Study of five schools or the curriculums published by three State Departments of Education (two neighboring states and your own) to discover if there is a pattern in

suggested areas of interest or areas of activity for each of the elementary grades. Collect the music materials for any two areas—songs to sing, songs to play, music "live" and recorded —and plan possible ways materials could be used and possible activity for developing the physical being, the emotional being, the intellectual being, the social being, the creative being that is a child.

2. From your examination of Courses of Study, list the areas where European style music is *foreign* music. Become well-informed about two non-European styles and decide how to direct listening so children can become informed. What idealized music is available in "your" styles? Compare it with the authentic. Aim to become an "expert" in relation to these areas and their music. Aim to become an expert in two other areas next year. Collect material and save it.

3. Acquire to a greater degree the skills listed for classroom teachers; for example, learn to play both chords *and* melodies on the Autoharp and harmolin; learn to use augmented and diminished chords as well as fundamental chords in improvised accompaniments; collect and record songs children make up while at play. If you are to be *judged* a superior musician, you must *be* superior in the areas where classroom teachers are competent.

4. And, you must keep abreast of the times, musically as well as in other matters. For many people in your community you are Mr. or Miss or Mrs. Music. You know everything about music! (?) When your sketch of the seating arrangement of a symphony orchestra is the conventional plan, taken from a book, and does not coincide with what youngsters saw on television last night, explanations will be in order. You *must* be informed about programs children are likely to see.

5. Workers in a huge industrial plan characterized their foreman by saying, "You can *talk* to him" or "You can *ask* him things when you don't understand." Discuss the implications of these comments as related to democratic leadership.

6. Plan your own "program" to use when you are introduced as the "new" music teacher. Build it around your area of greatest competency and be certain to include something the children can do or take part in.

Additional Aids

in Teaching Music

It is hoped that this book, with the suggestions, plans, and devices it contains, will be a major aid in teaching. Many other aids are available. However, mere availability does not assure their use nor their intelligent use. If the precepts of *teaching for appreciation* are constantly kept in mind, these aids are more likely to fulfill their promise of enlarging or crystallizing concepts, of promoting further study and investigation, and of stimulating learning.

Along with auditory, visual, and certain miscellaneous aids there is another group that is important for its inspirational, psychological effect. True, if "anything goes wrong" for the individual, the psychological effect remains, but it is definitely not "inspirational!"

PSYCHOLOGICAL AIDS

Although some of the aids not mentioned here do have or can have an inspirational effect, those listed have unusual possibilities.

Public Performance

Our society puts its stamp of approval on those who can perform well in public. For that reason "being in a show" or "being on a program" gives status to an individual. It is a mark of distinction. It sets him apart from, and a bit above, the crowd. Contribution to any part of the program is approved, too.

Attendance at Concerts

Inspiration often comes with hearing and seeing experts perform and sometimes results in a determination to do equally well. Standards of excellence can be gained; direction toward a specific goal can become more pointed; emotional satisfaction can be great.

Many people believe that young children, perhaps the five- to nine-year-old group, gain more from hearing and seeing competent children perform than they do from hearing adult artists. Some parents and teachers refute that idea by presenting evidence of the children's obvious enjoyment and appreciation of the artistry of adult performers. And, when these performers are near, instead of on a stage, the gains are greater for these little folks.

To make certain that some, if not all, inspirational, emotional, and intellectual delights are realized, it is an excellent idea to give children some definite things for which to listen: the accuracy of the pianist's (or the violinist's) fingers, the singer's breath control, the relation between the soloist and accompanist, the way the orchestra men watch the conductor, or the variations in the conductor's beat, and so forth. Familiarity with the music heard in a concert adds considerable pleasure.

A concert in the schoolroom or auditorium can give as much or more pleasure than the really formal one. Inspirational, emotional, and intellectual delight does not have to be accompanied by a long journey or late hours.

Special Music-Making Groups and Music Clubs

Children who are gifted musically have more opportunity to grow and develop by participation in special singing groups, choirs—for boys and for girls—and music clubs.

Song material for these singing groups is easily available. It is usually more difficult than that used in class. Standards for performance are higher even though it is readily acknowledged that some classes sing better than some glee clubs! Even so, choir performance is usually on a higher level artistically than is class singing.

An instrumental group in which any or all of the players of orchestral, pre-orchestral chording, and rhythm instruments perform together is possible. When it prepares to accompany group singing, practice then has motivation if motivation be necessary.

Music clubs offer additional opportunities for gifted students. When children themselves decide on the area in music to be studied, plan their own programs, and prepare their musical contribution independently (or with the help of their private teachers), they can have a rich experience. Ideally, should they decide to study the music of Spain, *they* would gather background material; *they* would search for examples of music; *they* would plan what the students would learn to play; and *they* would decide what recordings of which artists to use. Once started, such a group needs relatively little supervision, especially if the children have acquired independent work habits in their classes.

> *Note:* Sometime, though, someone somewhere is going to take those children who do not sing very well and whose sense of rhythm is not at a very high level of development and who are, therefore, not too welcome as members of the *elite* groups

and make a performing group out of them. Or, organize a music club for those not quite as interested as those mentioned above —organize it on a different basis, a do-it-yourself basis, for example.

The Music Assembly

An assembly devoted to music and activities related to music can have the same good psychological effects of concert attendance and public performance. It offers opportunity for special singing groups, music clubs, and grade groups to share their experiences with others in the school. Children who ordinarily might not be invited to "be on a program" have the thrill of appearing in public when their class contributes to a program. Program notes prepared and presented by the children are valuable for both the audience and the participants.

Assembly Singing

Singing with a large group can be a most satisfying experience. However, for it to be satisfying someone must give the activity some attention. Assembly singing must not be incidental or left to chance.

One important aspect of group singing often—in fact, too often—escapes attention. People cannot sing together unless they know the same songs. Song sheets, slides, the leader, books, or memories must supply the words. Children in the first and second grades cannot read well enough to use printed materials. Songs they know can be extended by adding simple descants or "drones" supplied by the leader.

In some schools, the first three grades and the upper grades have separate assemblies. The younger children learn their songs by rote.

Assembly time can be used to learn community and patriotic songs. A list of songs for the grades assembling together is prepared. They are introduced, discussed, and partially learned in the classroom. Sometimes a recording is used to insure no variation in interpretation of symbols by teachers. This list is amplified by the occasional popular song that delights children; or the list is augmented by songs groups enjoy in their classroom. Quite a bit of time and energy are wasted when songs enjoyed in one grade are never referred to or thought of again. Actually, they can serve as a reservoir of assembly song material.

Assembly singing can be so valuable and so pleasurable that it should receive considerable thought and attention.

USING AUDIO-VISUAL AIDS

Audio-visual materials as aids in teaching music are increasing yearly. The day of one record player and one piano (and one pitch pipe!) in a school is past. The general public as well as school personnel are well aware of the worth of these aids. The important consideration is: are they used to the best advantage? Much of the necessary equipment is expensive, and its purchase can be justified only in terms of its wide and intelligent use.

It is suggested that the purchase of equipment be the result of a teacher decision rather than of an administrator decision. After a demonstration of the equipment and some materials and after a discussion of the ways it could be used, teachers will have an idea as to whether it *would* be used.

The wide use of equipment and materials depends on its easy availability, and its intelligent use depends on teachers. Mere availability, however, does not assure that the potential value will be realized. Children go to the movies, watch television, and listen to the radio by the hour, read dozens of books, and play records in their out-of-school time and we know that all the potential learning therein is not realized. Upon the teacher, then, rests the responsibility for making these possible aids to learning *actual* aids.

Teachers must know the techniques of using these materials as teaching aids and *act* as if they knew, lest they be accused of being like the farmer who refused assistance in making his farm more productive by saying "I don't need help—I don't farm now as well as I know how."

To be able to direct conscious attention to specifics in material for the purpose of becoming aware of the implication of material, teachers must pre-audit and pre-view it as well as know how to manipulate the mechanical equipment by which it is presented.

Pre-Audit and Pre-View

Hearing or seeing material before it is to be used is the only way a teacher can know its value. Doing so will prevent certain situations that can cause embarrassment. Consider the experiences of a group that was studying American Indians. They were pleased when their teacher said they were going to see a film about Indians. They trooped happily into the room where it was to be shown. As they watched, puzzled expressions could be seen on their faces in the half light. Through this experience they became aware of the fact that the people of India are Indians, too. Their teacher had not pre-viewed the film.

Perhaps you have had the following experience: In the middle of a discussion about music, the teacher goes to the phonograph, picks up the playing arm, and puts it down, saying, "Here is an example." After the record plays for a few seconds, she picks up the arm and says, "No, that wasn't it, but here it is." This performance is repeated several times. If the record had been studied, pre-audited, and *marked*, this could have been avoided. (A red pencil can be used to mark records.)

Mechanical Equipment

When teachers know how to operate the available equipment correctly, material is more likely to be used at the moment of its greatest timeliness. It is not particularly exciting nor stimulating to hear: "Three weeks from tomorrow we shall see an example of this in a film." If three other people are necessary to help show a film, the psychologically right time may slip by. Most adults approach a phonograph or radio with little apprehension because of their familiarity with the mechanism. It is equally as easy to operate film-strip projectors, recording devices, and moving-picture projectors.

It should never be assumed that mechanical equipment is in working order. It is wise "to try it out" before starting to operate it for a group. It is a fact that when several people use equipment, the likelihood of damage to machines increases. For that reason, all persons who might need to use it *should be taught* to use it. Capturing the interest of children and enhancing their learning must not be circumscribed by limiting the use of mechanical equipment that can be repaired or replaced, if necessary.

Source of Materials

Many universities, colleges, museums, and libraries, as well as many school systems, maintain audio-visual libraries and services, and issue catalogues listing available materials. Often, the audio-visual center of the city school system is equipped to offer its services to neighboring communities.

But for wide and continual use, nothing helps more than having some materials and equipment always in the building— a *school* center for teaching aids and materials.

The area encompassed in the school program is now so vast an individual teacher can scarcely hope to keep track of materials that are known to be helpful and those that might be. Therefore, a collection, cooperatively acquired and for use by all, is suggested. A file of information is a necessary adjunct— the type suggested for records in Chapter 6. For example, it should be noted for future reference that the film *Dances Around the World* contains material on homes and national dress, as well as dances.

AUDITORY AND VISUAL AIDS

No listing of Aids in Teaching Music can be up-to-date because these aids are increasing daily in amazing and exciting numbers. After studying the available materials in the exhibits of the last Music Educators Conference, a teacher said: "If we don't do a good job of teaching music *now*, we have only ourselves to blame." That is true.

Creative teaching talent in conjunction with willing manufacturing talent is producing excellent materials to be used with excellent machines beyond the hopes and dreams of a few years ago. Although all items of material and equipment are not the finest, each represents the honest effort of someone to make an aspect of music-teaching more effective. There will always be some disagreement in evaluating materials but, since manufacturing costs are at an all-time high, *some* agreement must have been reached as to the worth of an item before manufacturers risked capital in producing it. Perhaps *you* wouldn't have it, but it may take care of someone else's need *exactly*.

Books for children and adults about music and musicians, collections of folk songs, and books of songs of almost all types are appearing with great frequency. More than four hundred companies are printing recordings.

Educational television stations are now a fact. Educational radio programs are more generally available.

This next statement is *not* meant to be facetious: It may be that each school will soon have to appoint a person to be the Acquirer and Cataloger, the Keeper and Disseminator of Information About and Information Related to Materials Available in the Area of Audio-Visual Aids for Music. Such a person would be the only one who *could* keep well-informed. Until that happens, it is suggested that others devote some time and study to material in at least one area, or to material about at least one source of information.

If we can learn to capitalize on even a few of these aids, children and music will surely be brought closer together.

Records

In the chapter on "listening," recorded music's possible contribution to learning was discussed.

In the bibliography, *Sources of Materials* contains information related to obtaining records. Information about records and music is a regular feature of the following: *Saturday Review, Parents' Magazine, Consumer Reports* [1], *Harper's, The Atlantic Monthly, Good Housekeeping,* the Sunday *New York Times,* the Sunday *New York Herald Tribune,* the Sunday editions of other newspapers, and the magazine and bulletins published by the Association for Childhood Education International.

Records are available for each book of each of the major song series, as are suggestions to teachers for using them. Folk dance music *plus* calls (directions) are available. Music of most of the world's ethnic groups has been recorded. The wealth of material in the archives of the Music Division of the Library of Congress is gradually being made ready for the general public. The publishers of the reputable Golden Books have prepared a set of Golden Records for children. Various state universities are recording and making available music of their own geographical areas as well as books about local music.

Films

The makers of commercial films are fully aware of the importance of using music to enhance mood. They use the works of classic, as well as contemporary, composers. However, many people in an audience do not consciously hear this music. The attention of elementary school children can well be directed to film music, and before seeing a movie in which well-known music is an integral and important part, they can become familiar with the selections that are used.

A teacher has more opportunity to pre-audit an educational film. As the result of the pre-audit, she is prepared to guide listening as she does the experience of listening to recorded music.

[1] Beatrice Landeck reviews records for children several times a year in *Consumer Reports.*

Recording Devices

Recording devices and play-back machines are invaluable aids in the areas of speech and vocal music. Pitch, tone quality, and precision of attack and release can be studied in recordings children make of their own singing.

In some schools songs recorded on a tape recorder are used by nonsinging teachers and for teaching songs to be sung in assembly by several classes. It has been used to record children's original songs.

Some teachers consider the tape recorder one of the most useful teaching aids. It has been used to record music for basic rhythms, to show the progress made by poor singers, to record stories with appropriate musical accompaniment, to furnish a consistent accompaniment for an all-school outdoor program—eliminating the need for moving the piano—and to provide a model for songs to be learned for assembly singing.

Pitch Pipe

A pitch pipe is the one teaching aid listed here that is indispensable. Even those few teachers who have absolute pitch can make many uses of it. The pitch pipe has been referred to many times in this book. Suggestions and directions for its use have been given. It is mentioned here *in the hope* teachers will be further impressed with its importance.

Radio

Radio is generally considered a better tool for motivating and supplementing learning than it is for teaching. Those who are best informed and most enthusiastic about classroom use of radio say its potential value is slowly being realized. The expanding use of electronics in FM (frequency modulation) is significant in developing radio education.

FM is a method of sending radio waves and has certain advantages over AM (amplitude modulation). These are: (1) greater fidelity of tone, (2) freedom from static, (3) opportunity for a large number of stations to operate without interference, and (4) relatively small expense in construction and maintenance of broadcasting and receiving equipment. FM permits schools to operate their own equipment without dependence on commercial stations.

Educational Television

Before many of us had learned how to use either an audio- or visual-aid effectively and to its fullest advantage, an audio-visual aid—television—was developed. At the end of 1959 there were television sets in eighty-six per cent of the homes across the nation. Before many of us had sensed its possible importance as a teaching aid, *educational* television had arrived. It is in its infancy but it has potentialities so great they stagger the imagination.

How did educational television start? What is its scope? What are its effects on learning? What are its effects on teaching? What are its potentialities?

The History of Educational Television. Permission to telecast (and broadcast) lies solely with the Federal Communications Commission, which licenses a station and fixes a designated channel within which it can operate. In 1945, the first thirteen channels were assigned to commercial telecasting stations. In 1948, the Commission "froze" the number of stations by refusing to grant new licenses when the demand for new stations became great. The Commission announced it would study the problem and formulate a policy for licensing new stations during the freeze. It was during this "freeze" that a movement started for noncommercial stations, providing educational and cultural programs for communities. The movement not only grew but it also became "vocal"—with the result that when the "freeze" was lifted on April 14, 1952, the Commission reserved two hundred and fifty-one channels throughout the nation for noncommercial educational use, a number sufficient for two thousand stations.

From the time the "freeze" was lifted until April, 1953, one hundred seventy-two new commercial TV stations were established—but no Educational Television stations. TV stations are expensive. ETV stations seem doubly so when the requirements for being granted a license are met.

A license is granted an ETV station on these terms: it cannot accept advertising—it is noncommercial, nonprofit; it must be run exclusively for the educational, instructional, and cultural enlightenment of the people; and it must be available to all qualified educational and cultural institutions within the reception area. $250,000 was the lowest estimated cost for establishing a station and from $100,000 to $200,000 or more was necessary to operate for a year. Thus, those who were interested in establishing ETV stations discovered considerable money was needed.

The Ford Foundation Fund for Adult Education made two important contributions at this time: money and expert assistance. The Fund set aside $8,000,000 and established:

1. the Joint Committee on Educational Television, which cooperates with and represents seven of the nation's leading educational groups and offers engineering and legal services to local ETV groups;

2. the National Citizens Committee for Educational Television, which aids local groups in organizing, raising funds, and publicizing ETV; and

3. the Educational Television and Radio Center, a clearing house for programs and ideas, housing and exchanging film and kinescope programs of the best that America's cultural institutions have to offer. This service thus makes it possible for local stations to maintain a high standard of programs.

Money was made available under certain circumstances by the Fund to help cover the capital costs of a station—often one dollar for each two raised locally. Where did the "two" come from? Local foundations, commercial TV stations, school systems, institutions and people—individuals and groups: clubs, PTA's, unions, and so on. Currently, thirty-seven per cent of the money for ETV comes from local contributions, thirty-five per cent from state tax funds, twelve per cent from boards of education and/or colleges and universities, and sixteen per cent from the Fund for Adult Education.

Some Facts of ETV. Let's consider some of the *facts* of educational television. As we consider, remember that (a) TV started in 1945, (b) the first ETV station—University of Houston—started telecasting in May, 1953 and (c) any listing in *this* area, particularly, is outdated the day it is made!

1. As of December, 1959, there were forty-five ETV stations on the air, eight were under construction and in ten communities there had been advanced planning toward construction and operation of ETV stations. And, negotiations were under way to tape or film a two-year college curriculum (fifteen courses) by 1964.

2. Closed circuit TV systems are numerous. They are used in two ways: instruction *in* TV and instruction *by* TV. The area of use is wide and varied: teaching all elementary and high school subjects, giving laboratory courses in TV and technical training and instruction in speech, observing teaching and children in laboratory and public schools, demonstrating surgical anatomy, training supervisory personnel in industry, training and instructing military forces, discovering TV teaching talent, teaching psychiatry and so on.

3. Over sixty-one million people live within broadcast range of ETV. There were 561 TV stations and 50,500,000 sets in use in the United States in December, 1959.

An Appraisal of the Facts. 1. In terms of ETV's short history those facts are amazing. They result from cooperation among groups of people: elementary and high school and college teachers; commercial TV personnel and college students and industry; the Junior League, unions, and the medical profession; PTA's, world famous museums and police departments; parents, professional musicians, and authors; guests in our country from around the world, university presidents, and the Atomic Energy Commission—just *some* of the groups making

ETV possible and just some of the groups making ETV programs possible.

2. People want to learn and to be informed. The response to courses offered for credit is one proof; the request for programs for special groups is another; and, the sought-for and received reactions is still another.

3. Teaching by television is effective. In some instances the same course has been taught by the same instructor to one group *via* television and to another group in the usual class situation. When both groups were tested, the one taught by television remembered more. The Army and the Navy and medical schools also testify to its effectiveness.

It is the consensus that televised instruction requires students to accept more responsibility for their own learning. Moreover, they use the library more than students in regular classes.

It is the consensus, too, that telecasts have been an important means of upgrading the level of teaching. The studio teacher not only helps the beginning teacher but has taught the best teachers new techniques.

Music on ETV. The following are *kinds* of music programs on ETV:

1. Learning to play the piano. Several series of such programs designed or planned for elementary school teachers were followed by high school students and young and older adults as well.

2. Demonstration of orchestral instruments—the making of instruments, the mechanism, how they are played, and so on. Performance by well-known artists, college students, and good child performers are aspects of the general pattern.

3. A class of five-year-old children in pre-instrument musical activities guided by an expert in this area of teaching.

4. Rhythmic activities of elementary shcool children in which children in school are invited to join.

5. Teaching elementary school children United States history through folk songs.

6. Demonstration of types of voices and the mechanism of singing.

7. Demonstrations of instrumental and vocal ensembles.

8. Concerts by local groups and individuals including the participants in state high school music festivals.

9. Learning to play the ukulele and guitar.

10. Filmed programs, featuring the finest professional musical talent. In some areas which do not yet have ETV these programs are being shown on commercial stations with a nonprofit agency paying the rental fee. The series of programs can be rented at a nominal fee from the National Educational Television Film Center, located in the Audio Visual Center of Indiana University, Bloomington, Indiana.

Teaching and ETV. Sight plus sound—television—is among the most effective media in conveying facts and concepts and in aiding memory retention. Experts agree, however, that in many instances viewing is not enough—doing must be related to viewing. When doing can accompany or coincide with viewing, learning is more certainly assured. Authorities agree, too, that regardless of the expertness of the teacher on television, the teacher of the class watching a telecast has a definite responsibility and a distinctive role.

It is the teacher's responsibility to prepare children for what they are about to see by relating it to what they know and to what they would like or want to know.

Having viewed a telecast, the teacher's role is that of "chairman of the meeting," helping children relate the material of the program to what they knew and what they wanted to know. A televised teacher cannot act as coordinator of information.

When doing is suggested to coincide with viewing, the teacher is a doer, too. An observer, also—with that extra pair of eyes mentioned previously in this book—but not an obvious observer.

Teachers must be informed as to the programs children see. It is impossible for each teacher to see each program each child sees. It is not impossible to know in general what programs are telecast and to view one of each series. Nor is it impossible to become informed about "favorites."

ETV can be the means by which the *art of teaching* is studied. Those teachers telecasting during school and after school are doing so because someone decided *they could teach.* Some of them are experts. Opportunity to study the *art of teaching* is the reason "observation of teaching" is included in the undergraduate and in-service teacher education program—but prospective teachers are not experienced enough and frequently do not have sufficient perception to sense the *art* in teaching. It may be that directing conscious attention, time after time, to artistry in teaching will develop perception. After teachers *start* teaching, it is possible for them to see more teachers-in-action in one month on ETV than in a lifetime of attending "demonstrations"—always a preferred and effective way of studying teaching. ETV can be the means by which the *art of teaching* is studied—it *can be,* when viewing is combined with doing. "Doing" here means "directing conscious attention to, thinking about and analyzing."

ETV is new. It is important. It can be revolutionary in its effect. Its very foundation is good teaching, artful teaching, skillful teaching. Its very life is good teaching: materials presented in an orderly fashion, emphasis on telling points, a change of pace precisely as needed, economy of word in presenting a wealth of ideas. If ETV does not exemplify good teaching it will die—good teaching in newscasts, good teaching in "how-to-do" programs, good teaching in presenting the third-grade chorus—teaching so skillful, in many instances, that only the alert and knowing will recognize it for what it is.

Some of the most popular and important current programs are conducted by teachers. Become so good yourself that you will be sought for a program. If you don't fancy yourself as a television artist, contribute ideas about programs and for programs. ETV is *our* job and *our* responsibility.

Film Strips

One of the advantages of the film strip is that the picture projected can be discussed for several minutes or it can be re-projected for comparison without delay or inconvenience.

Some film strips impose the responsibility for interpretation upon the teacher. Others do not.

Refer to Sources of Materials in this book for information about available film strips.

A film strip projector is relatively inexpensive and easy to operate.

Music Books in the Elementary School Library

Here "library" means a "collection of books." It does not refer to a means of housing such a collection.

There are books about music and musical instruments, as well as books containing music for both children and teachers, that should be readily available. The listing is constantly expanding.

Books for Children. The following list gives the areas of music and those pertaining to music for which books should be available:

1. Musical instruments
   The Making of Musical Instruments by T. Campbell Young Satis Coleman's books
   Drums, Tomtoms, and Rattles by Bernard S. Mason
   What Makes an Orchestra by J. B. Balet
2. Composers and their works
   Biographies of Composers by Opal Wheeler and Sybil Deucher
3. Stories of operas
   Opera Stories by Robert Lawrence (Metropolitan Opera Guild Edition)
4. Music and song books
   Collections of simple piano music
   Collections of folk songs
5. Encyclopedia and reference books
   Britannica Junior

History Sings by Hazel Kinscella
Growing Up with Music Series by Beatrice Perham

Books for Classroom Teachers. Books pertaining to the following areas should be readily available for teachers:

1. Folk songs of other lands
   Folk Songs of Many Lands by Hendrick Willem Van Loon
   Songs of Many Lands by Thomas Surette
2. American folk songs
   Folk Song—U. S. A. by John and Alden Lomax
   Collections by Ruth Crawford Seeger
3. Folk dances and music
   The American Square Dance by Margot Mayo
   The Folk Dance Library by Anne S. Duggan, Jeanette Schlott-
   mann, and Abbie Rutledge
4. Background information
5. Songs for children
   Copies of all the books in the major song series
6. Culture of various peoples
7. Teaching
8. Piano music
   Collections of piano music for various degrees of pianistic ability

Bulletin Board

In one class, a Music Bulletin Board Committee is appointed each month. Its duty is to collect and display materials in three categories: (1) Our Present Study, (2) Our Past Interests, and (3) Interesting Facts about Music. A notice is often placed on the bulletin board saying that a new book is in the library or that a magazine article on a certain subject or a collection of pictures is on the reading table. One day there appeared three short sentences on the topic, "Why I Like *Till Eulen-spiegel's Merry Pranks.*" Another time there was a listing of "Hit Tunes"—favorite class songs.

The collection of the materials on the Music Bulletin Board might well be assembled in a class scrapbook.

Individual Scrapbooks

Older children love to keep a music scrapbook. Sometimes,

the collector concentrates on finding pictures of composers, pictures of orchestral instruments, or pictures showing an artist's concept of a musical composition. More often, though, the material includes anything relating to the music that a collector fancies.

MISCELLANEOUS AIDS

The first two aids to teaching music that are discussed here might well have been included in the listing of inspirational psychological aids. However, they will be considered more as a result of, rather than a cause of, inspiration.

Orchestral Instrument Classes

Responsibility for teaching classes in orchestral instruments is usually assumed by specialists in that area to prepare children for the school orchestra. However, some classroom teachers have been eminently successful in teaching them. This means of teaching is sometimes used by teachers who do not sing well or with confidence. Often technical skill is not developed to an outstanding degree—but understanding and pleasure are.

The associated learning of such classes can pervade the whole music program. The fact that some children do not continue their study is not too important—they have had another contact with music even though they do not have the talent nor, perhaps, the interest to pursue their study further.

Pre-Orchestral Instrument Classes

The use of pre-orchestral instruments in the classroom has been suggested many times in this book. Such instruments include melody-making wind instruments and sets of tuned bells. Their merits are: (1) They are inexpensive; (2) satisfying skill can be acquired in a short time; (3) they can be taught by the classroom teacher; and (4) it is easier to learn to read music through these instruments than through the voice, since tones depend on mechanical manipulation and not on the musical memory.

It is essential that only those instruments that are accurately tuned be purchased. If the scale they produce is not exact and true, more damage will be done in establishing the wrong concept of tonal relationship than can possibly be overcome by all the good resulting from their use.

Piano

The piano is an important aid to teaching because it (1) can be used in each phase of the music program, and (2) makes possible a richer music experience for children in that it can produce both melody and accompaniment.

The possibilities of its contributions are limited only by the skill of the teacher, and whether or not it is kept in tune. The skill of the classroom teacher was discussed in Chapter 8.

The tautness of the piano's strings is affected by weather, use, and moving. But sometimes it is difficult to convince those who control the purse strings of the importance and the necessity of tuning. It is common knowledge that a violinist or a 'cellist tunes his instrument before playing. By directing attention to that fact, one can often convince those in charge that a piano must be tuned. Each school piano should be mounted on large rubber-tired casters for ease in moving and as an aid in maintaining pitch.

Autoharp and Harmolin

The Autoharp and harmolin are zither-like instruments with bars placed at right angles over the strings. When these bars are pressed, certain strings are automatically selected to make designated chords as the strings are plucked. Each bar is marked so that important chords of several keys can be played. The player needs only to know the chords he wants to play in order to use the Autoharp or harmolin.

They are useful as (1) accompanying instruments and (2)

a means of experimenting with tone. They can make some of the important contributions of the piano.

For Discussion

1. Under what circumstances could all music activities be psychological aids to learning?
2. Recall some good music assemblies about which you know.
3. Analyze your reactions to the program notes of a concert.
4. What are the two audio-visual centers nearest you? Audio-visual libraries? Do they offer recordings, films, film strips, tape recordings, projection machines, or experts to demonstrate material and equipment?
5. What programs for elementary children do the two FM stations nearest you offer? Are their booklets for teachers interesting?
6. What would be wrong with showing an educational film to a group in the morning and again in the afternoon with the period in between being used partially for discussing it? What would be good about such a practice?
7. Make two series of eight simple sketches to be used as material for a film strip to illustrate the mechanism or development of two musical instruments. Suggest some other related subjects for film strips.
8. What is the difference between the screen used for sound films and the one used for silent films? How much does each cost? How much does a projector for silent films cost? For sound films? What does 16mm mean?
9. Experiment with an inexpensive white window blind to discover its potentialities as a projection screen.
10. Learn to play a simple tune on your pitch pipe.
11. Experiment with an Autoharp. List its uses and potentialities against those of the piano.
12. Elaborate on the use of the tape recorder.
13. What educational television programs are available in your area? What suggestions have you as to how they would more nearly meet the needs of your children?
14. How many ETV stations are *now* telecasting? What courses for credit are *now* being offered in your area?
15. Become informed about your ETV station: how money was

raised; source of professional personnel; types of program—live and filmed; community participants; and so on.

16. Report on the educational programs presented by your nearest radio and TV stations. (Make your own definition of "educational"—your definition and the station's might differ.) Prepare a similar report on "Programs for Children."

17. Unleash your imagination. Within the limits of actual development, make your own list of the potentialities of ETV. Then, within the limits of three inventions *you* suggest, make another list of ETV's potentialities. Include music in each list. (Including the Ford Fund for Adult Education or its equivalent doesn't count!)

Music's Role in Under-

standing Other Peoples

"It's a small world!"—how rapidly that cliché has become a fact! Daily we are confronted with evidence. Transportation and communication have changed so that a once distant place can be reached within a matter of hours and headline news there becomes headline news here almost simultaneously. Our people go to those once "romantic" spots and their people come here. Thus, differences in a "way of life" are constantly brought to our attention. Our children must be conditioned to accept these differences and to understand that many of them are only superficial—not really fundamental.

THE NEED FOR UNDERSTANDING

This need for understanding has been reiterated by responsible groups in our society:

They (young Americans) need to know how people in other parts of the world live, what they wish for, what they believe. They need to know what is happening around the world today. These things the schools of this nation have taught for many years. They must continue to teach them if they are to remain true to their trust.[1]

The President's Commission on Higher Education has among those "goals which should come first in our time": "Education directly and explicitly for international understanding and co-operation." [2]

Article 26 of the "Universal Declaration of Human Rights" as adopted by the General Assembly of the United Nations on December 10, 1948 reads: "It (education) shall promote understanding, tolerance and friendship among all nations, racial and religious groups. . . ." [3]

Thus is the *need for understanding* stated. How can *music* help? Music has an important role to play in paving the way for and adding to the understanding of other nations, races, and religions.

The Need: Children and Music

Little children—bless their hearts!—*have* understanding. They have no consciousness of the national, racial, or religious backgrounds of other children. Those in a position to observe children of various groups playing and working together have told us time after time that children accept children as "nice people." They accept them and enjoy them until they run headlong

---

[1] Educational Policies Commission of the National Education Association, and the American Association of School Administrators; *The United Nations, UNESCO,* and *American Schools.* Washington: National Education Association, 1953.

[2] A Report of the President's Commission on Higher Education, Volume I, *Establishing the Goals.* Washington, D. C.: United States Government Printing Office, 1947.

[3] United Nations, *These Rights and These Freedoms.* New York: United Nations, Department of Public Information, 1950.

Although not relevant to the point of this chapter, Article 27 reads: *"Everyone* has the right freely to participate in the cultural life of the community, *to enjoy the arts* and to share in scientific advancement and its benefits." Of course, children in the United States are included in "everyone!"

into the folklore of groups and classes, rooted deep in dogma and prejudice transmitted from generation to generation.

But, instead of our imitating the ways of little children, we teach them to be like us; then, conscience-stricken when we see the error of our ways, we try to eradicate the effects of our efforts by re-establishing their habit of accepting individuals as individuals. Ironic? Yes, but that fact must be faced. And, we need to start eradicating early. The roots of prejudice go deep —so deep, in fact, that a DDT in the form of national prestige or even survival has difficulty in killing them. We *must* start early. The time of entrance into junior or senior high school or college is too late—many of our youth do not go to school that long.

The universality of music makes it an excellent medium for use in attempting to instill acceptance and understanding. *People* make music. So, if studying the music of a national, racial, or religious group can result in a sympathetic or objective understanding of the people, music will have, indeed, served an important purpose.

The Need: The Teacher and Music

The teacher is the link between our children and understanding of people through their music. It is the teacher who can direct children's thinking so they are at least "willing" to consider a way of life, a pattern of music, or a style of art that is different from their own. In this realm of "feeling," the teacher's role is important.

The teacher's role in consciously using music to bring about understanding is that of an informed, objective guide. Because she knows the way of life of a people, she can discuss their music in terms of their way of life and in terms children can understand.

The way of life of any group is called its "cultural pattern." Every group has language, provides for aesthetic expression and delight, and has standardized ways of behaving toward deeper problems—birth and death, perpetuating itself and its solidarity, and satisfying biological needs. *You* have a way of life, Australian Bushmen have a way of life. One of the facets of each way is music. That is one of the "realities of the physical and political world."

"Our" way of life has its roots in European culture. It is not based on an Oriental pattern. It is true, of course, that now the "American" way differs in many aspects from the culture on which it is based, but it is essentially European. The study of any other group whose culture had its roots in Europe will disclose that it is similar to our culture in many ways. For example, just as our music is based on European-style music, so is theirs. It is comparatively easy for teachers and children to discuss objectively a culture that differs only in details from "ours." There are, however, many people whose present way of life is based on a pattern that was developed independently of, and in most instances, long before, a European cultural pattern.

It has been stated succinctly that "one third of the people of the world eats with its fingers, one third with chop sticks, and one third with knives and forks." Actually those who eat with knives and forks (European culture) are the minority group. When a teacher who belongs to this minority group guides children who also belong to this minority group toward an objective awareness of the cultures of the majority, many people would say that is a wise course, indeed.

One of the best means of bringing about an objective awareness of the cultural pattern of any group is to prepare children for obvious differences and, then, to minimize them. What, for example, is the *real* difference between a ring in the nose and a ring in the ear? Between taking off one's shoes before entering the house and taking off one's *over*-shoes? Between streaks of blue on the cheeks and daubs of rouge? Between starting for new hunting grounds with one's wigwam and belongings piled on a travois and moving one's trailer to the vicinity of a new job?

The teacher of a group of children in the second and third grade in rural Georgia felt proud—and rightly so—of her success in minimizing differences. They were discussing the visitor expected the next day. He was an Oriental. The children had never seen an Oriental. How would they treat him? The children finally decided upon a pattern of behavior—they would "treat him like kinfolks."

This informed objective guide—the teacher—should be opportunistic in studying the music of any national, religious, or racial group represented in the community and in the class. Guidance in this area of children's everyday life gives opportunity to instill, in a concrete way, a sympathetic understanding of "differences." And, of course, the good effect on a child who belongs to any minority group of having the culture of his group enhanced in this manner cannot be measured.

The teacher must be informed and correctly informed, too—correct interpretations and correct names are important. Correct interpretation of the customs of religious groups and correct group names are vital in furthering better human relations. For example, Negroes prefer to be called by their correct name, "Negro"; any other name in song or conversation is anathema to them. People from China are "Chinese." Those born in Alaska, Hawaii, and Puerto Rico are not "foreigners" any more than those born in the continental United States.

Actually, teachers are accustomed to guiding children in the study of people of other cultures. Such study has been standard practice in our elementary schools for a long time. But, when music was used, it was almost exclusively to gain an understanding of a variant of European culture. The music of China or of India or of the North American Indian are non-European styles; they are rarely used in a study of the culture of the people who make it. And, for a very good reason, too. Non-European-style music is "different." Sometimes, the "difference" is rather overwhelming. For this type, especially, "specifics" are needed to guide listening.

The remainder of this chapter will be devoted to non-European-style music. This music will be discussed objectively to minimize "differences"; it will be discussed objectively in order to answer questions about the idealized non-European-style music with which there is familiarity—"What makes that music sound 'Chinese'?" or "Why does it sound like Indian music?" It will be discussed objectively in the familiar terms of European-style music—melody, rhythm, harmony, form, and instruments.

STUDYING NON-EUROPEAN-STYLE MUSIC

The music of the major groups that have developed their own system or style has been recorded, and for most children and teachers, recordings will, of necessity, be the source of information about it. Those same recordings have been the basis of the materials listed and discussed in this chapter.

There are two ways or two points from which to study the music of any people: (1) its place in the life of those who make it, and (2) an analysis of the music itself. Neither of these ways excludes the others.

For example, consider a Navajo *Corn Song.* If emphasis is placed on the *name,* thinking will be directed toward the importance of corn in the life of the Navajos, with discussions of their concepts of magic power and their religious beliefs. If a study of the music is the point of departure, the music will be analyzed in terms of "our" music in order to discover its general characteristics.

Each of these methods of study is objective, not subjective. Each is based on facts and not on feelings engendered by something new or different.

Objective Terms

What are the essential characteristics of melody, rhythm, harmony, form, and instruments upon which to base objective listening?

A *melody* has an ascending or descending trend, or both; it progresses scale-wise or by intervals, or both, with or without embellishments or trills; it does, or does not, contain tones of a specific scale.

Rhythm (movement) results from beats or pulses recurring, or not, in regular, repeated patterns. ("Fast" and "slow" are subjective terms; "uneven" is objective.)

Harmony refers to a planned relationship between tones heard simultaneously. ("Pleasing" is subjective; "familiar" is objective since a similarity to European-style harmony is implied.)

Form is the pattern made by the arrangement of melodies. ("Lacking in form" can mean "not a familiar form.")

Instruments (including the voice) are, or are not, similar to "our" instruments; they play either melody or rhythm predominantly and are made of certain materials. Sometimes, the *manner* of playing results in an important characteristic.

General Statements

1. The material that follows is background information for the teacher and (2) background for children when they have been judged *ready* for it. Much of "ready" consists of experience in discussing music objectively. The transfer from "idealized" to "authentic" is easy when objective terms are used. Although children in the lower grades cannot discuss music using all the suggested terms, they have a "feeling" for the elements, engendered by all the European-style music they have heard. For example, a child in the second grade said about Indian Music: "It is hollow—just the top and bottom with nothing in between."

2. Non-European music styles are not now exactly as they were a thousand or two thousand years ago. Even in isolation, the music of any group changed, but now the barriers that kept out influences of other cultures are rapidly disappearing, if they have not already done so. For example, in the recently recorded music of the Negro in Africa there is evidence of European-style music not present in material collected twenty years ago. Incidentally, because of the general availability of recorded music of this group, this is an excellent area for "re-

search" to discover for one's self the impact of one culture or another. Such a study is likely to be most satisfying. It will be most interesting, too, considering the impact an aspect of their culture had already made on ours.

3. It is interesting to note how ease in procuring food directly influences the music of an ethnic group. Ease in procuring food gives leisure to be devoted to placating and wooing the gods, which can be done most effectively in elaborate ceremonies with an elaborate system of music or sound. The Aztecs exemplify this way of life. Pygmies, on the other hand, struggle continuously for food. Their culture and their music are both the essence of simplicity.

4. Whether or not a style of music is "pleasing" is unimportant. It is likely to be found "interesting" when judged objectively.

5. In the large cities around the world a cosmopolitan European-style culture is evident. One characteristic of this culture is a series of concerts by world-renowned artists. The "folk-artists" are there—but in metropolitan centers music made by both groups is heard.

AMERICAN INDIAN MUSIC [4]

Musicologists have analyzed literally hundreds of Indian songs in order to discover the general characteristics of Indian music. The music of the Eskimo is the most simple—his leisure was limited because of the time and energy required to secure food, clothing, and shelter. The music of most other Indian groups reached a generally high level of development. Certain characteristics in this music have been noted. In any one recording of authentic Indian music, it is likely that only two or three of the characteristics listed below will be present:

Melody: Proceeds downward by intervals; use of tones smaller than half tones; chant-like sections; phrases of tune "lifted"

[4] A list of available recordings of American Indian Music will be found on page 328.

and sung on higher pitch; use of nonsense syllables as words —hi–hi–ho–ho–hu–hu; five-tone scale.

Rhythm: Lack of dominant rhythm; forced; nonflowing; short beat followed by long.

Harmony: None; if two voices sing two different tones simultaneously, it is accidental.

Form: Consistent repetition of short phrases or no repetition; endless wandering tunes; nonsense syllables used as a chorus; instrumental introduction; vocal grunts to signify end.

Instruments: Voice: manner of singing—harsh attack, forced tone, strong pulsation (vibrato), mouth almost shut, tight jaw (often there is no coordination between voice and accompaniment). Drums, rattles, bells, flutes.

THE MUSIC OF MEXICO [5]

There are three types of music in Mexico today: (1) In the urban center of Mexico City, the fine Mexican Symphony Orchestra, and the same series of concerts by world-renowned artists found in metropolitan centers around the world; (2) the folk songs and folk-dance music showing European influence; and (3) that music which clearly shows its heritage from pre-Columbian times.

Pre-Columbian Mexican Music

Information concerning the music of the Aztecs is available only because some of their instruments have been found by archaeologists or are shown in Aztec picture writing. Some of the instruments found still produce sounds. It is not known what the mass effect of these sounds (music) was, since, if the Aztecs devised a system of musical symbols, to our knowledge they did not record them.

The following ancient Mexican musical instruments are now in several collections:

[5] A list of available recordings of Mexican music will be found on page 328.

Conch shell: (consult a dictionary for a picture) a hole cut in the end of the shell serves as a mouthpiece; makes several sounds by varying pressure on the mouthpiece.

Notched stone: stone twenty inches long, ten inches wide, and two inches thick with notches in the long side; sound is made by passing a long, thin stone rapidly over the notches.

Ocarina: hollow, clay, elongated ball about the size of a small fist, with three or four holes in the top; sounds like a piccolo and is similar to the musical toy, the "sweet potato."

Bells: many shapes; made of metal; sometimes used in clusters as a style of rattle.

Flute: made of wood with small bell-mouth and fingerholes.

Drums: many shapes; one of the most interesting, perhaps, is the slit drum, found in many parts of the world. One is made from a solid piece of wood, two feet long and ten or twelve inches in diameter, carved in the shape of a crouching cat. There is a hole the shape of a six-inch H in the top of the back. Through this hole, the shape was hollowed with one side uniformly a quarter of an inch or so thicker than the other. Because of this variation in thickness, the drum produces two tones.

Mexican Indian Music

The music of the less sophisticated Mexican is a curious and fascinating mixture of native Indian and superimposed Spanish music. Since a school of music was established by the Spanish in Mexico City in 1523, it is surprising that any of the "old" can still be found. It is heard mostly in rural areas, in old Indian ceremonies. In dancing, it is not quite an accompaniment, because, in most of the available recorded music, the sound of the dancer's feet and the music do not synchronize. It seems as though the instrumentalists and the dancers just happen to be performing at the same time. The general characteristics of the music follow:

Melody: Consists of three or four tones; descending line heard more often in vocal than in instrumental melody.

Rhythm: Melody-playing instruments more often play rhythmically than do the percussion instruments; drum likely to play without pattern; two- and three-pulse measures often alternate.

Form: Repetition of short melody; little variation or variety.

Harmony: None.

Instruments: Voice: raucous, forced. Percussion: Notched stick or stick scraper, often rested on gourd that acts as amplifier; drums—variety, one of which is large gourd placed in a still larger one filled with water; rattles—seeds, shells, bells; clappers—two pieces of wood struck together (this may be a variation of a castanet). Wind: flute or trumpet made of metal—named for shape, not tone; whistles; small wooden flutes. String: not native; some bowed, some plucked; body often made of armadillo shell; some with loosely attached pieces of metal that vibrate sympathetically.

Manner of playing: Flute and drum are often played at once by same person: he rests the drum upright on his knee and holds it and the flute with his left hand, thus freeing his right for beating.

Carlos Chavez, the eminent Mexican composer, has used primitive Indian melodies and instruments in some of his symphonic works.

THE MUSIC OF THE NEGRO IN AFRICA[6]

There is no one cultural pattern for the Negro in Africa. Those who live in the east coast have been in contact with sailors from the East for centuries—their music and art have an Oriental tinge. Those who live in the north central area have been there since the days of the ancient Egyptians and Hebrews. Those living in the vast interior have been isolated and, until World War II at least, did not have many contacts with

[6] A list of available recordings of the Negro in Africa will be found on page 329.

European culture. Groups of Pygmies, isolated within isolation, have been the least influenced by outsiders and live much as they have for hundreds of years.

The seven-foot Watusi tribe has little in common with the four-foot Pygmy, less, perhaps than any group one can imagine —the most complex social structure versus the most simple; highly developed arts and crafts and vast material wealth versus a lone thorn stuck in the hair for an ornament and possessions so few they can be carried by a child when the group moves in search of food.

There is no one music, either. It runs the gamut from a four-tone melody repeated thirty-seven times without change to a symphony of sound played by five drummers.

In analyzing the music of Africa, the usual pattern will be varied by listing the characteristics in order of their complexity.

Melody: Chant on one tone with drop in pitch at the end; descending melody line consistent even in complicated melodies ("The American Indian steps his way down melodically while the African tumbles."); tones of tonic chord, five-tone scale; complete major scale.

Rhythm: No pattern of beats; simple unvarying pattern; syncopation; combination of last two played on drums; varied and complicated; five complicated patterns played simultaneously.

Harmony: None; two or three tones sung simultaneously; type of instrumental chordal accompaniment.

Form: Continuous repetition of four-tone melody; longer melody repeated; repeated with variations; vocal solo with group response; instrumental interlude in vocal solo.

Instruments: Bull-roarer (flat thin strip of wood twirled above the head by means of attached string); reed flute (produces one tone); sticks (rest on ground, held under arm with shell that acts as resonator); flutes—many sizes and materials; drums—amazing range in size and materials (slit drum); stringed—musical bow (large bow played in various ways), instruments with from one to twenty-seven strings; xylophone —from three to sixteen keys.

Miscellaneous: In some groups the melody results when each person produces *one* tone by voice or on flute or stick. Each player "comes in" at the correct time. Reeds or sticks are graduated in size. Clapping, stamping, and beating leather garments are used often as accompaniments. Sometimes a player hums a vocal accompaniment to his instrumental solo. Vocal quality varies from raucous to covered soft tone. The ensemble of some choral groups is excellent according to "our" standards.

THE MUSIC OF CHINA [7]

Chinese music is of three definite types: classical, folk, and that which is a mixture of both (perhaps "popular" is the best descriptive term).

Classical music is a highly developed science, completely enveloped in symbolism, the subject of philosophical discussion. Facts concerning their instrument, the ching (ch'in, chin [g]) will illustrate that statement. The invention of the classical ching was attributed to the legendary Yellow Emperor who lived in the year 2852 B.C. It measured 3.66 feet or 366 tenths of an inch because the year contained a maximum of 366 days. There were five strings to agree with the five elements. The upper part was round to represent the firmament; the bottom was flat to represent the ground. Classical Chinese vocal music is probably the most "different" of all non-European music.

However, the "people" of China have had and still have their own music. There are folk songs and dances. Popular music retains its characteristic color, with the melodies arranged in familiar patterns.

These are the characteristics of Chinese music:

[7] A list of available recordings of Chinese music will be found on page 329.

Melody: Pentatonic scale [8] predominates in folk music; in classical, all tones of the major scale are used in arriving at pentatonic scale tones; trills and ornaments are often heard, and melodies are long and ill-defined; vocal melody lies high in pitch but with wide range.

Rhythm: Not a dominant or outstanding feature; accompaniment frequently follows pattern of the melody.

Harmony: None.

Form: Phrases of irregular length (one reason for lacking dominant rhythm); phrase repetition not usual; classical music *has* exact form, but to Occidental ears it appears lacking; variety obtained by different instruments or voice repeating melody, often at higher or lower pitch; end or beginning of section marked by a percussion instrument.

Instruments: Voice: falsetto often used; harsh attack and quality; not natural voice, results from training. Strings: variety in number of strings; bowed and plucked; with or without frets; used as solo and accompanying instrument. Manner of playing: hand that stops strings *glides* from position to position, thus allowing intermediate tones to sound. Woodwinds: end-blown and cross-blown flutes; used as solo and accompanying instrument; often plays exact tones of vocalist. Percussion: bells, gong, clappers, chimes, wooden sticks and blocks, cymbals.

In general, there is only melody and accompaniment in Chinese music.

THE MUSIC OF INDIA [9]

The music of India is circumscribed by tradition and closely

[8] The Pentatonic scale is 1-2-3-5-6 of the major scale. To play it on the piano, place the thumb of right hand on the lowest of the three black keys and play five consecutive black keys. Suggestions for making a suitable accompaniment to Chinese music are given on pages 71-72 of *Music Fundamentals Through Song* by Louise Kifer Myers. Englewood Cliffs, N. J.: Prentice-Hall, Inc., 1954.

[9] A list of available recordings of the music of India will be found on page 329.

ked with philosophical thinking. The medieval music-makers bandoned the rigid pitches of their forefathers—dominated by inflexible stone chimes—and adopted instruments capable of a fluid and flexible style. Form and melodies are bound by rigid rules and regulations. For example, a *raga* is a type of composition of certain mood; and a *maquam* is a type of melody. Only a *maquam* of a certain type may be used in a certain *raga*.

It has been said that melody in Indian music has disintegrated. After hearing the music, that statement will have more meaning. Its characteristics are:

Melody: Some short and simple; fundamental tones rigidly fixed but enveloped by colaratura ("coloratura" is characterized by numberless shadings, slides, tremolos, twist, and turns); scale—tonal distance of the octave includes twenty-two tones; pentatonic sometimes used.

Rhythm: Strict adherence to pattern; regular repetition of generally complicated pattern; often, when rhythm is complicated, melody is simple, and vice versa.

Harmony: None; accompaniment often resembles a drone (deep sustained monotone).

Form: Strict but unrecognizable for the untutored; varied repetitions of melodies gives variety.

Instruments: Strings: variety in size and number of strings; bowed and plucked; some with loose, untuned extra strings that vibrate sympathetically. Winds: flutes of various sizes and tone quality; conch shell. Percussion: chimes, gongs, drums, wooden blocks with or without loosely attached metal discs; series of porcelain bowls (each producing one tone); series of small drums (arranged as bowls).

The music of India is pleasing and usually delights Occidentals.

MUSIC OF THE MIDDLE EAST [10]

The music of the Middle East shows the influence of boti India and Europe. The blending of these influences makes the Occidental comfortable as he listens to the music of Turkey, Rumania, Persia, Greece, Egypt, Armenia, and Russian Middle East.

Melody: Coloratura (see Music of India); short melodies in dance music; long, meandering melodies in art songs.

Rhythm: Repetition of simple or complicated pattern in dance music; in art songs, rhythm is determined by words.

Harmony: None; when instruments capable of making chords are used, they produce drone (see Music of India).

Form: Repetition of short melodies; variety obtained by use of different instruments playing melody alone or with others.

Instruments: Voice: not raucous, sometimes uncovered tone. Strings: plucked and bowed; variety in timbre; many with oboe- or viola-like quality. Winds: Flutes and pipes of assorted sizes and tone-color; accordion. Percussion: drums, bells, castanets, tambourine.

THE MUSIC OF INDONESIA [11]

In the distant past Java was influenced by the cultures of East Asia—Hindu and Islam. Then, in 1597, the Dutch came. Because Bali was better protected against influence, the Hindu-Javanese culture still occupies the high level it had achieved before the sixteenth century. Although the culture of Java has been somewhat influenced by the Dutch, in Bali musical instruments that have not been known in Java for generations are still in daily use.

The gamelan—an orchestra made up primarily of percussion

[10] A list of available recordings of the music of the Middle East will be found on page 329.

[11] A list of available recordings of the music of Indonesia will be found on page 330.

instruments—is a unique feature of Balinese and Javanese music. There are large and small gamelans, gamelans for accompanying men, and gamelans for accompanying women. There is no system of notation; each player learns his part by rote.

In the gamelan, instruments are divided according to their function: those that (1) play the leading melody, giving it character by simple strict rhythm (long-sounding kettle-gongs and metallophones); (2) are freely melodic and independent, hovering above main melody (voice, flute, violin); (3) are accompanying instruments, which sub-divide the melody into a network of smaller intervals (short-toned metallophones and xylophones); (4) punctuate or divide the melody into sections; and (5) are for rhythmical purposes (drums), frequently providing rhythm counterpoint.

A "metallophone" is a xylophone with metal keys ("xylo-" means "wood"). Most metallophones and xylophones have only four or five keys. The violin used is the Arabian *rebab*. A zither is used often as a melody, not as a chording, instrument. A bamboo flute is often heard.

In some areas there is a mixture resulting from the gamelan and "Oriental" and Indian music.

THE MUSIC OF HAWAII [12]

After Captain Cook discovered the Hawaiian Islands in 1778, the islands became a regular stopping place for world travelers. The Spanish and Portuguese sailors brought their guitars which were adopted and adapted by the natives. Note the similarity in shape of the ukulele and guitar. Today both are often used to accompany ancient chants or dances as well as modern songs and dances. It is this music that is usually referred to as "Hawaiian" music.

If, however, a reference to or a study of the Music of Hawaii is made, it must include not only "Hawaiian" music but the

[12] A list of available recordings of Hawaiian music will be found on page 330.

music of Japan, China, the Philippines, Korea and Tahiti. People from those lands are in Hawaii in numbers. While it is true that immigrants of "different" national and racial groups try to acquire the pattern of living and culture of the "at home" group—and try to erase their own—these people from those other lands are *now* "at home," and have been for years. Currently, efforts are toward making certain that their children learn or become aware of certain aspects of their great grand parents' cultural background! The succinct statement by a senior at Vassar summarizes the present political, cultural, and racial picture: "I am an American of Chinese ancestry born in the State of Hawaii."

Music of the areas from which many of these Americans came is discussed elsewhere in this chapter.

In "Hawaiian" music: a *hula* is a song; an *oli* is a chant. Each tells a story. The story of some olis and all hulas is made clearer by a dancer's interpretation. By now, the motions of a hula dancer are stylized, certain words being interpreted by definite motions—almost a sign language.

The modern hula is European-style music. The Hawaiian "flavor" results from the manner of playing the ukulele and guitar.

The characteristics of an *oli* follow.

Melody: Limited range ("born of words"); many with only one tone or hovering around one tone; sometimes *no* tones, just rhythmic speech.

Rhythm: Repetition of a regular, recurring pattern.

Harmony: None originally, but today the accompaniment may have harmonized interludes.

Form: Repetition of short melodies; variety obtained by chorus or instrumental interlude.

Instruments: Voice: soft, covered tone. Percussion: rattles (many kinds), stamping board, drums, bull-roarers. String: ukulele, guitar.

(The nose-flute is used in old ceremonies but has not been

recorded; the sound is made by using the breath of the nostril.)

THE MUSIC OF LATIN AMERICA [13]

Latin-American music is essentially European music. For example, the Argentine gaucho has his music, but in it are the rhythms, the scales, and the harmony of European music. He makes it on instruments brought from Europe. True, his songs can be divided and sub-divided according to form or tempo or subject-matter or use, but they are still European-style music. However, two non-European styles are found in Latin America—one, the music of a native people; the other, the music of a transplanted people. The latter has been the more influential.

The music of the Indian of the mountains is quite similar to the music of the Mexican Indian, except that he has pan-pipes, which neither the Mexican nor North American Indian have. Panpipes, flutes, drums, rattles, and clay trumpets were found among the artifacts of Pre-Columbian Incas. They are still used today. The Indians of the Amazon region have reed flutes, drums, and rattles.

In Haiti, Brazil, and Cuba the interestingly intricate and compelling rhythm of Africa is found. The samba, the rumba, and the calypso are dominated by African rhythm. Haitian songs and dances used in Voodoo *are* African. "Voodoo" comes from a West African word meaning "spirit" or "god." Today "Voodoo" means those religious practices and concepts not identified with the Catholic or Protestant Churches. Drums, bamboo stamping-tubes, mortars and pestles provide a rhythmic percussion accompaniment to the songs that are a part of the ritual of Voodoo (Voudoun).

[13] A list of available recordings of Latin-American music will be found on page 330.

AVAILABLE RECORDINGS OF ETHNIC MUSIC

Material in this area of music is multiplying rapidly. Not only are important collections of ethnic music being released by the larger companies but also several smaller companies are issuing single records. The best means of keeping informed about releases is to consult Schwann's record catalog.

Remember, it is not likely that *all* the listed characteristics for a type of music will be heard in any *one* record. While listening to a record, check the characteristics recognized against the listing given. (Use the list, too, in checking characteristics "borrowed" for idealized music.)

Vocal music of the non-European type may be too "different" for little children, but it can be used with older children when they have been *carefully prepared*. Remember that people, including children, snicker *and* giggle at what they don't understand! Preparation for listening and specifics upon which to center the attention are the keys for using ethnic music successfully.

Refer to "Sources of Materials," page 357, for information about where the listed recordings may be obtained.

Consider the "Note" at the end of this list.

American Indian Music

Indian Music of the Southwest. (Boulton) Folkways
Songs from the Iroquois. Library of Congress
Seneca Songs. Library of Congress
American Indians. Folkways
Eskimo. Folkways
Chant of the Eagle Dance. RCA Victor Library for Elementary Schools. (Other records in the album are idealized Indian music.)

Mexican Indian Music

Music of Indians of Mexico. (Boulton) Folkways
Folk Music of Mexico. Library of Congress
Indian-Yaqui and Mexican Tribes. Commodore

Mexico-Indian. Folkways
Sinfonia India by Chavez. Decca DL9527 (Some pre-Columbian
    instruments are used.)

The Music of the Negro in Africa

African Music from the French Colonies. Columbia Library
Equatorial Africa. Folkways
Belgian Congo Records. Commodore (Compare these with the
    chants in *Afro-Caribbean Songs and Rhythms,* Decca
    DL5336.)
Music of Africa-Kenya. London
African Music. (Boulton) Folkways
Music of the Ituri Forrest People. Folkways

Music of China and Japan

Japan. Monitor
Japan. (History of Music in Sound) Victor
Music of the Orient. Decca DX107
China. Monitor
Japan. Folkways
The Azuma Kabuki Musicians (Japan). Columbia 5ML 4925
Folk Music from Japan. Columbia SL 2k4

The Music of India

India. Folkways
India (Religious). Folkways
Indian Folk Music. Columbia Library
Classical Music of India. (Examples) Folkways
India. Monitor
India. Victor
Folk Songs and Dances of North India. Period
Indian Instrumental Music. Angel
Anthology of Indian Classical Music. London. Ducretet-Thompson,
    collected under auspices of the International Music Council,
    UNESCO

The Music of the Middle East

Music of the Orient. Decca
Music of the Middle East and Palestine. Folkways
Israel. Folkways

Great Russian Folk Dances. Epic
Folk Music Festival: Songs and Dances of Kazakhstan, Uzbekistan,
    Kirghizia, Georgia and Moldavia. Westminster.
Southeast Asia. Folkways
Moiseyev Dance Company. Monitor
Ethiopia. Folkways

Indonesian Music

Dancers of Bali. Columbia 5 ML 4618
Indonesian Music. Columbia Library
Bayanihan Philippine Dance Company. Monitor
Music of the Orient. Decca
Java and Bali. Folkways
Music of Laos. Monitor

The Music of Hawaii and Tahiti

Tahitian Chants. (Listen *only* to the old style chant and percussion
    accompaniments—*do not listen* to the harmonized sections.)
Souvenirs of Hawaii. Decca L 5319 (Same caution as above.)

The Music of Latin America

Afro-Bahian Religious Songs from Brazil. Library of Congress
Folk Music of Venezuela. Library of Congress
Folk Music of Puerto Rico. Library of Congress
Folk Music of Mexico. Library of Congress
Puerto Rico. Folkways
Music from Mato Grosso (Brazil). Folkways
Peru. Folkways
Haiti. Folkways
Afro-Caribbean Songs and Rhythms. Decca

Note: The following records are excellent if you can find them:
"Xochipili-Macuilixochitl" from *A Program of Mexican Music* by
Chauvez (Columbia); *Hindu Music* by Uday Shankar and His
Company of Hindu Dancers and Musicians (Victor).

Note: In addition to Decca's *Music of the Orient,* Columbia's
World Library of Folk and Primitive Music, and Victor's *History of
Music in Sound* (companion of NEW OXFORD HISTORY OF
MUSIC), there are Folkways' four important volumes: *Music of the*

World's Peoples (widely separated and unrelated areas being represented in each), the one volume, *World's Vocal Art* (illustrating vocal styles), and the one volume *Man's Early Musical Instruments* (selected by Dr. Kurt Sach).

All of these collections are important.

For Discussion

1. Give a specific example illustrating a first-grade child's concept of each statement relating to the "need for understanding."

2. Think about an incident in which you were ridiculed. Why were you? How did you feel?

3. Why are the "out" groups that you know so considered?

4. Read Ruth Benedict's *Patterns of Culture*. Make notes about how each group discussed regards the following: material wealth, birth, death, marriage, dance, "out" groups, success, lodges, cleanliness, adolescence, musical instruments, inheriting property, family authority. Compare their practices or reactions with those of your group.

5. There is an old admonition, "Man, know thyself!" Read an anthropologist's analysis of "Americans and American Life" in *Mirror for Man* by Clyde Kluckhohn.

6. Do you think people of other cultures have a point when they say we are "dirty" because we put a used handkerchief back in our pockets or that our women waste a lot of time and energy ironing sheets and towels?

7. Try singing a melody in the manner described in the section on African music. Suggest possible reasons for the development of that style of singing.

8. Play a pentatonic scale. Make up six tunes using those tones. For an accompaniment, play 1 and 5 of the scale together or any combination of those five tones that sounds "well."

9. What is the interval construction of the pentatonic scale? Play one on any C, D, E, F, or G on the piano.

10. List the instruments made of pipes in order of their complexity, from the single pipe to the pipe organ.

11. Find out about the use and importance of bells in China.

12. Look up the difference between lutes and zithers. Get the exact definition of "tambourine."

13. Who are the Melanesians, the Polynesians, the Micronesians? What are their distinguishing physical characteristics?

14. Which style of ethnic music do you like best? Why?

15. Why is a type of soprano voice called "coloratura"? Why is an orchestra called a "symphony" orchestra?

16. List the ways music is used in *your* cultural group. Discuss the items with older members of your group to discover changes. Compare your list with that of a person with a different background.

17. Tell of incidents proving that "children *have* understanding."

Bibliography and

Sources of Materials

BACKGROUND IN MUSIC

Bauer, Marion, and Ethel R. Peyser, *Music Through the Ages.* New York: G. P. Putnam's Sons, 1946.

> Good for an introduction in music history.

Bernstein, Leonard, *The Joy of Music.* New York: Simon and Schuster, 1959.

> This eminent musician shares some of his love and understanding with us. Excellent.

Biancolli, Louis, and Robert Bagar, *The Victor Book of Operas.* New York: Simon and Schuster, 1953.

> Detailed stories of the operas in the standard repertoire.

Boatright, Mody Coggin, and others, *Ballads, Tales and Talk*. Dallas: Southern Methodist University Press, 1953.
   The migration of ballads, stories, and speech are traced from one country to another—and finally to Texas.

Britten, Benjamin and Imogen Holst, *The Wonderful World of Music*. Garden City, New York: Garden City Books, 1958.
   This primer of musicology should whet any reader's appetite for this field. It is a beautiful book—its appearance compatible with its content.

Bronson, Bertrand Harris, *The Traditional Tunes of the Child Ballads*. Princeton, New Jersey: Princeton University Press, 1959.
   Francis James Child (1825-1896) made the first definite collection of English and Scottish popular ballads—the words but with only a few tunes. This collection has since been known as "Child's Ballads." Professor Bronson has collected the tunes for these texts. Thus, he can show the way of the folk with a tune—they adapt and adopt it. Interesting and exciting—and the most authoritative survey of the Anglo-American folk-song yet made.

Cardus, Neville, *Composers Eleven*. New York: George Braziller, 1959.
   A wise and affectionate book about the author's favorite composers. His enthusiasm is contagious.

Charters, Samuel B., *The Country Blues*. New York: Holt, Rinehart & Winston, Inc., 1960.
   This author has done for a phase of Afro-American music what Bronson did for Anglo-American ballads: he collected a wealth of fugitive material about the tap-root singers of these songs as well as recordings of their singing. These will be re-issued by Folkways. This is a vitally significant area of American music.

Chase, Gilbert, *The Music of Spain*. New York: W. W. Norton & Company, 1941.
   Chapter XVII—"Hispanic Music in America" has background material for a study of the music of the Latin American countries and the southwestern part of the United States.

Copland, Aaron, *Music and Imagination*. New York: The New American Library of World Literature, Inc., 1959.
   The author deals with the musical mind at work in its different capacities as listener, interpreter or creator.

Courlander, Harold, *Haiti Singing*. Chapel Hill, N. C.: University of North Carolina Press, 1939.

This is the story of music and its place in the life of the Negro peasant in Haiti.

Dudley, Louise, and Austin Faricy, *The Humanities.* New York: McGraw-Hill Book Company, 1940.

The work of art itself is the beginning and the end of study in this book in applied aesthetics. The material concerning music is well presented, but it is in its consideration of *all* art forms that the book is important. An integrated presentation of the arts.

Ewen, David, *The Complete Book of 20th Century Music.* Englewood Cliffs, New Jersey: Prentice-Hall, Inc., 1959.

"Music's interpreter to the American people" presents a comprehensive and analytical guide to some thousand compositions in all the major musical forms and includes biographies of composers and evaluations of many compositions.

Farnsworth, Paul, *The Social Psychology of Music.* New York: The Dryden Press, 1958.

The author believes that music must look for its explanations far more often to social science than to physical science—and makes his point. He includes an excellent review of music tests.

Folk Music. Washington: Library of Congress, 1959.

A listing of folk songs, ballads, dances, instrumental pieces and folk tales of the United States and Latin America from the Library of Congress' Archives of Folk Songs.

Hartog, Howard, editor, *European Music in the Twentieth Century.* New York: Frederich A. Praeger, 1957.

A source of information about lesser known composers.

Hughes, Langston, *Famous Negro Music Makers.* New York: Dodd, Mead & Co., 1957.

Short biographies.

Hunt, Sarah, and Ethel Cain, *Games the World Around.* New York: The Ronald Press, 1960.

Four hundred folk games with illustrations, costumes and traditions of the various countries.

Jacobs, Robert L., *Harmony for the Listener.* New York: Oxford University Press, 1958.

A clear understandable presentation of harmony for a *listener.* It could, however, enlighten students of traditional harmony.

Joh, Mary C, Kimm, *Folk Songs of Korea.* Dubuque, Iowa: Wm. C. Browne Co., 1950.

A Korean's desire to share Korean folk melodies led to the preparation of this book of songs with piano accompaniments.

Johnson, Edna, Carrie E. Scott, and Evelyn R. Sickles (Compilers), *Anthology of Children's Literature*. Boston: Houghton Mifflin Company, 1948.

    Included in this anthology is a chapter called "Folklore that Has Inspired Good Music." Seven tales are given, plus suggested recordings of music. Other stories are listed with the titles of related musical selections. Excellent.

Korson, George, (editor), *Pennsylvania Songs and Legends*. Philadelphia: University of Pennsylvania Press, 1949.

    A practical, authoritative, and entertaining account of Pennsylvania's folklore. One of the many regional collections of songs available today.

Loggins, Vernon, *Where the World Ends: The Life of Louis Moreau Gottschalk*. Baton Rouge: Louisiana State University Press, 1958.

    This American pianist-composer made several important contributions to the development of American music even though he wrote *The Last Hope*! Interesting.

Lomax, John, and Alan Lomac, *Folk Song—U.S.A.* New York: Duell, Sloan & Pearce, 1948.

    An important collection of songs by two well-known collectors. References, books for further reading, and recordings are listed.

Lundin, Robert William, *An Objective Psychology of Music*. New York: The Ronald Press Company, 1958.

    The reader is given a sound basis for selective listening and for appreciation of musical performance. The reactions of performer and audience are related to biological equipment, previous musical training, and immediate environment.

McPhee, Colin, *A House in Bali*. New York: The John Day Company, Inc., 1946.

    An entrancing account of a musician's life in Bali with an emphasis on explaining the *gamelan*.

Malm, William P., *Japanese Music*. Rutland, Vermont: Charles E. Tuttle Company, 1959.

    A wealth of information, both general and specific, making clear the structure of Japanese music, with accounts of Japanese instruments (their construction, history, and use), accounts of music's function in society, descriptions of religious music, court music, and popular music and folk musical arts. Comprehensive and important.

Myers, Louise Kifer, *Music Fundamentals Through Song*. Engle-wood Cliffs, New Jersey: Prentice-Hall, Inc., 1954.

A song-text-work book that follows the method used in *this* book for learning to read music and learning music theory.

Neal, Harry Lee, *Wave as You Pass*. Philadelphia: J. B. Lippincott, 1959.

The story of the trailer travels and life of the husband and wife duo-pianists. Perhaps you have heard them.

Nettl, Bruno, *An Introduction to Folk Music in the United States*. Detroit: Wayne State University Press, 1960.

What is it? Where does it come from? What purpose does it serve?

Pace, Robert, *Piano for Classroom Music*. Englewood Cliffs, New Jersey: Prenctice-Hall, Inc., 1958.

Teachers or prospective teachers learn to play material for the classroom as well as other music.

Peter, Hildemarie, *The Recorder: Its Tradition and Its Task*. Trans-lated from the German by Stanley Godman. New York: C. F. Peters Corporation, Agents, 1958.

The popular household musical instrument during the fifteenth through the eighteenth centuries is finding a new popularity. Interesting for the recorder player (you become one!) and to musicians generally.

Sachs, Curt, *A History of Musical Instruments*. New York: W. W. Norton & Company, Inc., 1940.

The impulses that gave rise to instruments in the world of the primitives are discussed first; then, the instruments of antiquity; the instruments of the Middle Ages; and finally, the modern Occident. An important work of permanent value which should be in all school libraries and in libraries of those interested in music and in people.

———, *The Commonwealth of Art*. New York: W. W. Norton & Company, Inc., 1946.

This comparative history of the arts is concerned with the ori-gins of music and the place of music in the Western Orient, in East Asia, in India, in Greece, and in Rome. It is in the Ancient World that the roots of the music of the West are exposed. Con-tains much of interest concerning music and musical instruments and the culture of groups.

Schreiber, Flora, and Vincent Persichetti, *William Schuman*. New York: G. Schirmer, Inc., 1954.

Mr. Schuman is an American, formed by American teachers, a product of the American scene, a composer, a force in today's music. There *are* composers with us today. Read about this one.

Spaeth, Sigmund, *Fifty Years with Music*. New York: Fleet Publishing Co., 1959.

A crisp and stimulating account of Mr. Spaeth's long-time love affair with music. Some of his happiness will affect you, too.

Stevenson, Robert M., *Music in Mexico*. New York: The Thomas Y. Crowell Co., 1953.

Not only are music and musicians discussed but music is related to the history and the society of the time.

Stringham, Edwin John, *Listening to Music Creatively*. Englewood Cliffs, New Jersey: Prentice-Hall, Inc., 1959.

Listening interest is evoked, personal taste is developed, and an awareness of the close relationship of the arts is created.

Tooze, Ruth, and Beatrice Perham Krone, *Literature and Music as Resources for Social Studies*. Englewood Cliffs, New Jersey: Prentice-Hall, Inc., 1955.

Some of the material listed is background for the teacher, but most of it is aimed at making children "knowing" citizens of the U.S.A. and of the world. Books for children to read and songs and recorded music for them to learn and enjoy are listed for each national and ethnic group in our country and in the world. Excellent. An important source of information.

UNESCO, *A Catalogue of Recorded Classical and Traditional Indian Music*. New York: Columbia University Press, 1955.

More than a catalogue since it contains information about the music, scales, and musicians of India, as well as pictures, and lists of available recordings. A person with casual interest will continue reading, while the student will be captivated.

Van Loon, Hendrick Willem, *The Arts*. New York: Simon and Schuster, 1937.

A history of the arts—painting, architecture, music, and the minor arts—written in Van Loon's personal, wise, nonreverent style and illustrated by him. Background in history, anthropology. Excellent, delightful—and, everlasting!

Waters, Edward N., *Victor Herbert, A Life in Music*. Ithaca, New York: Cornell University Press, 1955.

The biography of a beloved American musician who played an important part in American musical life during several decades at the turn of the century.

Vellesz, Egon, Editor, *The New Oxford History of Music, Vol. I. Ancient and Oriental Music.* New York: Oxford University Press, 1957.

A monumental survey of the history of music against the backdrop of history in all its manifestations. RCA Victor has an accompanying volume of recordings. Important.

Vold, Milo, and Edmund Cykler, *An Introduction to Music and Art in the Western World.* Dubuque, Iowa: Wm. C. Brown Company, 1958.

A picture of the chronological relationships between cultural, social, and economic history.

MUSIC'S ROLE IN UNDERSTANDING OTHER PEOPLES

Note: This section is intended for *all* teachers. It is not comprehensive; rather it gives a glimpse of possible readings about people of different cultural patterns, which will help individuals understand themselves and others and discover how music can fulfill its promise in helping to understand people.

Benedict, Ruth, *Patterns of Culture.* New York: Mentor Books, 1934.

Contains descriptions of the culture patterns of three groups, which, when compared with our culture, become even more interesting and informative. A *must,* when comparisons with our culture are made simultaneously.

Bouquet, Alan Coates, *Everyday Life in New Testament Times.* New York: Charles Scribner's Sons, 1954.

An illustrated study of how people lived in the world around the Mediterranean in the first century A.D. Considers houses, clothes, modes of travel and communication, meals, schools, and places of worship.

Burchfield, R. W., and E. M. Burchfield, *New Zealand.* (Lands and People Series). New York: The Macmillan Co., 1954.

This concise history of New Zealand describes the customs and achievements of the Maori and white races as they have lived together peacefully for eighty years.

Busch, Noel F., *Thailand: An Introduction to Modern Siam.* Princeton, New Jersey: D. Van Nostrand Company, Inc., 1959.

A small, informal and unpretentious book that provides gen-

eral information written by a representative of the Asia Foundation.

Caiger, George (Editor), *Australian Way of Life*. New York: Columbia University Press, 1954.

A handy, authoritative survey of an emergent nation that is
unique in its situation, history, economy, and culture.

Cameron, Meribeth, Thomas H. D. Mahony, and George E. Mc-
Reynolds, *China, Japan, and the Powers—A History of the Modern Far East*. New York: The Ronald Press, 1960.

Starting with a brief but genuinely illuminating account of the
older cultural traditions, it concentrates on the events of the
past two centuries. Interesting and important.

Densmore, Frances, *Yuman and Yaqui Music*, Bureau of Ethnology
Bulletin 110. Washington: United States Government Printing
Office, 1932.

Miss Densmore not only recorded the songs of these Indians
but she has also given us a concept of their culture. Descriptions
and pictures of musical instruments, customs, ceremonies, dances
and legends are included, as well as melodies and analyses of
melodies.

Fairservis, Walter A., *The Origin of Oriental Civilization*. New
York: The New American Library, 1958.

The history of early man in Asia—the beginnings of religion,
ethics, art, and technology.

Fitch, Florence Mary, *One God—the Ways We Worship Him*. New
York: Lothrop, Lee and Shepard Co., 1946.

A simple description of the traditional ways in which Jews,
Catholics, and Protestants worship the one God.

———, *Their Search for God*. New York: Lothrop, Lee and Shepard
Co., 1952.

A companion for the above book.

Greenbie, Sydney, *The Good Neighbor Series*. New York: Row, Peterson and Company, 1942.

The books in this series contain authentic and interesting material about Latin-American countries. Each is illustrated, each
has a pronouncing glossary. Upper elementary children and their
teachers will find background for music in these inexpensive
books.

Japan: A Packet for Teachers. New York: Japan Society, Inc., 1959.

A compilation of material and bibliography relating to the
culture, economics, history, and politics of Japan.

abir, Humayan, *The Indian Heritage*. New York: Harper and Brothers, 1957.

The broad course of Indian history showing broad movements of people rather than a date-by-date, name-by-name account.

eesing, Felix M., *Native Peoples of the Pacific World*. New York: The Macmillan Company, 1945.

An excellent book with which to begin a study of the diverse peoples scattered among the thousands of islands in the Pacific.

luckholm, Clyde, *Mirror for Man*. New York: Whittlesey House, 1949.

The relation of anthropology to modern life is pointed out. The facets of "our" pattern of living are explained and give light to some of the other cultural patterns. A *must* for an illumination and understanding of us and our society.

aves, Walter H. C., and Charles A. Thompson, *UNESCO: Purposes, Progress, Prospects*. Bloomington: Indiana University Press, 1957.

The genesis, development, achievements, and current status of UNESCO. Doubtless the best one-volume study of the organization.

inck, Orville, *A Passage Through Pakistan*. Detroit: Wayne State University Press, 1960.

A Fullbright lecturer (1956-57) attempts to help us understand why the East and West are a long time in meeting: the differences between the two in manners and mores, drives and motives, and political attitudes and educational advantages. Highly readable.

eeker, Oden, *The Little World of Laos*. New York: Charles Scribner's Sons, 1959.

This informative and entertaining book by a CARE official also includes material related to Cambodia, Thailand, and Vietnam.

etrauz, Alfred, *Voodoo*. New York: Oxford University Press, 1959.

A definitive study which charts accurately esoteric practices and beliefs.

ichener, James A., *Hawaii*. New York: Random House, 1959.

The beginnings of Hawaii as told by the author of *Tales of the South Pacific* in an epic novel.

intz, Sidney W., *Worker in the Cane*. New Haven: Yale University Press, 1959.

A Puerto Rican life history documenting the drastic social changes occurring there.

Morgan, Lewis Henry, *The Indian Journals, 1859-62*. Ann Arbor: The University of Michigan Press, 1960.
To know the Old West, read this eye-witness account of frontier life by the founder of anthropology.

Najafi, Najmeh, *Reveille for a Persian Village*. New York: Harper and Brothers, 1958.
The American-educated author returns to help her village people.

New Horizon's World Guide. New York: Pan American Airways, 1959.
Not the usual "travel" book, but a book of facts about people, places, and things all around the world. You'll discover the facts but in the process you'll probably discover you *must* go, if not immediately, sometime soon.

Nottinghan, Elizabeth K., *Religion and Society*. Garden City, N. Y.: Doubleday & Company, Inc., 1954.
Religion is treated in a broad universal and social sense rather than in an individual or theological sense.

Perspective of Indonesia. New York: Intercultural Publications, 1959.
This Atlantic Monthly Supplement is intended to help Americans learn something about one of their newest neighbors. Other anthologies in the series relate to India, Japan, Greece, and Brazil. Each contains suggested readings and a glossary.

Peterson, Frederick A., *Ancient Mexico: An Introduction to Pre Hispanic Cultures*. New York: G. P. Putnam's Sons, 1959.
Ancient Mexico as a background for the Aztecs.

Preston, Ralph C. (Editor), *Teaching World Understanding*. Englewood Cliffs, New Jersey: 1955.
For those desiring to develop in children an understanding of world cultures, this book offers descriptions, encouragement, and suggestions. One of the most important books in this listing. Excellent.

Richer by Asia. Chicago: American Library Association, 1959.
A selected bibliography of books and other materials recommended for promoting West-East understanding.

Rogers, George W., *Alaska in Transition*. Baltimore: The Johns Hopkins Press, 1960.

Highly readable, this account should be read by everyone interested in Alaska, including actual and prospective residents.

itwell, Sacheverall, *The Bridge of the Brocade Sash.* New York: The World Publishing Company, 1960.

A world traveler shares with us his delight in visiting Japan.

tark, Freya, *Riding to the Tigris,* New York: Harcourt, Brace & Co., 1960.

This traveler brings to us the sights and sound of the remote hinterland of modern Turkey. Beautiful writing—so beautiful, in fact, one reviewer likened it to the "speech of angels."

tefansson, Evelyn, *Here Is Alaska.* New York: Charles Scribner's Sons, 1959.

This revised statehood edition contains important changes and many new photographs.

eachers South Asia Packet: Ceylon, India, Nepal, Pakistan. New York: The Asia Society, 1959.

Selection of materials useful in teaching about these countries.

hompson, Elizabeth Marshall, *Other Lands: Other Peoples.* Washington: National Education Association, 1960.

Country by country fact book written primarily for Americans entertaining visitors from abroad.

——, *The Harmless People.* New York: Alfred A. Knopf, 1959.

The story of the African Bushman who lives in the Kalahari Desert as learned by Mrs. Thomas on three expeditions, not in the early 1800's, but *just before* this book was published. Read of a people who have as near nothing in the way of possessions as can be imagined. Some of the facts may revolt you—but what would *you* do in like circumstances?

unis, Edwin, *Indians.* Yonkers, N. Y.: World Book Company, 1959.

American Indian life before Europeans arrived.

on Hagen, Victor W., *The Sun Kingdom of the Aztecs.* Yonkers, New York: The World Book Company, 1958.

A colorful account of Aztec life prior to 1519.

——, *The Incas of Pedro de Cieza de Leon.* Norman, Oklahoma: University of Oklahoma Press, 1959.

A translation of the chronicles of Cieza, a boy of thirteen, who observed and wrote as he traveled.

Vilson, Edmund, *Apologies to the Iroquois.* New York: Farrar, Strauss & Cudahy, 1960.

A study of Iroquois history and currently resurgent nationalis tic spirit (with "apologies" for not knowing, before!). This boo includes, too, Joseph Mitchell's *Mohawks in High Steel*—an ac count of a colony of Mohawks living in Brooklyn who are steel workers. Excellent and fascinating.

THE ELEMENTARY SCHOOL PROGRAM

Note: This section is intended for the music specialist to help en large his awareness of the whole school program and where musi *fits*. Material related to teaching in areas other than music is in cluded in order to enlarge the specialist's concept of "teaching."

Archer, Clifford P., *Elementary Education in Rural Areas*. Nev York: The Ronald Press, 1958.

The author describes the school and the community and show why a knowledge of rural culture is basic in bringing about a educational program for the continuous development of rura children.

Association for Supervision and Curriculum Development, *194 Yearbook: Toward Better Teaching*. Washington: National Edu cation Association, 1949.

This report of current practices, written by teachers themselve *must* be read by every teacher. Excellent. Important. Indispen sable. *Still* new.

——, *1954 Yearbook: Creating a Good Environment for Learning* Washington: National Education Association, 1955.

Teachers diaries report, emphasize, and show the ways home school, and community can cooperate in improving the learnin environment. A *must* for all teachers.

——, *1959 Yearbook: Learning and the Teacher*. Washington: Na tional Education Association, 1959.

Intended for those who want to increase their knowledge an understanding of the teacher-learning process, this analysis c the nature of learning and its implication for educational work ers is a *must*. The emphasis is on the systematic skills used b teachers in stimulating children's intellectual development. E cellent—and reinforces the idea of "systematic" propounded i *this* book!

Craig, Gerald S., *Science for the Elementary-School Teacher*. Bos ton: Ginn & Co., 1958.

Supplies basic science information for teachers, pays attention to pre-school and primary children and suggests experiences to help children (and their teachers?) interpret the physical world.

le Francesco, Italo L., *Art Education: Its Means and Ends*. New York: Harper and Brothers, 1958.

A comprehensive study of every level of art education.

Gaitskell, Charles D., *Children and Their Art*. New York: Harcourt, Brace and Company, 1958.

A detailed discussion of both the theoretical and the practical aspects of rich varied art programs. Much of what is said about visual art can be said about sound art (music).

Gwynn, J. Minor, *Curriculum Principles and Social Trends*. New York: The Macmillan Company, 1960.

Current practices and methods, the influences operating to change them, new departures in the curriculum, and the areas in which it should be improved are described.

Harrison, R. H. and L. E. Gowin, *The Elementary Teacher in Action*. San Francisco: Wadsworth Publishing Company, Inc., 1958.

The scope and character of "good teaching" are explained by examining the best in principle and practice.

Heffernan, Helen and Vivian Todd, *The Kindergarten Teacher*. Boston: D. C. Heath and Company, 1960.

A study of the kindergarten child is followed by concrete suggestions for dealing with these children and their specific characteristics and needs. Excellent.

Hildreth, Gertrude, *Teaching Reading*. New York: Holt, Rinehart, and Winston, Inc., 1958.

This comprehensive discussion of reading in the elementary school, its processes, methods, instructional techniques, materials, and special problems has considerable import for would-be teachers of *music* reading.

Hurley, Beatrice Davis, *Curriculum for Elementary School Children*. New York: The Ronald Press, 1957.

The necessity for preparing today's children for meeting life's problems is the theme.

Johnson, Earl A., and R. Eldon Michael, *Principles of Teaching*. Boston: Allyn and Bacon, 1959.

A comprehensive coverage of the problems facing beginning teachers.

Kearney, Nolan C., *Elementary School Objectives, A Report Pre-*

pared for the Mid-Century Committee on Outcomes in Elemen- tary Education. New York: Russell Sage Foundation, 1953.

Eminent educational talent from all sections of our country prepared these goals. Part I of the study gives its background Part II consists of the recommended goals, and Part III, thei implications. The goals and expectations are listed for childrer about age nine, about age twelve, and about age fifteen—the goal for children to be taken into account by those concerned witl the education of children. The goals are in terms of (1) physica development, health, and body care; (2) social and emotiona development; (3) ethical behavior: standards and values; (4) so cial relations; (5) the social world; (6) the physical world; (7 esthetic development; (8) communication; and (9) qualitativ relationships. Even those on the committee say the goals ar too high—but why have goals already achieved? *This is probabl the most important book in this bibliography.*

McKim, Margaret, Carl W. Hansen and William L. Carter, *Learn ing to Teach in the Elementary School.* New York: The Macmil lan Company, 1959.

This book is designed to help beginning teachers translate pro fessional education into successful classroom practice. Excellen for new teachers and student teachers.

Mueller, Francis J., *Arithmetic, Its Structure and Concepts.* Engle wood Cliffs, New Jersey: Prentice-Hall, Inc., 1956.

This book is especially useful to the teacher who has no learned arithmetic with meaning and who wants to build up hi own understanding of number concepts.

National Society for the Study of Education. *Social Studies in th Elementary School. Fifty-sixth Yearbook, Part II.*

Excellent for an over-all view.

Ohlsen, Merle, (Editor), *Modern Methods in Elementary Educa tion.* New York: Holt, Rinehart & Winston, Inc., 1960.

With its emphasis on learner-centered teaching, a workabl program in each learning area is defined, major learning prob lems identified, and pre-tested techniques offered. Excellent.

Siks, Geraldine, *Creative Dramatics: An Art for Children.* Nev York: Harper and Brothers, 1958.

Methods and techniques for teachers.

Warner, Ruby H., *The Child and His Elementary School Worlc* Englewood Cliffs, New Jersey: Prentice-Hall, Inc., 1957.

The author is concerned with the child in his school world, hi needs, and how best to satisfy them. Excellent for a picture of good creative practices and experiences in all key areas of the curriculum.

LEARNING ABOUT CHILDREN

Note: This section is intended for those who hope to make their teaching more effective by studying and knowing children *as well as* by knowing subject matter.

Abraham, Willard, *Common Sense about Gifted Children.* New York: Harper and Brothers, 1958.
A warm human approach is used to cover every facet of dealing with gifted children. Important.

Caplan, Gerald, (Editor), *Emotional Problems of Early Childhood.* New York: Basic Books, 1955.
This book is based upon the papers presented to the International Institute of Child Psychiatry in Toronto in 1954. It provides an account of current thinking and practice in the areas of prevention, diagnosis, and treatment of those psychological disorders which are attracting the interest of child psychiatrists throughout the world. Twelve case histories are presented followed by a discussion of fundamental points as well as reports of relevant research currently in progress. The author of *this* book lists the publication in order that you can gain an insight into the way these scientists study and *not* so you can take a few notes and rush out and begin practicing psychiatry without a license!

Garrison, Karl C., and Dewey G. Force, Jr., *The Psychology of Exceptional Children.* New York: The Ronald Press, 1959.
Stressing the importance of viewing the child as a whole, the authors bring together a vast amount of material about exceptional children including recent research, new concepts and theories, and the latest developments.

Gesell, Arnold, Frances L. Ilg, and Louise B. Ames, *Youth: The Years from Ten to Sixteen.* New York: Harper and Brothers, 1956.
This is what youth are like—a complete study. Important.

Hutt, Max L., and Robert G. Gibby, *The Child: Development and Adjustment.* Boston: Allyn and Bacon, 1959.
Organized in terms of the central personality characteristics of each period of development, each aspect is discussed in terms of the child as a whole.

Ilg, Frances L., and Louise Bates Ames, *Child Behavior*. New York: Harper and Brothers, 1955.

These co-workers in the Yale Gessel Clinic of Child Development trace the year-to-year peaks and valleys of child development and give advice and suggestions to parents and teachers about what to do in relation to the basic cycles of behavior.

Jersild, Arthur T., *The Psychology of Adolescence*. New York: The Macmillan Company, 1957.

Adolescent psychology is related to all facets of human development—the childhood conditions influencing adolescence and *its* bearing on adult life.

Lane, Howard, and Mary Beauchamp, *Understanding Human Development*. Englewood Cliffs, New Jersey: Prentice-Hall, Inc., 1959.

A section on behavior in general is followed by discussion of growth and suggestions for studying children and young people.

Lee, J. Murray, and Doris Lee, *The Child and His Development*. New York: Appleton-Century-Crofts, 1958.

An excellent book in this area.

Lowenfeld, Viktor, *Creative and Mental Growth*. Third Edition. New York: The Macmillan Company, 1957.

This study on the interrelationship of mental development and artistic creativity is designed to give an explanation of the psychology and growth of human creativity.

———, *Your Child and His Art*. New York: The Macmillan Company, 1957.

A detailed account of the characteristics of a child and his art in each of five stages of development with the approximate chronological age at which each stage can be expected.

Prescott, Daniel A., *The Child in the Educative Process*. New York: McGraw-Hill Book Company, Inc., 1957.

The director of the Institute for Child Study, University of Maryland, shares some of the insights he and other consultants in the Institute have gained: the complexity and interrelatedness of certain factors which influence children's learning readinesses and perceptions.

Radler, D. H., *Success Through Play*. New York: Harper and Brothers, 1960.

How to help the pre-school child "get ready" for the first grade, and how to help the child having difficulty in school.

Strang, Ruth, *An Introduction to Child Study*. New York: The Macmillan Company, 1959.

Discussing the importance of developmental tasks and factors, the emphasis is on the dynamics of children's behavior—how they perceive the world and why they behave as they do. Important.

Sumption, Merle, and Evelyn M. Luecking, *Education of the Gifted*. New York: The Ronald Press, 1960.

The aim of the authors is to help provide a solidly based and well-thought-out program for gifted children.

White House Conference on Children and Youth, *The Nation's Children* and *Children in a Changing World*. Washington: White House Conference, 330 Independence Ave., S. W., 1960.

The first of many books resulting from the conference.

White, Verna, *Studying the Individual Pupil*. New York: Harper and Brothers, 1958.

The author outlines and illustrates methods that do not require special training or supplies or equipment.

Witmer, Helen L (Editor), *Personality in the Making*. New York: Harper and Brothers, 1952.

The fact-finding report of the Mid-Century White House Conference on Children and Youth.

Wright, Beatrice A., *Physical Disability: A Psychological Approach*. New York: Harper and Brothers, 1960.

The emphasis is on the kinds of social-psychological situations which confront a person with an atypical physique and how he copes with them.

TEACHING CHILDREN AND MUSIC

Note: This section is intended for all teachers as an aid in guiding child growth and development through music.

Andrews, Frances M., and Clara E. Cockerille, *Your School Music Program*. Englewood Cliffs, New Jersey: Prentice-Hall, Inc., 1958.

A music educator and a school administrator discuss the music program and develop the point that it cannot be developed apart from the general program. Excellent—and a *must* for music majors.

Andrews, Frances M., and Joseph A. Leeder, *Guiding Junior-High-School Pupils in Music Experiences*. Englewood Cliffs, New Jersey: Prentice-Hall. Inc.. 1953.

The teacher of upper-elementary children will find this book valuable, too.

Andrews, Gladys, *Creative Rhythmic Movement for Children.* Englewood Cliffs, New Jersey: Prentice-Hall, Inc., 1954.
Rhythms—a means of releasing the creative being that is a child.

Arbuthnot, May Hill, *Children and Books.* New York: Scott, Foresman and Company, 1947.
This is a *must* for those without an excellent background in children's literature.

Bailey, Eunice, *Discovering Music with Children.* New York: Philosophical Library, 1958.
An anecdotal record of musical growth in children aged four through seven without their "being taught." The easy, folk-like approach to coordinating music, poetry, art, dance, and dramatic play is telling in its effect.

Britannica Junior Study Guide, No. 15, *Music and Art.* Chicago: Encyclopaedia Britannica, 1947.
Material may supplement classroom activities or be a source for independent study. Directions for making instruments. There is a list of suggested studies in music.

Buck, Percy C., *Psychology for Musicians.* New York: Oxford University Press, 1945.
The terms of psychology are illustrated by examples in music teaching. A *must* for music majors.

Coleman, Satis N., *Music for Children.* New York: G. P. Putnam's Sons, 1931.
Mrs. Coleman is one of the teachers who pioneered in freeing children from a diet composed entirely of the science of music.

———, *The Drum Book.* New York: The John Day Company, 1931.
A history of drums and directions for making and playing them.

Ehret, Walter, *The Choral Director's Handbook.* New York: Edward B. Marks Music Corporation, 1959.
Advice in capsule form for the inexperienced conductor and a check list for the "veteran."

Geri, Frank H., *Illustrated Games and Rhythms for Children.* Englewood Cliffs, New Jersey: Prentice-Hall, Inc., 1955.
Activities for children in the lower elementary grades. It includes music, pictures, directions, records, words of songs. Comprehensive.

Harvey, E. P., *How to Make Your Teaching Easier and More Effective*. Davenport, Iowa: Teaching Aids Company, 1959.
Since, hopefully, this is what we're all seeking, let this author help.

Hughes, Langston, *First Book of Rhythms*. New York: Franklin Watts, Inc., 1954.
A poet's book for creative adults to share with creative children.

Ingram, Madeline D., *Organizing and Directing Children's Choirs*. New York: Abingdon Press, 1959.
This is important for church choir leaders as well as those teaching music in elementary and junior high school.

Jones, Betty Jensen, *What is Music for Young Children*. Kingston, R. I.: NANE Center, College of Home Economics, University of Rhode Island, 1959.
A publication of the National Association for Nursery Education.

Krone, Beatrice, and Max Krone, *Music Participation in the Elementary School*. Chicago: Neil A. Kjos, 1951.
The materials and methods for making music are presented. Perhaps you will profit, too, from the companion volume, *Music Participation in the Secondary School.*

Landeck, Beatrice, *Children and Music*. New York: William Sloane Associates, Inc., 1953.
The emphasis is on how music can be used to enrich the lives of children at home and in school. Excellent.

————, *Music for Fours and Fives*. Washington: Music Educators National Conference, 1959.
This was prepared by the Commission for Pre-School, Kindergarten and Elementary School.

McLaughlin, Roberta, *Music in Everyday Living and Learning*. Washington: Music Educators Conference, 1960.
Anecdotes demonstrating ways of correlating music with other school experiences.

Mathews, Paul W., *You Can Teach Music*. New York: E. P. Dutton and Co., Inc., 1953.
Mr. Mathews agrees with Mrs. Myers that teaching music is easy. Lists of song books. Illustrated.

Mayo, Margot, *The American Square Dance*. New York: Sentinel Books Publishers, Inc., 1948.

Contains calls and music, with descriptions of figures for folk and country dances. A list of recordings is included.

Morgan, Hazel Nohavec (Editor), *Music Education Source Book*. Chicago: Music Educators National Conference, 1947.

It is a *source* book.

————, *Music in American Education* (Source Book No. 2). Washington: Music Educators National Conference, 1955.

Reports of MENC Committees during 1951-54. Important.

Music Education Materials. Washington: Music Educators National Conference, 1959.

A selected bibliography by music educators for music educators.

National Council of Teachers of English, *Language Arts for Today's Children*. New York: Appleton-Century-Crofts Co., Inc., 1954.

Many of the successful teaching procedures in the four language arts can be adapted to the four areas of music—listening, singing, reading, and playing. Discover the principles and adapt and adopt the procedures.

National Society for the Study of Education, *Fifty-seventh Yearbook, Part I, Basis Concepts in Music Education*. Chicago: University of Chicago Press, 1958.

This cooperative project with the Music Educators National Conference is a major addition to our field—basic, timely, significant and comprehensive. A *must* for music majors.

————, *Thirty-fifth Yearbook, Part II, Music Education*. Bloomington, Illinois: Public School Publishing Company, 1936.

A pertinent example of the fact that theory is always ahead of practice. Most of this material is definitely *not* out of date.

Nelson, Mary Jarman, and Gladys Tipton, *Music for Early Childhood*. New York: Silver Burdett Company, 1952.

Its delightful songs, specific techniques, accompanying records, attractive illustrations, and its sound philosophy make this a most important contribution to pre-school education and to pre- or little-experienced teachers. Excellent.

Oberndorfer, Anne Faulkner, *What We Hear in Music*. Camden, New Jersey: Victor Division of RCA, 1943.

This book is valuable for its analysis of music often used in elementary schools. Excellent background material. Lists music of many areas.

Salt, E. Benton, Grace Fox, and B. K. Stevens, *Teaching Physical*

Education in the Elementary School. New York: The Ronald Press, 1960.

Among the many activities and methods for teaching them are included rhythms and dances. Teachers of music should know what is basic to teachers of physical education—and be able to "understand" them. The reverse is true, too!

Sheehy, Emma D., *Children Discover Music and Dance.* New York: Holt, Rinehart &Winston, Inc., 1959.

The author's successful methods of teaching and developing the love for music are extended into the area of the dance.

———, *The Fives and Sixes Go to School.* New York: Holt, Rinehart & Winston, Inc., 1954.

Living and working with five- and six-year-olds as it is done by creative, resourceful teachers. About children, the program, activities, materials, and teachers. A *must* for music people.

———, *There's Music in Children* (Revised Ed.) New York: Holt, Rinehart & Winston, 1952.

"Proof positive" that children are musical. Mrs. Sheehy accepts that fact—and plans their development.

Taubman, Howard, *How to Bring Up Your Child to Enjoy Music.* New York: Hanover House, 1958.

Advice to parents which ought to be of interest to teachers.

Timmerman, Maurine, *Let's Teach Music in the Elementary School.* Evanston, Illinois: Summy-Birchard Publishing Co., 1958.

An excellent guide with extensive lists of reference books and sources of materials for units.

Wilson, Harry Robert, *Artistic Choral Singing.* New York: G. Schirmer, Inc., 1959.

To students of the choral art, (including choral art in the first grade) a master and devoted director has much to say.

AUDIO-VISUAL MATERIALS AND METHODS

Note: This section is prepared for all teachers in the hope they will become adept in using these media as well as alert in taking advantage of their possibilities.

Brown, J. W. and others, *A-V Instruction: Materials and Methods.* New York: McGraw-Hill Book Co., Inc., 1959.

A thorough survey of materials with emphasis on the teacher's role in presenting and relating them to classroom instruction.

Dale, Edgar, *Audio-Visual Methods in Teaching*. New York: Dryden Press, 1956.
> Many suggestions related to materials and activities that will make teaching more effective.

Educational Film Guide. New York: H. Wilson, 1959.
> This publication is revised annually.

Educator's Guide to Free Films and Free Filmstrips. Randolph, Wisconsin: Educators Progress Service, 1959.
> Sixty-one films in the music category are listed.

Hartsell, Horace C., and Henry R. McCarty, *The Cooperative Approach to Audio-Visual Programs*. Washington: National Education Association, 1960.
> A guide for communities desiring to establish an area center for materials.

Indiana University Audio-Visual Center, *The 1960 Educational Motion Picture Catalog*. Bloomington, Indiana: Audio-Visual Center of Indiana University, 1960.
> This catalog replaces the 1956 issue and the three supplements following.

Jordan, Robert Oakes, and James Cunningham, *The Sound of High Fidelity*. Chicago: Windsor Press, 1958.
> Believing "an investment in information should always precede an investment in equipment," the authors give valuable guides to the use and purchase of material.

Mayer, Martin, *Hi-Fi*. New York: Random House, 1958.
> Non-technical language and numerous illustrations are used to take one into the world of high fidelity.

National Film Board of Canada, *Music for Children*. New York: Contemporary Films, Inc., 1960.
> A film presenting a novel technique in teaching children and music.

National Society for the Study of Education, *Fifty-third Yearbook, Part II, Mass Media and Education*. Chicago: University of Chicago Press, 1954.
> A summary of knowledge in the area and suggestions for using the press, movies, and broadcasting in teaching. Important.

1960 Supplement to the National Tape Recording Catalog. Washington: National Education Association, 1960.
> Information on recorded programs and those available for recording.

Sheridan, Lee, *How to Get the Most Out of Tape Recording.* Flushing, New York: Robins Industries Corp., 1958.

A guidebook for the uninitiated, with descriptions of recommended tape recorders.

Sources of Visual Aids for Instruction in the Schools. Washington: U. S. Office of Education, Department of Health, Education and Welfare, 1960.

Lists sources of films, pictures, maps, exhibits and so on.

Thomas, R. Murray, and S. G. Swartout, *Integrated Teaching Materials: How to Choose, Create and Use Them.* New York: Longmans, Green and Co., Inc., 1960.

Following a discussion concerned with the best method for conveying ideas, audio-visual materials and their making and use are presented.

Wittich, W. A., and C. F. Schuller, *Audio-Visual Materials: Their Nature and Use.* New York: Harper and Brothers, 1957.

A full discussion of materials, relating them to problems of instruction and showing how they are most profitably used.

MISCELLANEOUS

Cramer, R. B., and Otto E. Domian, *Administration and Supervision in the Elementary School.* New York: Harper and Brothers, 1960.

A cooperative attack on the problems of elementary education is proposed.

Eye, G. G., *The New Teacher Comes to School.* New York: Harper & Brothers, 1956.

Helpful suggestions for meeting the needs of the new teacher.

Fine, Benjamin, and Vivienne Anderson, *The School Administrator and the Press.* New London, Conn.: Arthur C. Croft Publications, 1956.

This how-to-do-it public relations manual presents numerous practical techniques for building increased community understanding and support for education.

Flanagan, John T., and Arthur Hudson, *Folklore in American Literature.* Elmsford, New York: Row, Peterson and Company, 1958.

An anthology presenting the rich legacy of folklore in American literature.

Franseth, Jane, *School Supervision as Leadership.* Elmsford, New York: Row, Peterson and Company, 1960.

"Supervision" means the leadership that results in improvement. A survey of recent findings and a report of supervisory experiences. Excellent.

Free and Inexpensive Learning Materials. Nashville: Division of Surveys and Field Services, George Peabody College for Teachers, 1959.

Revised often, this is an invaluable source of information about the wealth of free materials available today.

Hermann, Edward T., *The Music Teacher and Public Relations.* Washington: Music Educators National Conference, 1959.

A serious treatise with a light touch.

Lawrence, Mortimer W., *The Rocket's Red Glare.* New York: Coward-McCann, Inc., 1960.

A report on the first real steps into the space age and of the centuries of preparation making these steps possible. Teachers, many children already know the mechanisms of rockets, so you might as well become informed, too.

Lindsey, Gruhn, *Student Teaching in the Elementary School.* New York: The Ronald Press, 1957.

A guide to student teaching in the elementary school.

Mandell, Muriel, and Robert Wood, *Make Your Own Musical Instruments.* New York: Sterling Publishers, 1956.

A how-to-do-it book for children and their teachers.

Moore, Sallie Beth, and Phyllis Richards, *Teaching in the Nursery School.* New York: Harper and Brothers, 1959.

A comprehensive and informally written text.

Muldoon, Mary Warren, *Learning to Teach: A Handbook for Beginners.* New York: Harper and Brothers, 1958.

Guidance for both the prospective and the beginning teacher. Excellent.

Redefer, Frederick L., and Dorothy Reeves, *Planning a Teaching Career.* New York: Harper and Brothers, 1960.

The questions of beginning teachers and those seeking advancement are answered.

Snyder, Keith D., *School Music Administration and Supervision.* Boston: Allyn and Bacon, Inc., 1959.

This publication covers the major problems.

Taubman, Howard, *How to Build a Record Library.* New York: Hanover House, 1953.

Mr. Taubman suggests the most important works for both a starting collection and a more advanced one, and lists the single best recording of each from the standpoint of performance and technical reproduction.

What Research Says to the Teacher. Washington: National Education Association, 1960.

A series of informative and concise booklets—each written by an authority in his field—brings to teachers the answers to many questions and problems.

Zirner, Laura, *Costuming for the Modern Stage.* Urbana: University of Illinois Press, 1957.

Many suggestions for solving the problems of costuming.

SOURCES OF MATERIALS AND INFORMATION

Information about the records listed in Chapter 12 may be obtained from your local dealer.

The Young Peoples Record Club and the Children's Record Guild are at 100 Sixth Avenue, New York 13, New York.

Music Minus One, 719 Tenth Avenue, New York 19, N. Y., issues recordings of instrumental music in which one instrument is missing, and you, at home, are supposed to play the missing part. Catalog.

Music Appreciation Records, a branch of the Book-of-the-Month Club, Inc., 345 Hudson Street, New York 14, New York, issues the *Music Appreciation Educational Album* with a Teaching Guide and teaching aids.

American Handicrafts Co., Inc., 33 East 14th Street, New York, N. Y., is a source of do-it-yourself-handicrafts materials.

Orientalis, Inc., 11 East 12th Street, New York 3, New York, specializes in books on the East. Its catalog is so interesting it is difficult to decide what books to order even though one is only moderately interested in this field.

Notes, a magazine devoted to music and its literature, with bibliographies and reviews of books, records, and music is published by the Music Library Association, Music Division, Library of Congress, Washington 25, D. C.

The Long Player, Long Player Publications, Inc., 233 West 49th Street, New York, New York publishes a monthly record catalog containing Abner Levin's selection of the finest recordings available.

W. Schwann, 137 Newbury Street, Boston 16, Massachusetts, publishes a monthly listing of available long-playing records. New releases are so marked. An excellent source of information.

Keyboard *Jr.*, 1346 Chapel Street, New Haven 11, Conn., publishes bulletins discussing music on radio and television and in films and reviews records for use with children.

Bibliography, resource units, information for various grade levels about Asia, Africa, China, Japan, and the Middle East may be ordered from World Affairs Materials, Brooklyn College, Brooklyn 10, N. Y.

Columbia Records contribution to non-European style music is contained in The Columbia World Library of Folk and Primitive Music.

Contemporary Films, Inc., 267 West 25th Street, New York 1, N. Y. rents "The Lady from Philadelphia," the film of Marian Anderson's singing tour of the Far East in 1957.

Folk Music Guide USA, a magazine listing folk events, concerts and festivals may be obtained from I. G. Young, 110 McDougal Street, New York 12, New York.

Music Masters, an excellent series of fifteen long-playing records in which a Master's major works are woven into a narration of his life, are issued by Vox Productions, 236 West 55th Street, New York 19, New York.

Folkways Records & Service Corporation, 117 West 46th Street New York 36, New York, publishes authentic folk music (from all over the world, literally) films and filmstrips, as well as records—including *The Science of Sound* produced by Bell Telephone Laboratories. *Folkways Records*, the catalog of the corporation, is a *must* for school libraries and individuals interested in ethnic music.

Sing'n Do records and related materials may be obtained from Sing'n Do Company, Inc., P. O. Box 279, Ridgewood, New Jersey.

Sing Out is a regularly-published folksong magazine, issued five times a year, containing songs, articles, news, and so on. Sing Out, 121 West 47th Street, New York 36, N. Y.

Teachers Packet on Korea may be ordered from the Korean Pacific Press, Washington, D. C.

The Harmolin Chord-Harp may be obtained from Harmolin Inc., P. O. Box 244, La Jolla, California.

The Jam Handy Organization, 2821 East Grand Boulevard, Detroit 11, Michigan, distributes color filmstrips with correlated musical recordings.

The Metropolitan Opera Guild, 654 Madison Avenue, New York 21, New York distributes color filmstrips of operas.

The World of Folk Dances is RCA Victor's series of folk records. Young Audiences, Inc., 645 Madison Ave., New York 22, N. Y., presents small groups of professional musicians in informal concerts for school children all over the country.

Rhythm Band Instruments and Autoharps may be obtained from the major band instrument companies, from the large mail-order houses, and from Peripole Products, Inc., 51-71 Rockaway Beach Blvd., Far Rockaway 91, Long Island, New York.

Index

Index